Comments fr~~

in Edu

have often puzzled how creativity can be related to international education. Now they have the answers, and more. This is a collection of well chosen essays that link the local with the global, theory with practice, and both with rich peda-gogical implications. International educators did always "know" that exposure to other cultures is a way to unleash creativity. Now it comes documented through hundreds of well-chosen references that Dr. Bleedorn weaves through her text and connects to her major themes, creativity and critical thinking, lead-ership, education, and business. This book is a delight—and a must—for all who seek the unity of knowledge, entrepreneurship outside of business, under-standing of complexity, synthesis of paradoxes, and grasp of global issues that impact our lives every day. For international educators the book has additional insights about transfer and production of knowledge and maintaining key inter-disciplinary and multidimensional concepts from ours and other cultures.

—J. A. Mestenhauser
Professor and Coordinator
College of Education and Human Development
University of Minnesota

Bee Bleedorn is a seminal thinker in the area of creativity. She possesses an unending belief in the value which creativity brings to society. The depth of her knowledge, the wisdom of her years, and the passion of her spirit are evident in each chapter of this book.

Superseding today's tendency toward "fad" tools and techniques of creative ideation, *The Creativity Force* postulates a series of well documented, provoca-tive wake-up calls for the public and private sectors of today's society. It clearly speaks to the need for synergy, the value of diversity, and the importance of syn-chronicity in today's ever-changing world.

—Craig W. Bakken
Global Training Manager
Honeywell Inc., Center for Leadership and Learning
Minneapolis, Minnesota

Many years ago, a character in an E.B. White story predicted "a bright future for complexity in the United States of America." He was right; and the growing complexity demands of us all what Berenice Bleedorn calls a "higher order" of understanding—an enhanced creativity, based on rational thinking but sparkling beyond its reach.

Berenice Bleedorn, who is both a reflective practitioner and a practical academic, has been successfully teaching creativity for two decades. Her book shows that creativity, which we all need to learn in order to cope with complexity's bright future, can also be taught—attractively, persuasively, creatively.

—Harlan Cleveland
President, World Academy of Art and Science
Minneapolis, Minnesota

Bee Bleedorn's book, *The Creativity Force,* presents a strong case for the teaching, fostering, and practice of creative thinking in education, business, and life. I love the interweaving of examples from the lives and work of a wide range of people, from Einstein to people in prisons with genius in them that went unrecognized in conventional schools; from poets such as Blake who saw through the illusion of a false heaven promised in his time by a burgeoning industrial revolution and revealed a deeper promise in the universe and souls of people; to businesses that thrive because they enable rather than stifle creativity among managers and employees. Good reading. Important advice.

—Dr. Patricia M. Mische
President, Global Education Associates, New York

Bee Bleedorn's vast experience in the discipline of creativity and creative problem solving provides her with an extremely rich background for this book. It pulls together in one place her best thinking over the many years. Readers will be challenged by her depth of understanding of the many aspects of creativity, innovation, and leadership in education, business and all aspects of life.

—Sidney J. Parnes, Ph.D.
Professor Emeritus and Founding Director
Center for Studies in Creativity, Buffalo State University College

Berenice Bleedorn is a "seed woman" par excellence; just as Johnny Appleseed tried to seed trees, she spent a lifetime "seeding" people and nurturing their variety of potentials. Nobody who truly meets her stays unaffected by her message that human diversity should just as zealously be protected as bio-diversity if our species wants to survive, and that the key to this is creative and critical thinking. Reading her book, with its urgent wake-up call to all education, one can only wonder how much more must be done before a paradigm shift will finally take place.

—Dr. Piet Muller
World Chairman and Founder, Dr. P. J. Muller and Associates
Pretoria, South Africa

This volume effectively communicates the message that creativity is a powerful force, but that it is a potential force, and one which thus requires mindful effort. The real virtue of this book may be that it communicates that message—and then follows it up with practical ideas for fulfilling creative potentials and translating research in creativity into action.

—Dr. Mark Runco, Editor
Creativity Research Journal
Professor, California State University

Dr. Bleedorn's book is an interesting combination of experiences from both a business and educational perspective. Based on my experience with students in our master's degree and undergraduate minor program, these two contexts are the primary ones from which student populations are drawn and to which text or instructive material should be appropriately addressed.

—Dr. Mary C. Murdock
Center for Studies in Creativity
Buffalo State College, Buffalo, New York

Dr. Bleedorn has been a very strong proponent of the practical approach to creativity for a number of years, for all walks of life—including business and education.

Her knowledge of the field is well expressed in this book and will be a valuable resource for everyone—managers, administration, specialists, teachers, and members of any organization.

—Dr. Min Basadur
Center of Research and Applied Creativity
Ancaster, Ontario, Canada

As the title of this work proclaims, Berenice Bleedorn does indeed send out an urgent message. At a time when the social/political climate pressures the schools to focus on the transmittal of factual data, to treat students as buckets to be filled, educators—and the business community—need to be concerned more with the wise and prudent facilitation of the fullest possible growth of each child. This process can only be achieved by a creative, risk-taking company of scholars/specialists in cooperation with, and enjoying the support of, parents and business men and women, who will reap a rich reward for their collaboration. That reward will be a generation of young men and women who will aggressively, imaginatively and productively lead our society in the new millennium, who will use wisely and build inventively, and who will establish an exciting synergistic environment in which some of us may be fortunate enough to share. The alternative would be a tragic waste of the human spirit.

Listen to Dr. Bleedorn's urgent message.

—William E. Salesses, Ph.D.
Professor and Former Dean, School of Education,
University of St. Thomas, St. Paul, Minnesota

The Creativity Force embodies critical insights for business and entrepreneurial endeavors. It raises creativity and innovation to new levels, bringing author Berenice Bleedorn's scholarly, gifted, and expansively creative mind directly into the heart of today's and tomorrow's strategic business issues. Read it carefully!

—David L. Braun
Inventor and Corporate Scientist
Carlton Award Winner
3M Company, St. Paul, Minnesota

THE CREATIVITY FORCE
IN EDUCATION, BUSINESS, AND BEYOND

AN URGENT MESSAGE

The Creativity Force in Education, Business, and Beyond

An Urgent Message

Berenice D. Bleedorn, Ph.D.

1998
Galde Press, Inc.
PO Box 460, Lakeville, Minnesota 55044–0460, U.S.A.

First Edition
First Printing, 1998

Cover design by Irene Vande Moore

Edited by Dr. Patience Dirkx

Library of Congress Cataloging-in-Publication Data
  Bleedorn, Berenice D. Bahr.
       The creativity force in education, business, and beyond : an urgent
  message / Berenice D. Bleedorn. — 1st ed.
          p.   cm.
       Includes bibliographical references.
       ISBN 1–880090–57–0
       1. Creative thinking.   2. Creative ability in business.
  3. Creative thinking—Study and teaching.   I. Title.
  BF411.B54   1998
  153.3'5—dc21   97–52788
                                                                CIP

Galde Press, Inc.
PO Box 460
Lakeville, Minnesota 55044–0460

For my daughters
Joan Barnes and Bonnie Sample
with love

Contents

Acknowledgments

Without the treasured friendship, moral support, and extraordinary talents of Dr. Patience Dirkx, there could have been no finish to this book. The mysterious process of bringing the written word through the final editing and formatting has been totally outside of my own line of interests or abilities. Patience, with her complete mastery over the complexities and vagaries of electronic systems, made those skills available to me from the start. Not only that, but her quiet stability and approval sustained me through countless moments of doubt and uncertainty. I am intensely aware of the critical value of the talents and wisdom of this good friend, whose consistent wisdom, professional judgment, and modesty are so exceptional and who was in the right place and right time for the preparation of my book.

I also wish to acknowledge the influence of Dr. E. Paul Torrance, Professor Emeritus, University of Georgia, who has been a mentor and inspiration since my first encounter with his work and leadership in creativity at the University of Minnesota in Minneapolis in 1965. It is a rare privilege to be one of the countless students throughout the world who have followed his leadership and vision for education and the future of human society.

In addition, I have had the invaluable support and service of Steve Dahlberg, a colleague whose friendship began when, as a sophomore at the University of St. Thomas, he enrolled in my course on Entrepreneurial, Creative Thinking and Problem Solving. His response and commitment to both the philosophical and practical development of creative studies brought him into the arena of my work, first as a work study student and, later, as a total scholar and practitioner.

Anna Fellegy deserves recognition for her service and judgment in the first editing of the manuscript. Her recommendations and observations provided both encouragement and the establishment of standards of quality in the preparation of the manuscript.

Finally, a full measure of gratitude is due Dr. Piet Muller, Pretoria, South Africa, friend and colleague, working to provide leadership in creative studies for education and business in his country. It was his review of my papers that caused him to insist that I make a selection of them for publication. His enthusiasm caused me to embrace the task that is now complete, and I thank him for his confidence in my ideas.

So many other students, scholars, practitioners, colleagues, and inquirers into the nature of my teaching have been constant in their expression of interest in my writing and have sustained me in the long process. Most of all the enthusiasm of students and community for the discipline of creativity and its influence in their personal and professional lives have been a source of satisfaction and energy. I thank them all.

In addition, I will always be grateful to a few special scholars who, along the way, were a major influence on my search for understanding and for avenues of service:

Dr. Harlan Cleveland, Professor Emeritus, Hubert H. Humphrey Institute of Public Affairs, University of Minnesota, and Director, World Academy of Art and Science. From the time that I became aware of his work, the extraordinary nature and scope of his world vision have been a fundamental guide to understanding.

Dr. Anwar Dil, United States International University professor and co-author with Buckminster Fuller of *Humans in Universe*. As chair of my doctoral committee and favorite professor, Dr. Dil opened the doors of perception to more than a glimpse of universal human realities.

Dr. William Salesses, professor and former dean, College of Education, University of St. Thomas, St. Paul, Minnesota. He was the college administrator whose insightful leadership made possible my entry into a service of almost twenty years in the academic design and teaching of courses and programs in Creative Studies in both education and business departments, graduate and undergraduate.

For the inspiration and encouragement of these scholars across the years I will be forever thankful.

Foreword

The tides of global change have indeed become enormous. The rate of these changes has become ever more rapid. These changes offer a powerful challenge in both education and business. Neither education nor business can prepare anyone for tomorrow. This does not mean that either education or business can afford to stop teaching the knowledge and skills needed in jobs. Creativity is a force that must be added. When anyone encounters a problem for which they have no known and practiced solution, some degree of creativity is required.

Fortunately, all people have within themselves this creative force. Furthermore, many techniques have been developed for strengthening and eliciting creative thought and expression. This force and its development are the subject of this book, and such development addresses the needs of both education and business. The author gives special attention to making connections between business and education.

Also, fortunately, research and experience in the last forty years have produced a vast quantity of new insights about creativity and the skills and knowledge that release creative solutions in response to change. In fact, these new insights have moved far ahead of performance, as the author points out in the introduction. This gap must be reduced but doing that also requires creativity.

In the changes that are experienced daily, the open-endedness of the problems and their solutions must be maintained. Many of the features of creative problem solving, as it is being taught and practiced, are designed to solve this problem. The techniques of creative problem solving should be taught in schools, colleges, universities, and professional schools in every subject. This is true for even the retired and elderly.

The author rightly points out the necessity for training teachers in the skills and techniques of creative thinking and creative problem solving. Open-ended learning and thinking experiences are needed and should be used. I believe this book will give educators motivation to accomplishing this task.

This book gives examples of devices that others have usually ignored. One of these is the use of humor in facilitating creativity and in healing. The practical demands of business for new kinds of leadership is emphasized and discussions of spirit, loyalty, teamwork, initiative, and risk taking are considered.

Attention is also given to the need to create a work environment that facilitates creativity and creative problem solving. There is urgency for translating insights into action and for futuristic thinking. We must move forward the universal trend toward an evolving change of mind and make possible the dreams of world peace and justice.

—E. PAUL TORRANCE
Pioneer and International Authority on Creativity
Professor Emeritus, University of Georgia

Preface

This book has been written many times in my head during periods of reflection in the past thirty years. My years of educational and business involvement with equal parts of theory and practice of creativity have a singularly independent and paradoxical nature. The book's content reflects those qualities. At the same time, it is focused and random, sequential and systemic, realistic and visionary.

Specifically, the book's purpose is to argue for an extension of the interpretation of creativity as a specialized feature of individual thinking and behaving to a perception of creativity as a powerful potential force, a natural endowment of all humanity, and a significant vehicle for speeding the evolution of human intellect and consciousness to a higher level. It follows that if education everywhere were designed for the teaching and development of improved qualities of creative and other higher orders of thinking (with an eye to human diversity), the hope for a better, more peaceful, global future would become more realistic.

My observations as an educationist in creative studies with academic and practicing ties to business and entrepreneurship have persuaded me of the difficulty with which the quantitative science of business and the qualitative studies of human behavior integrate the emphasis on their differing, often polarized value systems. A career as part-time faculty member of a university for seventeen years gave me the opportunity to design and teach graduate and undergraduate courses in creative studies at the same time that I was engaged in creativity programs in the business community. The experience was a continuous exercise in perceiving a unity of opposites.

In the academic setting the enthusiastic response of students to courses in creative studies testified dramatically to the value they placed on their learning experience. As founder and director of the Institute for Creative Studies at the University of St. Thomas in Minneapolis, I witnessed the effect of programs in integrative creative studies for the general public. Participants across a broad range of disciplines found the interrelationship of other perspectives enlightening and enriching to their own specialized field. The result was an aptitude for avoiding the absolutism of labels and categories based on assumptions and an increased capability for systemic thinking.

The capacity to perceive oneself as a significant part of a broad, all embracing system at the same time that one acknowledges the personal, unique value of each single contribution is a quality of thinking much to be desired whether it be in large or small social systems, competitive business settings, the political arena, or the vast mysteries of the dynamic universe.

This book is an invitation to readers to move beyond their current perception of the place of creativity in their life and join in the growing effort to liberate the creative forces of the world awaiting expression in education, business, and beyond.

Introduction

A powerful force is coming down the track of educational reform, and it promises to affect the nature of business and every institution struggling to find a new pattern of operation for a new kind of world. It is the creativity force, present naturally to some degree or another in all humans, in all cultures, and at every age. It is central to the human sense of personal identity and significance. It is a force that seeks and deserves expression.

Arrival of the information age with its emphasis on science and technology has brought about an imbalance of attention between technology and humanology—the study of human behavior and individual differences. Now educational institutions are beginning to recognize the fact that standardization and computerization of learning is effective for some students for some knowledge and skills, but that something has to be added to formal education that serves the great diversity of learners and protects the human urge for individuality and growth. Transition to new ways of thinking needs to move beyond pronouncements to practice, and from good intentions to bold and specific action.

Forty years ago the domain of creativity that had been the purview of philosophy and scientific discovery began to develop a discipline of creative studies within the fields of educational psychology and behavioral sciences. Pioneers in the study of human development and the creative potential introduced convincing research and theoretical argument to the academic community for serious attention to the specific teaching of the full range of thinking processes available to the human intellect. A persuasive case was made for better understanding of the creativity force and its application in formal education. In spite of the authenticity of their case, academic programs in creativity moved with difficulty into official educational circles.

As an observer of educational practices from every level and perspective for most of my lifetime, I can report that enlightened, dedicated, visionary, student-oriented educators are evident everywhere in growing numbers. Teachers of creativity and other higher level thinking processes are appearing in schooling at all levels; however, most of the conditioning for creativity and innovation in business goes on within the business organization in training and development seminars for personnel who finished their academic degree without benefit of courses in creative studies.

One of the hindrances to formal education for creative development is the assumption by the uninitiated that the concept of creativity applies only to the arts. A familiar response is, "Well, I'm not at all creative. I can't even draw a straight line." Most people have to be persuaded that creative studies is a discipline with a well-established body of knowledge based on both quantitative and qualitative research (Isaksen et al. 1993, Joyce at al. 1995). Because of the scope and complexities of the term, countless attempts have been made to define it. The most comprehensive is by Clark Moustakas. He says that creativity is the experience of expressing and actualizing one's individual identity in an integrated form in communion with oneself, with nature, and with other persons. Another definition says simply that creativity is the capacity to develop new capacities.

However it is defined, the discipline of creativity is consistent in its attention to four fundamental factors of study identified collectively as the "Four P's." They are:

Studies of the creative person. What are the cognitive (thinking) and affective (attitudinal) domains of the creative personality? How do you identify the behavior and attitudes characteristic of highly creative personalities? Can you use the Torrance Tests of Creativity to measure levels of creative thinking?

Studies of the creative process. What are the brainworks of creative thinking? How does the brain/mind create ideas? Make remote connections? Perceive relationships? Produce original work? How can the creative force be set free in individuals, in organizations, and throughout society?

Studies of the creative product. What are the differences between primary and secondary creativity? Who determines the level of creativity in a product? Does a product have to be of use to be creative?

Studies of the creative press. What are the characteristics of an environment that encourages and supports creative thinking? How can a business organization establish a climate for the production and effective management of new products and ideas? How can all organizations make maximum use of human capital, especially of the thinking power randomly scattered among the levels and labels of the organizational charts?

These and other questions often raised by scholars awakened to the power of the creativity force as it impacts on education and business will be addressed in the articles that follow.

It would be a denial of the urgency of the message if action were to wait until all the questions have been answered. The creativity issue is like a powerful locomotive announcing its arrival boldly through the mists and steams of its own energetic emergence. Now that the call for educational reform has reached a critical mass, demands for radical changes in the delivery of formal education are on track, up front, and "in the face" of the old traditions. In spite of years of educational counting and measuring, researching and publishing, higher salaries and smaller classrooms, statistical analyses and scientific reductionism, achievement scores are down and school dropout rates are up. Bright, independent thinkers are often lost to the system. It would seem that the federal, state, and local monies allocated for education are failing to produce a system that serves learning and thinking differences in a new kind of society with a new global dimension, subject to the quickening changes inherent in a dynamic Information Age.

The inflexibility of some of the bureaucratized educational leadership has an example in the experience of a consultant for gifted and talented in a state department of education. In an effort to integrate the services of the separate offices, a suggestion was made to the foreign language consultant for a cooperative program that would teach a second language to gifted elementary students with a language aptitude. The response was swift and absolute: "Are you kidding? Do you know what a problem that would be for high school teachers of languages when those students showed up in their class?"

It is not difficult to draw the conclusion that, for some educators, schools are organized more for the convenience and benefit of teachers than for the learning and development of students. The inclination of many professors to focus only on their particular discipline deprives education of the exercise of integrative learning and thinking, leading to the art of thinking in terms of the total system and an individual's place within it. A professor of critical issues in contemporary education demonstrated his bias against creativity when he wrote on a final paper: "This is an excellent paper for a proponent of creativity" and assigned a grade of B. For him, excellence outside of his personal bias didn't rate. Students are offended by professorial pomposity. Education is better served by professors who are student oriented and who, in addition to imparting their knowledge, explore ideas with students in a climate of trust and mutual respect. With the advent of electronic information systems and independent learning, the time is long gone when the teacher is the absolute and only authority in the classroom.

All of the articles in this book call for educational reform that opens the doors of learning to include more individualistic, humanistic, qualitative factors in the formal learning experience without sacrificing standards. The teaching of creative thinking invites habits of mind that honor diversity and, at the same time, discover individual identity in its relationship to the whole human system. University students have an enthusiastic response to courses in creative thinking. Course evaluations give high praise to the value of the course immediately and to its subsequent application to careers in the changing, twenty-first-century workplace.

The experiential learning strategies necessary to the teaching of creativity require a climate of trust in the classroom. Teaching creativity to undergraduates in a university can provide genuine intergenerational insights. The negative reputation that "Generation X" has had could change if educators asked students, "What do you think?" The educator might learn that students may prefer (as one student suggested) to be labeled "The Y Generation" (translation: The *Why* Generation because they are inquirers into the nature of things.) The maturity of thinking among serious young people often reveals an impressive belief system realistically and idealistically balanced.

All of society, both inside and outside of the educational arena, has a stake in what happens within the ivy-covered walls. Poised on the threshold of a new millennium, the business world has an increasing awareness that new ways of thinking throughout the organization are critical to the success and prosperity of the company in a competitive, global economy (Russell and Evans, 1992). The practice of creative thinking and behavior in teams and leadership roles leads to other, higher-level thought patterns that include:

- Critical thinking (assessing the facts of the case and making fair, thoughtful, unbiased choices.
- Systemic, "Big Picture" thinking (seeing the relationships of the parts to the whole and the value of each individual part to the total system).
- Visionary thinking (thinking ahead, speculating on possible future effects of present trends, having a sense of aim and purpose for time forward).
- Paradoxical thinking (the capacity to hold two opposing ideas in the mind at the same time and still continue to function).
- Transformational thinking (that solves problems and creates/actualizes positive change).
- Relationship thinking (perceiving how two factors are related through their differences, commonalties, or cause and effect).

The human right to think and be heard is a basic principle of democratic government. As the world and its affairs become more complex, a more sophisticated, integrative kind of thinking is required if the system is to work. Education has a responsibility to bring the quality of thinking up to speed. The natural, slow-paced process of the evolution of the human brain/mind needs help from institutions of learning.

The explosion of public attention to the creativity factor in personal development and effectiveness is a matter of record. A recent count located one hundred ninety books on creativity, fifty-five web sites, forty-five computer programs, seven annual conferences and six academic journals dedicated specifically to the discipline of creativity (*The Economist,* August 17, 1996). What is needed is a public perception of the power of the creativity force permeating the totality of the human condition at this breakpoint time in history. The reality of that force needs an expanding expression beyond personal development through groups and teams, organizations, institutions, cultures, and ideologies, to the universal search for peace and justice in the world and beyond. (Fig. 1)

Traditional habits of mind fail when they organize their services into a highly structured, strictly labeled, compartmentalized system with specific fixed levels of identity and authority. The zeitgeist of the new century calls for thinking and acting within the interactive, interrelated systems while being attentive to the function of the individual in behalf of both self and total system. The "trickle down theory," with its vertical hierarchical direction, no longer applies to the process of change. In the case of the creative force, the action is best seen as a "trickle out process" that encompasses all levels of human activity simultaneously like self-organizing systems (Wheatley 1992), including the conscious release of the unconscious mind. At the threshold of a new century, a surge of collective mental energy is breaking through old habits of thinking. A network of new thinking is forming across space.

This book is organized around three separate sections, all interrelated in an open-ended system.

The first section on creativity and education addresses the fundamental need for vigorous educational attention to creative studies as essential in the preparation of citizens of a democracy for participation in and contribution to a radically changing, diverse, and challenging world of local, national, and global dimensionalities. Education at all levels is a crucial key to unlocking the powers of the mind for creating and responding positively to change and for functioning responsibly in the practice of both local and global citizenship.

The second section relates to creativity in business and the trend to move away from traditional, hierarchical, closed systems of leadership toward a more flexible, open system of transforming leadership and followership. Connections between education and business become evident in discussions of the emergence of a work culture where the thinking levels and patterns of every player are important for the achievement of organizational goals, especially in the expanding, competitive, global marketplace.

A final section presents a collection of articles that demonstrate the insistent presence of creativity, both ancient and current. In each case there is a reminder of the search for understanding that testifies to the human urge to recognize that which lies deep within the human psyche, often neglected, but a determining factor in our separate lives and in our collective destiny.

I have written these articles with a focus on the creative thinking force in its service to the integration of differences and the richness of its connections to the subtle and mysterious realities of the human brain/mind. It is my hope that the ideas in these pages will connect with the thinking of educators and others concerned with the urgency of action for educational reform and the natural relationships between what is taught in school and what is required in the workplace in a changing world.

Creativity and Education

A Wellspring of Change and Growth

Dr. E. Paul Torrance (1979) made a prophetic statement when he said :

The genius of the future will be the creative mind adapting itself to the shape of things to come. This will require "Satori" bursts of new insights. The skills of creative thinking must be recognized as mankind's most important adaptability skills. Such skills must become basic to the curriculum of schools, homes, business and other agencies. (p. 9)

Observations and reflections as an educator with ties to the business community have brought about an overriding perception that the required years of traditional schooling have neglected the obligation to prepare citizens not only for creativity and innovation, but across the entire spectrum of intellectual processes. Formal schooling has a responsibility to specifically cultivate higher levels of quality thinking (creative, critical, paradoxical, systemic, visionary, global) as a major objective for teaching and learning. It is happening randomly in scattered educational settings, but not fast enough. What is needed is vigorous leadership and support from centers of power.

Quality thinking serves not only individual identity needs, but also the needs of fully functioning groups, organizations, and ultimately the shared hopes for a peaceful global human commons. Creativity can "just happen" or it can evolve in the slow-paced natural evolution of human thought. However, the singular demands of the dynamic present and the unpredictable future depend upon specific attention in curricula at all levels of schooling for the teaching and practicing of strategies that set free the priceless art and science of creative thinking for meeting new challenges and solving new problems (Torrance 1995).

Successful education for creative development depends upon students' direct, purposeful involvement in open-ended learning and thinking activities. Specific teaching of creative and other thinking processes enrich and illuminate traditional teaching with its familiar focus on memory and convergent or one-right-answer thinking.

The specific teaching of creative and other thinking processes will be speeded up when teacher preparation programs bring significant attention to metacognitive issues and less delay to the application of research findings in the studies of creativity. Government efforts at educational reform can help by adding creative studies to their call for smaller class size and higher teacher salaries. Fewer students and more money do not of themselves convert ineffective teaching to effective facilitation of learning in the classroom.

Structured, open-ended strategies for teaching that invite creative and critical thinking are relatively unfamiliar and unnatural to tradition-based educators. Academic bureaucracies with their organizational patterns based on separate disciplines respond haltingly to opportunity for creative, integrative curricula. In the world of human affairs, for which education prepares students, there is an accelerating need for habits of mind with capacities for integrating and interrelating information and ideas. The workplace requires it. The new kind of transforming leadership demands it.

Cultivating habits of thinking beyond our region and beyond our time is a fundamental art for a new kind of society. Thinkers like R. Buckminster Fuller and Anwar Dil (1983) and Harlan Cleveland (1993) have been giving us the message for a long time. Education is in a preferred position to bring about an essential new level of quality thinking and behaving, since everything we do "depends on our habits of thought."

Processes of thinking can be taught. The good news is that the human intellect is one resource in the world that is unlimited. If thinking about thinking and bringing new educational ideas into action were a popular academic practice, we would raise the percentage of applied brain potential from a speculated 25% to unlimited heights (Botkin, Elmandjra, and Malitza 1979).

The articles in the section on education are intended to provoke a measure of urgency to the generally slow pace of positive change in education. After all, that is where most people in the world spend at least twelve years of standardized learning in the company of his/her peers, where attitudes of comparative personal worth and significance, based on the level of respect for individualistic learning and thinking, have a fundamental importance in the world of work and oftentimes in a total personal lifetime.

Evolution of Education and Learning: An Urgent Message

Can we all graduate fast enough from the resolution of rising expectations to the evolution of rising responsibilities?

—Harlan Cleveland

Can it be that the natural evolution of the mind to higher levels and complexities of thinking is finding expression in formal, institutionalized education? It would be comforting to discover that, indeed, the evolutionary force for growth and change in development of the brain/mind is being aided and abetted by schools everywhere. The purpose here is to report and consider evidence that focuses on the evolving nature of learning and the need for a greater effectiveness of its delivery during the formal years of schooling. The argument is for the development of specific attention in education to the entire scope of processes of thought, including the function of intuition and other manifestations of the role of higher consciousness in human affairs.

Learning/Thinking Styles and Labels

Has formalized education failed? Yes. Evidence grows that, for many students, Margaret Mead's parents had the right idea. "They didn't send her to school. They didn't want her learning to be interrupted." As a lifelong educationist with background in a long list of educational vantage points, I suggest that there may be some justification for their startling statement. In spite of educational changes since Margaret Mead's time, standardization, competitive grading, and inflexible organizational policies in many places ignore the individuality and complex nature of the learner.

Now studies of human differences in learning and thinking styles have brought us to the place where, in assessing human intellect, we can look at a theoretical model of intellect and identify 150 separate and distinct ways of being smart (Guilford 1977).

Traditionally, measurements of IQ and achievement have been based on standardized tests, limited in scope and with little regard for evidence of alternative thinking excellences. The numerical record and standardized test scores of a student may show evidence of comparatively low intellect, whereupon the student is fixed with an official academic label by the system. Many highly creative intellects and minds of specialized thinking talents with important potential for service to society go unrecognized and unfulfilled.

My Teacher Thinks I'm Dumb

All learners are perceptive and alert for signs of approval or disapproval from authorities and peers. Psychological damage is done when a learner's perceptions of self-worth are based on the judgment and messages of authorities with limited input. A middle school student identified as a student at risk because of poor grades and lack of motivation represents a case in point. He confided to a university student/mentor that his teacher "thinks he's dumb." The fact that he was a brilliant chess player had not registered with the teacher as evidence of "smarts." Such a student will either be permanently persuaded that he is stupid or will be left in the disabling state of cognitive dissonance, confused by the contradiction between his perceived "official" label and his own sense that he is "smart." Opportunities for the demonstration and acknowledgment of creative and complex thinking can be a real boost in teacher perception of students and in student self-esteem. School programs that allow for the expression of a diversity of talent have particular value in culturally different student populations (Torrance et al. 1998).

Creative Students at Risk

Poverty, dysfunctional families, cultural differences, and a variety of psychologically-based problems are recognized impediments to success in school; they signal the classification of "student at risk." Another "risky" population on the school scene is the highly creative, "right brain" student in a highly standardized, "left brain" system. There is no end to case studies of highly successful, professional adults with dismal histories of low motivation and achievement during their school years. Many creative students are, by their nature and appetite for independent learning (according to their own style) able to transcend the established order, maintain their self-respect, and create interesting, productive lives and careers. Many, by reason of their perceptive thinking patterns and problem-solving abilities, are especially well prepared for the responsibilities of citizenship in a changing world and workplace.

Other "at risk" students blessed (or cursed) with a highly creative nature do not fare so well and become troubled and troublesome to society. According to Jose Arguelles, problems of violence can be related to the lack of creativity and self-expression in a person's life. He suggests that when we are deprived of the power of expression we express ourselves in a drive for power.

Populations of prison inmates and juvenile delinquents in detention centers could provide revealing data for a research study on the relationships between creativity and community offenders. To quote Mary Richards: "We have to realize that a creative being lives within ourselves, whether we like it or not, and that we must get out of its way, for it will give us no peace until we do" (p. 27).

Improving the Quality of Thinking

A few years ago a major conference at Massachusetts Institute of Technology attracted a huge cross-section of professionals from all over the globe with the title "Improving the Quality of Thinking in a Changing World." The program was organized around modules specialized for education (K-12), higher education, business, health care, technology, and general interest. The central issue throughout the conference was the urgent need for adding the deliberate teaching of processes of thinking to educational and training experiences everywhere. Sessions on creative thinking, critical thinking, paradoxical thinking, systemic thinking, futuristic thinking, and creative problem-solving skills addressed both theory and hands-on application. The discipline of creative studies dominated much of the program.

The module on "Thinking Initiatives in Business" attracted a major proportion of participants, and was a reminder that radical changes in the workplace and throughout society demand that every player in the system is being called upon to think in new ways. If the transition to a truly global society of peace and justice is to be accomplished, then the years spent in school need to result in a quality of thinking well prepared for the achievement of personal potential and beyond that for genuine, responsible participation in the larger system.

The Art and Evolution of Thinking

Vincent Ruggiero (1988, vii) said it best: "Thinking is an art with its own purposes, standards, principles, rules, strategies, and precautions. And it is an art well worth learning, for every important thing we do is affected by our habits of mind."

One thing is certain in these uncertain times. New ways of thinking will have to be specifically added to the teaching of content and basic skills if differences between people, religions, cultures, and ideologies are to be resolved in peaceful, productive mutuality at a paradoxical level of thinking. Talking with teachers about the importance of the specific teaching of thought processes and the evolutionary nature of the human mind often results in deadlock. Trained and certified teachers, as well as many professors of specialized disciplines, seem to feel that thought process is incidentally taught along with content. It is assumed that exceptional teachers may well elicit higher orders of thinking from students in their classes. However, the need is too critical to be left to chance.

The business community would profit from an influx of new workers whose formal education included new ways of thinking for a changing, complex marketplace. The corporate world with its traditional conditioning for a focus on profit line and numbers is opening the doors to the realities of the workplace not so measurable (Kastenbaum 1987, Fellers 1996). Corporations in many places are beginning to understand the importance of accounting for the uncountable. Creativity and other unlimited resources of the human mind and spirit are coming in for an increasing share of attention. The creative process, when shared with persons of differing perspectives and opinions, can serve as a "circuit maker" that looks for commonalties and harmony rather than polarities and discord. Training and empowering workers to think in new ways contributes to team-building and translates effectively to the corporate profit line.

It's Happening, But Not Fast Enough

Society and its institutions are at a breakpoint time in human history. Radical social and political change demands changes in the way people think. Creative, innovative thinking and problem solving are potential talents in every human being. New ways of thinking can be taught; blocks to new ways of thinking can be overcome through understanding and practice.

The early work of authorities, like Dr. E. Paul Torrance (Millar 1995), on the identification and teaching of creativity is being promoted in enlightened school programs worldwide. As in most institutions, student or client oriented change has a history of "bubbling up from the bottom" of the organization rather than being initiated from top levels of authority.

With the traditional emphasis on quantitative rather than qualitative-based research, and with faculty status strongly influenced by faculty research projects, applied changes in teaching and learning often wait a long time for research findings to reach the learner. Records often show that allocation of funds for educational reform find their way to teacher salaries and improvement of the physical plant, while long-established standardized teaching methods lock creative students into an unmotivated history of low achievement scores and ultimate dropout.

Centers of learning are positioned to speed the natural evolutionary process of brain/mind development beyond the practice of memory, analysis, and classification toward more complex patterns of thought. Evidence grows that the zeitgeist of our times reflects a serious search for meaning and personal identity throughout the population. Growing public interest in spirituality and the understanding of levels of consciousness signal the human urge for growth and enlightenment. The evolution is happening, but not fast enough.

Education can help by increasing its attention up, down, and sideways across the full range of individual differences to the recognition and deliberate teaching of higher levels of thinking. It can be done. It is being done. But the system needs the "fast forward" command.

The New Century Needs Quality Thinking

No great improvements in the lot of mankind are possible until a great change takes place in the fundamental constitution of their modes of thought.
—John Stuart Mill

One of the arguments being made in recurring discussions of educational reform is a case for the importance of understanding the effect of emotions on learning. There can be little dispute with the idea that the affective or feeling domain exerts a powerful influence on the learning process. Effective education recognizes the need for a learning environment that is comfortable and "learner friendly," free of fear and undue stress.

I propose an addition to the appeal for understanding the emotional component of learning. I am suggesting that teaching practices for effective learning need to add very specifically the metacognitive understanding and practice of the whole range of thinking processes as they have come to be understood in recent years.

Current literature, not only in the field of education, but also in journals related to business and human effectiveness, is calling for new and higher levels of thinking for a new century and a new, more complex and challenging world. Authorities on the changing nature of leadership from the traditional pyramid model of authority to a more enlightened, more "organic" model of transforming leadership remind us that in a complex, dynamic world or workplace every player needs a capacity for thinking beyond the familiar and obvious.

If educational systems really want to prepare students to function effectively and productively in a democratic, society and/or workplace, they will have to add to their curricula the specific teaching of thinking processes. They will teach the metacognitive skills that give students an understanding of their own thinking and learning style, along with plenty of practice in the art of thinking creatively, critically, and in problem solving modes. They will provide a learning climate that invites the discovery of student potential to think globally, futuristically, and with a talent for recognizing the reality of the interactive nature of all organizations. The capacity to think beyond the level of categories and labels, to recognize the reality of relationships and connections, and to think paradoxically (in ways that create a unity of differences) will give learners both within school and throughout the workplace a sense of their own role and its place within a changing, self-organizing system. The teaching of thinking processes will have a significant place on the list of learning objectives in institutionalized education everywhere.

The worldwide teaching of creative and other higher order thinking processes in educational as well as in business settings is a well-established reality. For example, the deliberate application of new ways of thinking socially and politically are producing in South Africa what has been termed a miracle. Their redesign of a country into an integrated diversity of cultures is being perceived as a model for places faced with the demanding challenge of unifying long-established differences. Evidence of creative education in another part of the world reports an Institute for Creative Studies in Shanghai and a pilot program for teaching creative thinking in schools in Singapore. A recent convocation listed more than twenty leaders from creativity centers and institutes in the United States and places all around the world.

Along with the well-developed strategies for practicing more creative ways of thinking and problem solving is the increased attention to the teaching of critical thinking and conflict resolution. Creative and critical thinking processes lead naturally to the cultivation of minds that can pass the test of a "first rate intelligence" described by F. Scott Fitzgerald as "the capability of holding two opposed ideas in the mind at the same time and still retain the ability to function."

That kind of intelligence requires the practice of deliberately thinking about thinking, a new trend among serious students and scholars who wonder about the intellectual preparation we have made for our time and its unique place in human history. The current world zeitgeist demands intellects capable of absorbing floods of new information and processing it with equal parts of imaginative vision and practical reality. New ways of living together harmoniously with all of our diversities intact are within our reach. Educational programs and human development training can confront the challenge of improving the quality of thinking for every citizen. In a democracy, the thinking processes of the entire population are contributing to the creation of the twenty-first century.

Many years ago the scientist philosopher, Teilhard de Chardin (1959), reminded us of the "incontrovertible evidence" that human kind was entering upon the greatest change period the world has ever known. Today those changes are happening to the whole structure of human consciousness. A fresh kind of life is starting with fresh demands on thought levels that reach beyond our immediate region and beyond our current time.

Perspectives and attitudes expressed by the separate communities of business and education have traditionally reflected a highly competitive if not antagonistic relationship. Realistically, the two opposing disciplines are coming closer together in their shared need for reform. Enlightened educational leadership is working to recognize and develop a broader, more inclusive array of human talents for meeting the challenge of the increasing diversity of learning and thinking styles in student populations. In the world of business there is a surge of interest in understanding the value of the human resource and especially the "intellectual capital" present in the work force that contributes so substantially to the "bottom line."

The obvious commonality of the two opposite forces is the realization that the unlimited resource of the human capacity to think and contribute has been too long neglected. Countless hours of research have produced countless stacks of evidence that moves at a snail's pace into educational practice. What we have learned about human differences and human potential is overdue for application in both education and business settings.

Some colleges and universities have moved more quickly than others to incorporate the teaching of creative thinking and problem solving processes into their programs. It is easier for many traditionally disposed professors to continue to repeat the past. More creative factors of flexibility, risk taking, awareness, vision, and integrative thinking among higher education faculty would help to initiate and support positive change in the preparation of an effective workplace.

The message is clear. Few observers have to be reminded of the radical changes in the workplace in response to new developments across the entire spectrum of society. The Information Age, with its dramatic developments in technology and communication systems drives and demands constant change (Cleveland 1997). The explosion of human affairs into a complex global system opens doors to new challenges and opportunities in the marketplace of new ideas. Many skills and talents required in the shifting complexities of modern business are found to be lacking among workers at all levels. Such a lack translates readily to lower productivity and limited profit.

Educational programs designed to prepare students to function effectively in the "real world of business" have traditionally focused on skills and practices of a fairly familiar quantitative-based system. Thinking creatively and critically has, in many cases, been left to chance. New ideas have traditionally met with organized resistance. The world of work has often seemed to be "proud of machines that think, and suspicious of men and women who think." Now business is calling for innovative, creative problem-solvers and risk-takers. Entrepreneurial workers are granted more freedom to think and to produce new ideas for the marketplace. Corporations are increasing the teaching of problem-solving, creative thinking, teamwork, and other "basic skills" in training and development programs.

Managers and administrators will not have to wait for on-the-job training and development in thinking if educational entrepreneurs recognize and seize opportunities to provide leadership in the design and introduction of formal courses in thinking up, down, and sideways.

Peter Drucker, respected authority on management, had words of advice for educators in "How Schools Must Change" (1989). He urged schools to start equipping students with the skills to work effectively in organizations, where most Americans now make their living. He said:

The trend in business, as well as in all of society's institutions, is toward a reinterpretation of leadership that will be less stratified and more egalitarian and dependent on individual responsibility, initiative and constant, open communication between individuals, regardless of organizational rank. Direction and discipline will come from within, not from above, through interaction among colleagues at all levels (p. 18).

New understandings of human potential and the value of human differences in an interactive, integrated organizational operation are studied and discussed in business journals with increasing frequency. The call for creativity and innovation in bureaucracies is a call for serious reminders of the theoretical nature of investigations into human behavior. The study of human behavior underscores the good news that much of what is needed in times of intense changes is available in the unlimited capacities of the human mind set free to think, to communicate new ideas, and to contribute to the common good (Bleedorn 1987).

The potential for creative contributions to organizations and institutions of all kinds is unlimited. A major task is to remove the limitations on the creative mind and spirit imposed by society, education, and employers. Human behaviors and differences have been measured, analyzed, and compartmentalized with little insight and application to the larger systemic vision of fully functioning, creative minds working together to meet organizational goals.

Both education and business are on the threshold of new realities. One of the components of the paradigm shift is the activation of the unlimited thinking potential available (Gelb 1995). A major challenge for both business and educational institutions is the freeing up of human resources from the organizational constraints that prevent their full participation and contribution. Business schools need educational entrepreneurs who recognize the importance of formal courses and course components in thinking processes and who can promote a place for them in college and university programs.

The case for improving the quality of thinking can be taken to a level beyond education and business to the emerging question of planetary survival. Jonas Salk (1983) said it this way:

> Therefore it is in the best interest of the species, from an evolutionary point of view, for individuals with problem solving attributes, as well as those possessing other creative and innovative traits, to be recognized. This requires an attitude and a system directed to the selection of those who would also serve the species' interest and not only the interest of the individual. The present serious human predicament requires all our creative energies for its resolution (p. 70).

Creative and Critical Thinking: Integrating the "Mind Field"

The principal goal of education is to create men and women who are capable of doing new things, not simply of repeating what other generations have done....men and women who are creative, inventive discoverers. The second goal of education is to form minds which can be critical, can verify and not accept everything they are offered.

—Jean Piaget

Bleedorn (1993) made an argument for the integration of creative and critical thinking by stating:

> The evolutionary development of the art of thinking at higher, more complex levels is joined in current times by the deliberate study of processes of thinking, not only as separate and distinct classifications, but especially as integrated, interrelated, and interactive systems. Dynamic, global changes in human affairs require creative and critical thinking directed toward new, more complex thought patterns and collective behavior. (p. 10)

She advances the proposition that the separate studies of two thinking processes (creative and critical) can be integrated since they have a "naturally integrative propensity and that what may be perceived as opposites or 'contraries' has the potential for productive mutuality" (p. 10).

Promoting the art of thinking at higher, more complex levels relates directly to the call for changes in American education, a familiar theme in both education and business. Arguments are made for the deliberate teaching of processes of thinking in addition to the traditional teaching of content and basic skills. It is argued that since science and technology have made possible a limitless storehouse of information, it is incumbent on educational services to provide understanding of the full range of thought processes for maximum use of that information in a changing, complex, and interrelated global society.

Today emerging attention to metacognition and a better understanding of one's individual "mind field" is evidence that a better balance between the teaching of content and the teaching of thought processes is under way in education. Thinking about thinking serves the personal urge to understand oneself as well as the need to better understand the diversity of thinking styles in any group, social or professional, working to achieve a common purpose.

Since the teaching of creative thinking processes has been established academically, and the discipline of creative studies has been slowly making its way into curricula in institutions of higher education throughout the country, the case being made here is for capitalizing on the pioneering efforts of the early leadership and speeding up the deliberate teaching of creative thinking and problem-solving processes at all levels of learning.

In the case of critical thinking, teaching that process in college philosophy courses has traditionally been based on studies of logic and deductive reasoning. As suggested by Bleedorn (1993), current studies of critical thinking

> have extended well beyond the classical concepts of critical analysis and logical, sequential thought. They have developed into a body of knowledge and recommended teaching activities designed for educational settings with the purpose of promoting responsible, fair-minded, critical thinking and decision-making. Although the history of their separate developments may cause creative and critical thinking to be perceived as separate and distinctive processes, their most effective applications are exemplars of highly integrative, sophisticated, and paradoxical thought. (p. 11)

Cleveland (1987), in his preface to *The Knowledge Executive,* referred to the ability of the human mind to integrate what William Blake called "the contraries." He said:

> The human brain delights in the balance of contrasting thoughts. The most effective rhetoric often exploits an apparent paradox. Truth seems often to come wrapped in small, paradoxical packages. I have come to believe that effective rhetoric often exploits an apparent paradox. The art of executive leadership is, above all, a taste for paradox, a talent for ambiguity, the capac-

ity to hold contradictory propositions comfortably in a mind that relishes complexity. (pp. xv-xvi)

Creative thinking can be critical even as critical thinking can be creative. They are not separable when operating at their best level. The joint assumption that both processes can be taught (understood, discovered, set free, cultivated) can be observed increasingly in educational literature and conferences, often under the banner of "creative problem solving." The creative and critical thinking patterns practiced in creative problem solving promote integrative thinking. Integrative thinking can open the "doors of perception" and speed the natural evolution of the mind and its exercise at all levels of society.

At the Individual Level. The freedom and encouragement to produce and communicate creative ideas, to be recognized for thinking "outside of the square," and to discover intellectual talents "way beyond the IQ" provide new insights into personal identity and individual significance. The question becomes not so much "how smart are you?" but "how are YOU smart?" Once the fact that everyone is creative (albeit in different ways) is recognized, students testify readily to the positive changes in their self-concept and in their confidence for creating and responding to change. Confidence begets risk taking and risk taking begets discovery and growth.

At the Group Level. The challenge of integrating a variety of specializations into a harmonious pattern for the accomplishment of the shared goal is served when characteristics and processes of creative and critical thinking are understood and applied. Creative factors such as flexibility, originality, risk taking, humor, and a perception of one's place and responsibility within the whole system all work together to get the job done. In interpersonal relationships, the creative flexibility of mind that allows for the mutuality of differences, coupled with the critical thinking of fair-minded judgment, engages thought patterns of harmony rather than polarities and conflict.

At the Larger Level of Society. Faced with the challenges of discrimination and stereotyping that ignore individual identities, a paradigm shift that values individual differences can be served by schooling that de-emphasizes labels and generalities, and capitalizes on the capability of the human mind field to integrate not only the subject matter in one's own mind, but also the diversities of human talents in all of society. Human attitudes and behaviors depend upon human thought. The deliberate teaching of thinking processes, beginning with creative, critical patterns of thought, supports efforts to achieve a harmonious, pluralistic, more fair and ethical society. Possibilities for the creation of self-organizing systems as described by Wheatley (1993) will depend for their success upon the ability of all the players in the organization to think in new ways and at higher levels.

At the Level of Global Awareness and Planetary Citizenship. The question of world peace and quality of life across space and time has direct relevance to the ability to create new departures, not only from "business as usual," but from "thinking as usual." Especially on the part of designated leaders of all nations and institutions, a mental capacity to create a unity of differences grows in importance as hardware for conflict and global destruction grows in sophistication. Of equal importance is the capability of undesignated leaders (everyone) to think holographically. A prepared mind can have a national identity and loyalty at the same time that it can perceive the reality of its global citizenship. This time in history presents an opportunity for the practice of integrative thinking to bring nations together to correct the abuses being visited on their shared planetary environment and on each other. There are no frames or boundaries on the air and the seas and outer space. Now and for generations to come, this is necessarily a shared project, and integrative thinking a shared responsibility.

A 1992 issue of *Time* asked the question, "Can we all get along?" The answer is relevant to questions of creative and critical thinking, and especially to the thinking processes of their paradoxical realities. Mikhail Gorbachev (1992) made a positive prediction: "Man remains capable of finding a way out of any crisis as long as he is allowed to explore, to think, and to be creative" (p. 42).

An example of the political and social influence of information and training in new ways of thinking is being played out in the Union of South Africa. The task of unifying two distinct and separate cultures following the end of apartheid has been a formidable one for leadership and for the entire population. Public information and creativity training, including annual conferences at the University at Bloemfontein, are helping to move the public mind forward toward the goal of national unity. The first period of progress in the transition has been called a "miracle" and a world model for the unifying of diversities.

According to Bleedorn (1993):

If creative and critical thinking has the potential to produce new and positive behaviors among people of difference who are learning to get along together, the question arises, 'Can it be taught?' Studies of new understandings and scenarios of new and expanded applications and resources testify to the fact that almost anyone can learn to develop his or her innate creative and critical thinking abilities. This writing is intended to contribute to the extension and expansion of interest in new ways of thinking and behaving appropriate to new global realities and visions of the future. The shift from an emphasis on separate parts and components to a more configurative perception of the 'whole pattern' is inherent in the creative and critical thinking qualities that become more thoroughly teachable as they become better understood. (p.19)

It was Buckminster Fuller who predicted that if the world's people were to move beyond their crisis of transition to a new level of mutuality it would be due to the growing numbers of individuals who are doing their own thinking.

The thinking of every person/citizen/worker is conditioned by the twelve or more mandated years in a formal, institutionalized educational experience. One of the greatest contributions that education can make to the quality of life in a community, nation, or planet is the addition to the required curriculum of the deliberate teaching of thought processes along with the teaching of knowledge and basic skills. The following list of ideas is offered as a cumulative argument and summary for that proposition.

We have changed almost everything in the world except the way people think. Educating students to new ways of thinking for a complex, interrelated world is a basic challenge of the future.

Higher levels of thinking, according to the Guilford model of the structure of intellect, include: thinking in systems, in relationships, in transformations, and in implications, way beyond the simple learned, memorized, right-answer response.

The discipline of creative studies is an accumulation of more than forty years of study, research, and practice related to the discipline of educational psychology and the full use of the human capacity to think and to solve problems. Creativity has been called "a new psychology."

Creative and critical thinking processes can be formally and specifically taught and integrated into the teaching of any subject matter. Methods and materials are in ever increasing supply. Students respond enthusiastically to a climate of organized freedom for the development and expression of their own advanced levels of thought and speculation.

Schools have a responsibility to develop more effective ways of teaching thinking skills to more students if this country is to compete in the world of new ideas and products. Schools everywhere in the world have the same responsibility if the global family and future generations are to have a reasonable quality of life on our shared planetary home.

Many teachers, especially professors of higher education, have been reluctant to give up the familiar, safe, routine teaching style that maintains their position of absolute authority in favor of more open-ended inquiry and discovery methods which stimulate independent creative and critical thinking and excite the minds of learners.

Real learning, especially for certain learning styles, is best internalized when based on direct, purposeful experiences which then lead students to understandings of abstract concepts, patterns, systems, and new connections.

The critical nature of threats to our global environment and the shared responsibility of citizen stewardship of the planet provide excellent motivation and opportunity for hands-on creative learning experiences in the real world for teaching across the disciplines and with attention to their integrative nature.

In the ideal learning environment that perceives the student as subject, new knowledge about individual learning and thinking styles underscores the need for a diversity of teaching methods. Students who, by their nature, are highly creative and independent in thinking and behavior patterns are best served when learning is perceived as relevant and intellectually stimulating. Students who distinguish themselves academically on standardized tests often need experiences in the use of "whole brain" thinking that includes creative production of original ideas.

Growing attention to the seven intelligences identified by Howard Gardner in *Frames of Mind* (1993) is a reminder of the limitations of IQ scores in identifying talents and intellectual strengths of individual students. Many of the brightest, most complex thinkers and imaginators are unrecognizable in traditional educational settings, are often misunderstood and lost to society. The world needs their talents in whatever special way they excel (Gardner 1993).

The discipline of creative studies is attracting more and more sensitive, enlightened, and concerned educators. Balancing the teaching of processes with the teaching of skills and content is a formula that is long overdue. It is too important to be left to chance. Bold new initiatives and models for teaching a diversity of learners are of the highest priority. Dedicated educators are prepared to provide the leadership necessary to overcome the constraints of old centralized, bureaucratic systems.

A lack of basic scientific understanding tends to produce a population of leaders and followers who are unable to make rational judgments on issues of environmental importance. Computer specialists with interest and insights into environmental studies as a "real world" vehicle for teaching and learning could be an important resource in the preparation of programs and specific curricula for effective, reality-based learning. Creative teaching and learning provides thinking practices in forming and testing hypotheses, interpreting results, drawing conclusions, observing, speculating, and plotting courses of action. Teaching creatively sets teachers free to design lessons and programs suitable for their particular group of students, based on current and meaningful content, integrative and collaborative.

Gradually, the myth that creativity resides exclusively in the graphic arts is giving way to the fact that creativity is a natural and essential part of human identity that can have expression in a rich variety of modes from creating computer systems all the way to performing in an improvisational jazz trio.

Resources and materials on creative teaching strategies from the work of authorities like E. Paul Torrance (1977) and Frank Williams (1970) have for years been providing effective guidelines for classroom teachers in developing original and timely learning experiences.

The transition to a reasonable and peaceful global society requires citizens with a capacity for creative, critical, systemic thinking. It is happening, but not fast enough.

Creative Education: Freedom to Think and Be Heard

Everyone has, simply by existing, a right to be intelligent. And to be provided with a way to become consistently more intelligent. This is a right that must be recognized and held sacred. Above all, the necessary conditions for the exercise of this right must be available. This is society's mission and the primary obligation of its leaders. All of them.

—Luis Machado

Background

At the First International Dialogue on Transition to a Global Society at Landegg Academy, Wienacht, Switzerland, in 1990, the influence of education on the world problematique was a recurring theme. At the academy's subsequent International Dialogue on Transition to a Just Society (1992) Frederico Mayor, Director General of UNESCO, called for a global approach to "engender the necessary change in thinking particularly within the educational system, as well as in social, political, scientific, and cultural affairs," and suggested that the time for action (worldwide *peristroika*) had arrived. Ilya Prigogine spoke of "freeing ourselves" from old patterns of thinking and aiming instead at a "new utopia." Implicit in these remarks was the genuine issue of the realization of human potential and the evolution of human intellect in educational planning everywhere in the emerging world order. The ideals of liberty, equality, and fraternity apply to all persons, or they apply to none, in the global schema. This discussion focuses not on acknowledged differences, but on the common human potential for "opening the doors of perception" to new, more visionary, creative habits of mind (Buzan and Buzan 1994). Educational purposes and possibilities will need major rethinking if learners are to prepare for participation and leadership in the paradigm shift to greater democratization in the world.

Paper presented at the Third International Dialogue on Transition to Global Society: The Transition to a Just Society. September 7–11, 1992, Landegg Academy, Wienacht, Switzerland.

This discussion is intended: (1) to argue for the importance of understanding, teaching, and practicing the full range of human thinking potential as a fundamental force for the transition to a just society and (2) to report examples of developments in the "politics of ideas" and actions that are providing leadership in education and business, especially in the growing attention to the teaching of creative thinking.

Thinking Process for a Just Society

Some time ago, I attended a showing of two documentary films at a small theater in Minneapolis, Minnesota, both of which related quite directly to the issue of justice. One film reported the trial and sentencing of an American Indian accused of shooting an officer on an Indian reservation in South Dakota. The other reported a union/management dispute and strike at a meat packing plant in a small town in Minnesota. Viewing them was a powerful reminder of the human urge for justice and the value conflicts inherent in the process of transition to a just society. Tensions between a sense of justice and personal self-interest contribute to difficulties in perceptions and negotiations. In viewing both of the films the impression grew that much of human behavior demonstrates an inability of the popular mind to think beyond absolutes and polarizations of opposites to a more empathic unity of differences. Decisions based on preconceived assumptions and prejudices fall short of the mark of justice whenever, wherever, and by whatever gender decisions are made or behavior is determined.

U Thant (1977), Secretary General of the United Nations from 1961 to 1979, recognized the obligation of educational systems in the teaching of higher level thinking processes. He argued especially for the development of the process of thinking at the level of paradox when he wrote:

I consider that the primary task of the educationist everywhere is to dispel certain age-old assumptions. It seems to be assumed, for example, that there are no more than two sides to a problem. As a matter of fact, almost every problem has more than two sides. It is also fallacious to paint human beliefs and human societies in terms of pure black and white. There are various shades in between; and there are human commonalties. Problems of racism and intolerance for differences could be reduced if attitudes and behavior had the benefit of a level of thinking that looks for those various shades in between. (in Bleedorn 1985, 156).

As early as 1979, Botkin et al., in a report to the Club of Rome, called attention to the "dichotomy between a growing complexity of our own making and a lagging development of our own capacities" (1979, 7). The Club of Rome is an international group of scientists, educators, and government leaders concerned with the enormous problems associated with energy, food, and population. The demands of future leadership and responsible participation in a pluralistic global society require new understandings, new perceptions, new skills, new behaviors, and, critical to all the rest, new ways of thinking. The increasing number of international conferences is bringing into focus the thought of our common humanity and the universally shared hope for a just and peaceful world.

Common, also, to most cultures and religions is a maxim admonishing the people to behave toward others in ways that they would like others to behave toward them. Such common spiritual guidelines take on cosmic dimensions in an American Indian definition quoted by Charlotte Black Elk at the Nobel Peace Conference at Gustavus Adolphus College in St. Peter, Minnesota: "God is a sphere, the center of which is anywhere and the circumference of which is everywhere." The scientific genius says it this way:

> The more knowledge we acquire, the more mystery we find....A human being is part of the whole, called by us the Universe, a part limited in time and space. He experiences himself, his thoughts and feelings as something separate from the rest, a kind of optical illusion of his consciousness. This delusion is a kind of prison for us, restricting us to our personal desires and to affection for a few persons nearest us. Our task must be to free ourselves from this prison by widening our circle of compassion to embrace all living creatures and the whole of nature in its beauty. (Einstein in McGaa 1990, iii)

The relevant role of education in society's transitions is readily acknowledged. Designing education that deliberately creates thinking patterns supportive of a new, interrelated, fair, humane, just global society is a staggering task. Beginning steps for such a "ministry of liberation" are increasingly in evidence throughout institutionalized education by enlightened, committed teachers and/or special programs, but not, to any great extent, by the institutions themselves.

Education and the Teaching of Thinking Processes

The deliberate teaching of processes of creative and critical thinking as a crucial additive to the traditional teaching of content, skills, and "right answers," has been developing with increasing momentum. The relationship between habits of the mind and the need for a paradigm shift to more creative ways of thinking for the increasingly complex nature of human society is underscored in a statement in the introduction and repeated here by E. Paul Torrance (1979):

> The genius of the future will be the creative mind adapting itself to the shape of things to come. This will require "Satori" bursts of new insights. The skills of creative thinking must be recognized as mankind's most important adaptability skills. Such skills must become basic to the curriculum of schools, homes, businesses, and other agencies. (p. 9)

Although critical thinking may seem to be the opposite side of the coin from creative thinking, the two processes are well interrelated. Critical thinking has often been perceived in a negative sense; that is, the obligation to point out only the faults and weaknesses of new ideas, products, or procedures. In a more current and enlightened interpretation, a distinction is made between weak, narrow-minded critical thinking based on selfish and biased motivations and strong, fair-minded critical thinking with an understanding of the total system and organizational goals. Strong, fair-minded critical thinking can be defined as the process of "thinking clearly and accurately with a view to judging fairly." Higher levels of thinking that go beyond the immediate personal focus to a perception of the system and implications for the future, at such a level thinking can be creatively critical and critically creative. At that level, relationships are mutualistic and ethical thinking and decision making become possible (Paul, Richard, 1993 ABS, 31–39).

Nature of the Discipline of Creativity

An accumulation of research studies has provided insights and understanding that form the basis for the teaching of creativity. Traditionally, the factors of creative person, process, and product were addressed. In current times an additional factor is being added. The factor of "press" or environment for creative, productive thinking and behaving is becoming a critical consideration.

A major contribution to the understanding and development of the creative thinking process are the *Torrance Tests of Creative Thinking,* published by Scholastic Testing Service in Bensenville, Illinois. They have been translated into over forty different languages and used in over 2,000 research studies. The tests measure four cognitive factors of creative thinking: fluency, flexibility, originality, and elaboration.

The discovery and practice of the creative talents for flexible thinking have particular relevance for a diverse, pluralistic global society searching for ways to find unity in cultural and ideological differences. It has been said that unity without diversity is uniformity; diversity without unity is chaos; justice is served when unity and diversity exist together in creative tension. Ervin Laszlo (1992) reminds us that the creative interplay of diversification and integration is a feature of the contemporary world that is of unparalleled relevance to the future of humanity. Without diversity, the parts could not form an entity capable of growth, development, self-repair and self-creativity. Without integration, the diverse elements could not cohere into a dynamic and unitary structure.

Injustice and intolerance grow when thinking processes are limited to a fixation with a single, preconditioned habit of mind based on superficial labels and prejudice. The recognition and practice of flexible thinking talents encourage the art of thinking at a level of paradox which practices the art of seeing two opposites as one harmonious integration. Such thought levels, if readily available, would result in more understanding and less fighting. Each position could understand and empathize with opposing positions instead of locking horns, wasting time competing for the floor, and solving nothing.

Love of homeland is not opposite, but is compatible with planetary citizenship. Genuine solidarity and respect for differences can coexist. It is time to acknowledge the concept that wars and injustices begin in the minds of men and women and that the human family is overdue for a major mind change. Our common humanity can transcend the violence that comes from differences if people can be educated to become better thinkers. Edward de Bono (1992), international authority and teacher of creative thinking, believes that our methods of thinking are antiquated. Our style of argument was set up by the famous Greek gang of three—Socrates, Plato, Aristotle. De Bono says that arriving at the truth by arguing and attacking each other's case is an extremely inefficient method of getting anywhere. Creative flexibility of mind finds ways to accommodate polarized differences in the shared, genuine search for unity.

In addition to flexibility, the factor of originality in thinking processes is recognized and encouraged in the teaching of creativity at all levels of learning. Strategies for overcoming blocks to creative thinking imposed by conforming, standardized educational practices, cultures, emotions, and hostile environments stimulates the production of new ideas for solving problems and meeting challenges. *The Creative Problem Solving Process* (Parnes 1981) teaches the fundamental concept of deferred judgment throughout its five-step process. A mind set for allowing new ideas and alternative ways of behaving to be carefully considered before making critical judgments is a mind set for greater fairness in relationships and less prejudged polarization of opposites.

The Guilford (1968) model of the structure of intellect which gave momentum to the study of creative, divergent thinking, lists the products of thinking in ascending order of complexity: from units up through classes, relationships, systems, transformations, and, finally, implications or the art of visionary thought. New problems and challenges call for new and original solutions. Society's escalating information base demands greater balance and equality with a thinking base that crosses the entire spectrum of human intellectual potential. Without a mental capacity for selective application of information overload the data bank of the mind remains simply a massive collection of facts.

Innovative educational practices based on creative and critical thinking processes are giving increased attention to the metacognitive understanding of the variant powers of the mind, the limited use to which they have been put (fifteen percent by estimate), and the critical need for their greater activation. Fritjov Capra (1990) suggests that the most critical issues of our time have been

excluded from the political dialogue because they cannot be adequately addressed within the current mode of thinking. Our present world view is based on a perception of reality that has dominated our society for the past three hundred years and that has become institutionalized and vested with power, but that is now incapable of conceiving new solutions. Ultimately, all these problems are facets of one single crisis, which is essentially a crisis of perception. (p. 64)

Perceiving and thinking at higher levels of systems, transformations, and implications as presented by Guilford's model is teachable. The teaching of futures studies as advocated by the World Future Society engages the highest level of thinking in terms of implications. Students identify observable trends related to social, technological, economic, environmental, and political issues of the day; they investigate the past development of the trend, and make predictions about the probable, possible, and preferable future of the trend if it continues. Depending upon the positive or negative perceptions of long range predictions, recommendations are made for leadership strategies that would encourage positive trends and intervene in cases of negative trends. Such a use of the mind makes possible the perception of things to come based on recognizable, studied present realities. Strategies for avoiding perceived negative futures can avoid catastrophic crises, and problem solving becomes pro-active rather than reactive.

In addition to the measurable factors in the cognitive domain of creativity, the affective or attitudinal domain of the creative person has relevance to survival in and contribution to a changing, complex world. Creative qualities of independence of thought, risk taking, tolerance for ambiguity, curiosity, and sensitivity mark the creative individualists who have been said to be "the conscience of the crowd." The thoughtful minority voice with the standards of a mature conscience has often been recognized as more ethical, thoughtful, flexible, and fair in judgment than the unengaged conformist when strong differences and disruptions arise. Recognizing and rewarding such qualities of mind where they already exist and teaching systemic, visionary and transformative thinking processes to learners at all levels and in all educational programs could provide support to the natural time consuming evolutionary growth of human intellect.

In fact, in his writing about the psychology of man's possible evolution, the philosopher P. D. Ouspensky (1973) had this to say:

Our fundamental idea shall be that man as we know him is not a completed being; that nature develops him only up to a certain point and then leaves him to develop further by his own efforts and devices, or to live and die such as he was born or to degenerate and lose the capacity for development.

Evolution of man (and woman) [parenthesis added] in this case will mean the development of certain inner qualities and features which usually remain undeveloped and cannot develop by themselves. (p. 8)

Examples of Creative Trends in Universal Education

More than twenty years ago a report to the Club of Rome called attention to the "dichotomy between a growing complexity of our own making and a lagging development of our own capacities" (Botkin et al. 1979). There is growing evidence that the capacity to think creatively and at higher levels is beginning to be specifically addressed in learning opportunities at all levels and across the spectrum of education, business and society in general.

In recent years the global dimension of the trend has been evident in the president's annual convocation held during the annual Creative Problem Solving Institute in Buffalo, New York. Persons engaged in educational leadership in creative studies from Spain, South Africa, Norway, United Kingdom, Mexico, Brazil, Canada, Netherlands, China, Chile, and the United States have attended and continue to network.

In December 1991, the Third European Conference on Creativity and Innovation met at Nordwijk aan Zee in the Netherlands with participants from most European countries as well as from the United States and other parts of the world. Participants represented both educational and business professions. In September 1992, the International Creativity and Innovation Networking Conference was hosted by the Center for Creative Leadership in Greensboro, North Carolina.

A directory of colleges and universities offering a formal course in creativity, developed at the University of Oklahoma, 1991, lists 126 institutions of higher learning from across the United States. It is reasonable to assume that colleges in other parts of the world reflect some of the same trend. Educational programming at elementary and secondary levels has been promoted for many years through the availability of resources and materials for creative thinking and problem solving, led by national and international efforts to stimulate higher level thinking in populations of identified gifted and talented students. Recent trends support the application of creative thinking principles for all students. The right of an individual to create new ideas and to expect a respectful, supportive climate for their expression is a human right too often ignored.

Thinking Talents for an Enlightened Populace

Arieti (1976) suggested that whether it is considered from the viewpoint of its effects on society, or as an expression of the human spirit, creativity stands out as an activity to be studied, cherished, and cultivated.

A great deal of talent important in the transition to a just, global society is lost in the world when creative expression and potential in all persons is discouraged. Characteristics of creative individuals identified in a study by MacKinnon (1978) include: a high level of effective intelligence, an openness to experience, a freedom from crippling restraints and impoverishing inhibitions, an esthetic sensitivity, a cognitive flexibility, an independence in thought and action, an unquestioning commitment to creative endeavor, and an unceasing striving for solutions to ever more difficult problems they set for themselves.

The demands of human participation in the advancing order of global complexity require new understandings, new perceptions, new skills, new behaviors, and, critical to all the rest, new ways of thinking. Freedom of thought, conscience, and religion/ belief is a right proclaimed in Article 18 of the Universal Declaration of Human Rights adopted by the United Nations General Assembly in 1948. The human right to think and be heard at higher, more complex and mutualistic levels is a necessary added freedom if diversity of religion or belief is to be guaranteed for the diverse human family. Luis Machado's *The Right to Be Intelligent* was published in Spanish in 1978 and in English in 1980. He believes that "everyone has, simply by existing, a right to be intelligent and to be provided with a way to become more intelligent. That right must be recognized and held sacred. Above all, the necessary conditions for the exercise of this right must be available. This is society's mission and the primary obligation of its leaders."

Educational Leadership for Creating Change

Why does educational attention to the formal teaching of creative thinking in colleges and universities proceed so slowly? A report of a survey of American colleges and universities (McDonough 1981) provides insights into some of the possible reasons:

1. It is a difficult challenge for traditional colleges to deviate from standard courses.

2. A course in creativity requires the professor conducting the course to surrender the position of authority to assist students in releasing their creative ability. It can be a difficult challenge for some faculty to give up that traditional role of authority.

3. It is possible that some faculty and college administrators may look upon a course in creative thinking processes as lacking traditional academic values.

4. Conducting a course in creativity requires the encouragement of a high level of student involvement, an attitude of flexibility, playfulness, and the enthusiastic commitment and belief in the concept that everyone possesses a creative ability. These requirements may not fit the style of some faculty members.

5. It can be difficult to be specific in classifying and providing a letter grade to the student's knowledge of creativity.

6. Generally, the faculty member who is enthusiastic about creativity develops and promotes the course and not the college administration. That type of person may not be at each college.

7. It is easier to continue to do what has been done in the past.

As is often the case, the role of education in the task of the transition to a just, global society is "long on diagnosis and short on prescription." The role of the educational entrepreneur, often working as a "minority of one" to bring the teaching of creative, critical and other higher orders of thinking into a recognized position requires patience and persistence. It also requires courage, risk taking, and initiative. Colleges and universities organized around the structure of departmentalized, special fields based on content and skills find difficulty with integrating into the official curriculum the interdisciplinary nature of the teaching of thought processes. The role of the change agent, especially in the structured, bureaucratic environment of many institutions of learning, relates well to Harlan Cleveland's (1984) analogy of the leader as the "first bird off the telephone wire" (p. 1).

Cleveland, in an address to the Regional Conference of the World Future Society in Minnesota in August 1991, spoke of the importance of the dialectic between leaders and masses. He suggested that initiative for change and reform comes not from the top down, but that it originates with undesignated leaders and that designated leaders, when they determine the direction of public force for change, provide the organization and codification that help to implement the ideas. The ideal prescription for change would revolve around the harmonized efforts of undesignated leadership initiatives and official, designated influential leadership with power to implement new world view thinking on a grand scale. Cleveland's reference to the role of students in the process of social and political change is a reminder of the responsibility of educationists to design curricula at all levels that will educate the masses to think for themselves. Creative thinking styles and attitudes reflect his list of qualities to be encouraged: a generalist mind-set and lively curiosity, interest in other thinkers, attitudes for risk, a sense that crises are normal, a sense of personal responsibility, and "unwarranted optimism."

Creative Leadership for a Global Future: Studies and Speculations (Bleedorn 1988) reports results of a survey on perceptions of talents critical to effective leadership for a global future and the degree to which such talents were being currently addressed in American schooling. The talent for creativity was perceived to be most important; in general, the highest ranking talents were perceived to be least addressed. A like survey with more global participation and conducted against the backdrop of the current zeitgeist could have significant results. If educational change is to go forward, talents for creative leadership that challenges educational norms are prerequisite.

Summary

It has been said that on Spaceship Earth there are no passengers. Everyone is crew. When systems for freedom and democracy function according to stated design, everyone involved bears responsibility not only for knowledge, but also for processing information creatively and critically to arrive at participation in judgments that perceive beyond self-interest to the common good, beyond our region and beyond our time.

Since society's capacity for change depends upon the thinking capacity of individuals who make it up, enlightened universal education will have to foster learning that will produce planetary leadership talents, while at the same time protect the national and cultural diversities of the global family. Although some of the planet's resources are finite, the reason for unwarranted optimism is that the human mind is unlimited in its capacity to think, grow, plan ahead, and act in terms for the common good. The role of education is critical to the challenge (Botstein 1997).

Ervin Laszlo, in his presentation to the Third International Dialogue on the Transition to Global Society in 1992, had the message:

> In the rapid transformation produced by globalization and informatization, the role of the individual is crucial. Individual creativity must unfold to its fullest extent, and it can unfold only if the individual has the optimum—which is never the maximum—freedom of thought, expression and action.... encouraging the creativity of individuals and enabling the fruits of such creativity to penetrate to the full social organism. For this reason freedom in thinking, in expression, and in action is a paradigmatic requirement of transition to a just global society. (p.21)

Developing Leadership With Vision

*No system can stay vital for long unless some of its leaders remain suffi-
ciently independent to help it to change and grow.*

—John Gardner

If talents for leadership were a part of our genetic heritage, educators wouldn't be
faced with the educational challenge to produce leaders. Further, if leadership talents were constants to history there would be established formulae to guide education. Such is a luxury and security that education does not have. The
development of talent for leadership with vision and a sense of the system in a
global future is a responsibility of education. The questions arise: What are those
talents? Does anyone know? Who has the vision to perceive them?

Changes in technology have brought humankind to new dimensions in their
perceptions of reality. Pictures of the earth from space are scattered throughout our
consciousness. Earth no longer has frames or boundaries. The message is clear. We
are a global commons. It doesn't require much reflection to realize that technology
and communication systems have interrelated the global family socially, environmentally, economically, technologically, and certainly politically.

A less obvious, but equally dramatic, development is the paradigm shift in the
talents seen as critical for effective leadership and followership in a global, futuristic, rapidly evolving spaceship earth. A goal of education is to prepare its citizens to function in their society. The time has come to perceive societies as
extending beyond narrowly perceived nationalistic borders and to envision an
integrated, interactive, dynamic planetary system that includes individuals,
groups, organizations, institutions, global realities (Mestenhauser 1997).

In an effort to develop guidelines for educators to join in the effort to educate
for leadership with vision, a survey was conducted to determine public perceptions
of qualities and talents critical for functioning effectively in roles of leadership
and followership with a mind for the world as it is coming to be (Bleedorn 1988).
Three disparate populations were surveyed to determine a cross-section of perceptions. A total of 105 subjects (educators, college students, and business leaders)
were asked for their perceptions of high priority talents for effective leadership in

37

a global future. In addition, they were asked to indicate their perception of talents that were currently addressed in American educational practices.

The results of the survey left no doubt that many of the talents perceived to be important were not being addressed in education in proportion to their perceived priority. A major finding was the group's placement of creativity as the number one priority rating. According to the data, the degree of attention given to the development of creative talent by the schools was out of sync with its order of importance. Observations of traditional school programs suggest continued need for creative reform.

The complexity of the world has broadened the scope of information and thinking processes needed by the citizens of a country, and deliberate measures for updating the learning experiences are in desperate need of attention. Traditional transactional leadership is being replaced by transforming leadership in which leadership and followership meet in interaction to achieve a common purpose (Burns 1978). According to the concept of situational leadership, the style and function of the leader depends upon the conditions of the particular situation. The leader needs to have the skills to function appropriately in each mode: authoritarian, consultative, participatory, and laissez-faire.

What, then, are the talents to be recognized and cultivated so that needs of leadership for a new age will be productively and harmoniously served? The question requires insight and vision. Although there were marked differences among the perceptions of the three groups in the survey (Bleedorn 1988), the composite ratings have significance as representative of a cross-section population. Ranked in order of priority, the top five perceived talents were:

1. Creativity
2. Change agentry
3. Academic skills
4. World focus
5. Pluralistic attitudes

Lowest ranking talents (lowest listed first) were:

1. Visionary talent
2. Multi-lingual talent

3. Listening ability

4. Sense of humor

5. Curiosity (p.73)

When respondents were asked to indicate their thoughts as to which of the talents on the list were being addressed in current educational practices, they named:

1. Academic skills

2. Communication skills

3. Goal-directed skills

4. Information retrieval skills

5. Organizational ability (p. 77)

The respondents identified twelve of the talents that they perceived as not being effectively taught in schools. Those talents were:

Tolerance for ambiguity	Multi-lingual talents
Commitment to service	Other-directed attitudes
Curiosity	Spiritual awareness
Empathy	Synthesizing skills
Humanistic attitudes	Visionary talent
Moral/ethical talents	Talent for world focus (p. 77)

According to the perceptions of those in the study, it was clear that they saw sequential, logical thinking skills forming the bulk of the learning experience in schools. The talents associated with creative thinking were not perceived by this group to be emphasized in educational programs. Such qualities as flexibility, respect for differences, and a general capacity to be comfortable, fair, and productive in a rapidly changing, complex, often unpredictable society were, according to this group, rarely touched upon by schools.

The nature of the times requires an educational effort to recognize and develop *processes* of thinking along with the traditional teaching of *content*. Creative thinking (the number one priority according to those surveyed in this study) has been finding its way into in-service seminars for educators as well as training and development programs for business and social services. The teaching of creative problem-solving, decision-making, and conflict resolution skills is becoming a somewhat familiar practice within schools and corporations alike. But not fast enough or intense enough if the world is going to be looking at the next generation for its leadership. The cultivation of the appropriate skills needs attention now, not only in the United States but worldwide. The predictive identification of those skills is an early step in their actualization.

Adding the teaching of thinking processes to the standard curricula of information and skills requires deliberate educational entrepreneurship and maybe even courage. The fixed organizational patterns and powers in many educational establishments present formidable challenges to change agents within the system. In spite of the challenges, new directions in learning and thinking are being designed and introduced at all levels by teachers committed to the teaching of metacognitive concepts and their application.

An example from a new offering in a university entrepreneurship program makes the case. Following the successful teaching of a course on creative problem solving, at the request of students a follow-up course was designed, tested, and approved by the curriculum committee. The course was designed to take students well beyond the teaching of creative thinking to an expanded perception of a new view of the world as a dynamic, integrated system dependent on the quality thinking of its people.

The basic objectives of the course were stated as follows:

To recognize current trends in the emerging global society and to practice predictions of possible, probable, and preferable futures.

To study the concepts of change and breakpoint as they apply to speculations regarding the twenty-first century.

To practice thinking processes that help to integrate and interrelate issues regarding social, technological, environmental, economic, and political futures.

To contribute to understandings of the importance of the unity of differences in a culturally pluralistic global society.

To participate in the productive exchange of ideas and opinions in the development of group learning.

To prepare for responsible participation in a twenty-first Century arena of human affairs and career activities.

To develop thinking (creative, critical, paradoxical, visionary, global, and systemic) appropriate for life in a changing, dynamic, complex world.

Two texts were required: *Breakpoint and Beyond: Mastering the Future Today* (Land and Jarman 1992), and *Birth of A New World: An Open Moment for International Leadership* (Cleveland 1993). Class periods focused on active participation in individual and group thinking and learning activities. Requirements included field trips, interviews, mind mapping reviews of readings, think pieces, and individual and group final projects.

The course evaluations testify to the serious nature of university student thinking in spite of much of the negative perception of attitudes of Generation X. They also suggest that students appreciate the opportunity to think and be heard when the issue relates so directly to their own life. Excerpts from the narrative course evaluations provide these comments:

"Excellent because it goes beyond the needs of business and indeed of the U.S. and encourages, even requires us, to view issues from a global perspective which will probably be the most valuable tool we can bring into the twenty-first century."

"Truly a revolutionary, forward thinking, amazing experience. Why isn't education always this much fun and this rewarding? I really want to know."

"The way the class was structured and the stimulating class discussions made for a great class and a great learning experience."

"The concepts taught in this course are some of the most important I have learned in my time at this university. This program should be a required part of the business major and perhaps any major. The ideas are so valuable."

"I love classes that give students a chance to enhance their creativity, draw in guest speakers, and allow presentations and group interaction."

"This course was excellent in helping me to develop a better understanding of where the world was in the past, how it is in the present, and how it will be in the future or twenty-first century."

"An excellent course that all students should be required to take."

"This was a good follow-up to 250 (Creative Problem Solving). The topics were talked about in a more in depth conversation."

"I hope all that was discussed throughout the semester somehow affects the life we're living now and as we progress into the twenty-first century. In my eyes I know this has been one of the best experiences I've had."

Time and global change are set on the fast forward button. Space shots of the earth are reminders that the "little blue marble" that is our earth is a tiny, vulnerable part of an immense universe that depends upon the vision and judgment of its leadership and followership for its quality of life and maybe even for its survival. Educators worldwide are key players in the leadership scenario that will do much to shape the future of the human species and their planetary home.

Values, Laws, and Ideologies in the Context of Creativity

Humanity, the spirit of the earth, the synthesis of individuals and people, the paradoxical conciliation of the element with the whole, of the one with the many: all these are regarded as utopian fantasies, yet they are biologically necessary and if we would see them made flesh in the world, what more need we do than imagine our power to love growing and broadening till it can embrace the totality of men and of the earth?

—Teilhard de Chardin

The following definitions and observations on the subject of values, laws, and ideologies serve to provide a philosophical base for the exploration of connections between them and the emerging discipline of creativity.

I. Observations on Values from the Literature

The concepts of value are profound and difficult exactly because they do two things at once; they join men into societies, and yet they preserve for them a freedom which makes them single men. A philosophy which does not acknowledge both needs cannot evolve values, and indeed cannot allow them. (Bronowski 1965, 55)

These are the measures we call indices of the social values. It is through their use that we are able to determine systematically the degree of value distribution affected by any of our institutional practices. They are power, respect, rectitude, affection, well-being, economic security or wealth, skill, and enlightenment.... Transcendental or transsocial values which are highly prized among millions of people, are not considered in this framework, since they are not subject to systematic observation and appraisal. (Arnspiger, Rucker, and Preas 1969, 32–36)

When I use the term, "values," I shall be referring to those "standards (of behavior) which you have in your mind." (Gardner 1968, 28)

I then go on to show how the other values derive from truth. There are the personal values—respect, sensitivity, tolerance—without which science could not be carried on. They are the "is" values—the values of the man working by himself. And then there are the communal values, the "ought" values—honesty, integrity, dignity, authenticity—which bind the scientific community together. (Bronowski 1978, 132)

I am thinking about their lives—their personal relations, their loves and rejections, their community with themselves and with others. These are the values that industrial society destroys. And in their place it puts nothing: a blank. (Bronowski 1965, 110)

Values are rooted in the very conditions of human existence—hence our knowledge of these conditions (the human situation) leads us to establishing values which have objective validity, existing only with regard to the existence of man. Outside of him there are no values. (Margenau 1959, 151)

 All values come from unselfish motives…everything we judge to be of value…is all of God. (Suzuki 1959, 95)

II. Observations on Laws from the Literature

Justice is probably the oldest and most universally professed value…. Nature is unjust, humans are often unjust, yet we refuse to live in a world without the idea of justice…. We want justice mainly for ourselves, but commitment to the value is to be measured by our efforts to ensure that justice is done to others….even to those with whom we disagree—the value takes on meaning only when we build justice into social institutions….for the continuing growth and evolution of values, the generations must mingle. (Gardner 1968, 31)

 The whole structure of values, beliefs, laws, and standards by which a society lives must be continuously restored, or it disintegrates. It will survive and flourish only if people continuously renew the values and reinterpret tradition to make it serve contemporary needs. (Gardner 1968, 23)

As soon as the law becomes a device, then the whole relation between "law of nature" and "law of man," between "is" and "ought" is lost. The distinction is lost as soon as the law becomes a means of manipulating people into jail.… Once you introduce the system of the law as a device (the protection of the status quo by legal means) you finish up not with society against criminals, but with two gangs: one called the police and the other called criminals.… Having said those things about the general tendency for the law to become an entity of its own beyond justice, what I call "the insolence of office"…I come back to the central point about the cement of science which I now believe is the cement for any lasting community. (Bronowski 1978, 135–136)

Legislation is too limited in its purview to establish the most embracive, moral, aesthetic, and logical values—not to speak of the philosophic uncertainties which still becloud the scene of jurisprudence. (Margenau 1959, 45)

Law-binding custom or practice of a community; a rule or model of conduct or action formally recognized as binding by a supreme authority or made obligatory by sanction; a means of redressing wrongs.… Natural Law: Body of law derived from nature and binding upon human society in the absence of or in addition to institutional law. (Unabridged Dictionary 1968)

The moral law is man's own essential nature appearing as commanding authority. If man were united with himself and his essential being, there would be no command. But man is estranged from himself, and the values he experiences appear as laws, natural and positive laws, demanding, threatening, promising. Nevertheless, it is not a strange, heteronomous power which gives authority to the law; it is man's own essential being. (Tillich 1959, 195)

III. Observations on Ideologies from the Literature

In general there are two distinct and separable meanings of the term, "ideology," the particular and the total. The particular conception of ideology is implied when the term denotes that we are skeptical of the ideas and representations advanced by our opponent. They are regarded as more or less conscious disguises of the real nature of a situation, the true recognition of which would not be in accord with his interests.… In the more inclusive total conception of ideology…we refer to the ideology of an age or of a concrete historic-social group, e.g., of a class, when we are concerned with the characteristics and composition of the total structure of the mind of his epoch or of this group.… Neither relies solely on what is actually said by the oppo-

nent in order to reach an understanding of his real meaning and intention…not taken at their face value, but are interpreted in the light of the life-
situation of the one who expresses them. (Manneheim 1968, 49–50)

The term "group ideology"…can only mean that a group of persons, either in
their immediate reactions to the same situation or as a result of direct psychic
interaction, react similarly…and are subject to the same illusions…every
individual participates only in certain fragments of this thought system
(Weltanschauung), the totality of which is not in the least a mere sum of these
fragmentary individual experiences. (Manneheim 1968, 52)

Ideologies are the situationally transcendent ideas which never succeed de
facto in the realization of their projected contents. Though they often become
the good-intentioned motives for the subjective conduct of the individual,
when they are actually embodied in practice, their meanings are most frequently distorted. (Manneheim 1968, 175)

Ideology: Visionary speculation; often idle theorizing; impractical theory or
system of theories; a systematic scheme or coordinated body of ideas or concepts, especially about human life or culture; a manner or the content of
thinking characteristic of an individual, group, or culture; the integrated
assertions, theories, and aims that constitute a sociopolitical program; an
extremist sociopolitical program or philosophy constructed wholly or in part
on factitious or hypothetical ideational bases. (Unabridged Dictionary, 1968)

The only way to settle questions of an ideological nature or controversial
issues among the people is by the democratic method, the method of discussion, of criticism, of persuasion and education, and not by the method of
coercion or repression. (Mao Tse-Tung in Schram 1967, 28–29)

Values, Laws, and Ideologies Relationships to the Discipline of Creativity

To embark on a personal interpretation of values, laws, ideologies, and their
interrelationships is to confront the dilemma of their essence—the translation into
communicable form that which lies so deeply within one's consciousness as to be
inarticulable—that state of mind which has been referred to as the "dancing sys-

tem." The term is said to have its origin in the dance of Shiva from Hindu mythology. In a paper presented at the World Futures Conference in Toronto in 1980, Richard Bergeron introduced the concept of dancing systems when he said that often education is a hindrance to understanding these systems. Susuki Roshi, a Zen master, would tell his students that in the beginner's mind there are many possibilities, but in the expert's there are few (Zukav 1979). These systems may be understood at times, but they are impossible to describe verbally, logically, or mathematically.

Time, Trends, and Possibilities

Any synthesis of definitions and concepts drawn from the literature represented in this discussion will need to add the dimension of time beyond and time forward; i.e., the time beyond the dated literature up to the present, as well as time forward as a speculation into the future. The recent years have placed increasing emphasis on the disease of valuelessness and philosophy of meaninglessness (von Bertalanffy 1959) pervading contemporary society. People whose energies and expectations form the fabric of that society, feel torn away from any fundamental union with nature, as the age of science and technology widens the gap between rapid advances in machine/man-made environments and the growth of human consciousness with its potential to deal positively with the increasing complexities and demands of the present age.

The escalation of change in science and global communication systems has heightened awareness and produced conflicts, the resolutions of which are beyond established guidelines. Law lacks the ability to transform itself. The letter of the law is inflexible. Legalistic theory does not provide standards for the increasingly interdependent ethical and moral affairs of daily life. Eric Fromm (Fromm and Xirau 1968) has suggested that if values are vague, and if they are always too broad for the concrete and specific case, the only thing left is to trust our instincts. Certainly this is a time when differences between values and behavior and the gradual disintegration of familiar customs, traditions, and communities have created uncertainties and stress in our lives and institutions. The effort to insure the social values indexed by Arnspiger et al. (1969) through language, exhortation, and law continue to fail. Selfish ambitions and single-issue politics clash and compete. Power and authority are abused, and nepotism displaces excellence—

where a virtuous exterior may clothe piety or duplicity (Gardner 1978) and where young people are said to think of the state of public affairs not as a "credibility gap," but as a "hypocrisy gap."

The progress and direction of these discouraging trends is difficult to determine. There are hopeful signals that a reversal may be in process and in acceleration. As might be expected, the leadership toward a new age of being and becoming stems, not from institutions, laws, and bureaucracies, but from the ranks of the people, from scholars and from those with creative, altruistic urges reflecting the idealized, mutualistic laws of nature. Such laws are not foreign to human beings, as cynics might suppose, but are natural expressions of the emergence of a new symbolic universe of values (von Bertalanffy 1959).

Growth of Consciousness

If we can believe, in spite of our observation of the primary, more ubiquitous, particular values, that humans are in the process of evolving to a higher level of consciousness with capabilities for thinking in systems, for dealing effectively and comfortably with the complexities and contradictions of the world—then we can act together on the principle that "values are not rules, but are those deeper illuminations in whose light justice and injustice, good and evil, means and ends are seen in fearful sharpness of outline…. the values by which we are to survive" (Bronowski 1965, 94).

Creative Balance in Human Potential

The vigorous assessment of man's potential from the writing of Eric Fromm (1968) are reasons for faith that man's urge to transcend the role of creature to creator, to grow beyond passivity and apathy toward a sense of identity with the systems, both immediate and cosmic, within which he finds himself, and to become oriented in the world intellectually; all these predictions and expectations are well founded. Allport tells us that the individual desire for personal status is insatiable. Motivations for status cause individuals to spend energies in a variety of directions and intensities. Maslow (1959) sees needs as values. He suggests that although some values are common to mankind, idiosyncratic needs generate idiosyncratic values, and that capacities clamor to be used, and cease their clamor only when they are used sufficiently. Western society, with its value and reward system firmly placed on left brain processes of analysis, quantifications, and rationality, has traditionally deprived itself, through social and educational institutions, of the influence and values of right brain creative, intuitive, holistic urges (Ornstein 1977). Metaphysical insights and excursions into the transcendental wisdom of Eastern philosophy also need to be incorporated into the pragmatism and specificity of the West.

One of the idiosyncratic needs inherent in the human organism is the need to create, to bring order out of chaos. Where the chaos identified is of a social nature and the urge to confront the task is strong enough, leadership emerges. Bronowski (1965) reminds us that independence and originality are qualities of the mind, and when a society elevates them to values, as ours has done, it must protect them by giving a special value to their expression. The endorsement of dissent by bureaucratic institutions is a major hurdle in the necessary course of a moral transformation of humankind and the man-made universe. Human nature is capable of creative altruism. A paradigm shift from a competitive society based on materialistic values and hierarchies of power to a cooperative society based on material/spiritual balance and symbiotic, synergic power is imperative for the future of the global family.

Such a transformation would be possible if understandings of human differences in thinking and learning styles were honored and applied in centers of power. Whether recent developments in the psychology of consciousness (Ornstein 1977) are perceived neurophysiologically or metaphorically, the actualization of right/left hemispheric balance in educational and social leadership is fundamental to an enlightened value system for a new age.

Values in Transformation

Marilyn Ferguson, editor of *Brain/Mind Bulletin,* continues to provide a support system for creative altruism. *The Aquarian Conspiracy: Personal and Social Transformations in the '80s* (Ferguson 1980) is a reminder to individuals concerned with the need for social transformation that they are not alone in their efforts to contribute to positive change. Her book is a broad and detailed record of a dynamic network of individuals, social groups, and organizations representing the "conspiracy," silent but understood, and so identified from the dictionary definition of "conspire—to breathe together." Personal growth and social growth are not mutually exclusive. We develop ourselves to show others how to develop themselves. The sum of individual styles forms a culture, and when individual growth reaches a critical mass, the culture reforms itself.

The penultimate aim is for a conspiracy based on a passage of love between men and women of good will. General Systems theories advanced by Teilhard de Chardin (1964) provide a construct for the process of growth (personal, cosmic, and everything in between) from divergence to convergence to emergence.

Leadership

With confidence in the laws of nature to produce growth and evolution in all living forms over time, we can dare to perceive the beginnings of transformation in the phase of divergence and the testing of alternative values preliminary to convergent choice and the resulting emergence to a new age. For this massive paradigm shift in society to occur, leadership values of action and risk taking, modeling, tolerance, and self-forgiveness need visible expression.

A shift in educational patterns is critical to necessary shifts in social values. Leadership is needed in the understanding and actualization of new educational paradigms:

From	**To**
Emphasis on content, acquiring a body of "right" information once and for all	Emphasis on learning how to learn, how to ask good questions, and pay attention to and evaluate new concepts
Learning as a product, a destination Priority on performance	Learning as a process, a journey Priority on self-image as a generator of performance
Emphasis on analytical, linear, "left-brain" rationality	Striving for whole-brain education, thinking augmenting "left-brain" with holistic, nonlinear and intuitive strategies
Concern with norms	Concern with individual's performance in terms of potential (Ferguson 1980, 289–291)

The list suggests a shift in the educational value system toward the student as subject and away from student as customer in a highly organized, standardized, categorized, competitive, quantifiable operation. If leadership, in the urge for transformation, continues its expansion and influence, there is reason to hope that the zeitgeist or volksgeist of the coming age will reflect a social value system based on a unity of consciousness-dynamic and in constant process of becoming.

Personal Definitions

From the foregoing, it must be reasonably clear that my personal belief system leans toward positiveness. Such a position must have its base in the idealistic assumption that we are capable of continued growth toward mutuality, change and transformation; in fact, that our biological destiny is to grow or die (Land 1973). There is a necessary tentativeness in my commitment to the following personal definitions, derived from lectures, readings, and reflections:

Values. The principal component of choice, decision, and behavior in both reflective and/or spontaneous response.

Laws and Systems. Both natural and man-made, which attempt to organize and balance interactions between inner and outer space.

Ideologies. Stated visions of utopia incapable of practical implementation when acted upon by time and other realities.

In spite of the esoteric nature of a discourse on values, laws, and ideologies, educators would do well to consider their relationship to the familiar pragmatic purpose of education. Schools are called to lead the public mind to new philosophical dimensions that reflect our values, respect our laws, and determine the ideologies that define collective global aspirations.

Creativity and Business

Human Capital and the Profit Line

Acquaintance both with schools of education and with schools of business and entrepreneurship has positioned me to recognize the critical nature of relationships between studies of human behavior and the practical concerns of the business "bottom line." Traditional polarizations between qualitatively and quantitatively based disciplines are already giving way to the force of creativity as an integrative process for mutuality and growth. New challenges in a globally competitive marketplace have greater need than ever of creative, innovative thinkers and doers.

There is a strong possibility that the practical demands of business for new leadership will be the force that will overcome the old perceived polarities between specialized fields of education and business. Impressions have been that education and the behavioral sciences exist in one camp and the world of dollars and cents in another. Education is too theoretical for serious business attention and the practical down-to-earth business operation is often disdained by educators as too simplistic. The science of business has seemed to hold that nothing is real unless it is measurable and countable, researched, analyzed, surveyed, and translated to numbers. The uncountable factors of worker loyalty, flexibility, and commitment to excellence don't often make it into the success formula. Now with changes in the work culture and a new importance assigned to the quality of work life by employees, a better understanding of individual human differences and talents becomes fundamental to the art of leadership, efficiency, productivity, and profit.

A new reality is finding its way into leadership strategies that acknowledge the unlimited creativity present and largely ignored and wasted in traditional hierarchical systems of management. Absolute labeling and categorizing of jobs and people have had a seriously limiting effect on motivation in the workplace, especially among highly creative thinkers and innovative workers. Enlightened corporations and institutions are opening new doors and removing old barriers to the creative energies ready to contribute to the well-being and growth of the system. Discussions of spirit, teamwork, initiative, and risk taking are joining the meeting agenda dealing with figures, charts, reports, and tabulations.

Integration of the countable with the uncountable, the quantitative with the qualitative, is heralding a new interpretation of leadership. *Intellectual Capital: Realizing Your Company's True Value by Finding Its Hidden Roots* (Edvinsson, L. and Malone 1997) is among the more recent and relevant titles addressing the issue of the profitable reality of the uncountable in business. In its more advanced applications, the transition to an increasingly humanistic workplace includes recognition of soul and spirituality at work. A current best seller has the provocative title of *Chicken Soup for the Soul: 101 Stories of Courage, Compassion, and Creativity in the Workplace.*

This section on creativity and business is designed to point out the need for creativity and innovation in business for moving the workplace into considerations of human capital as a constant resource to be recognized, cultivated, and rewarded. Concepts of forces for change and growth are not new to the business community. Authorities like Tom Peters (1987) have, for some time, been pointing out to management the power of creative habits of mind at all levels of authority, up, down, and across. There remains an urgency for translating intentions into actions.

Creativity Has Countable Value

We can build systems which facilitate creativity, rather than be preoccupied with checks and controls on people who are motivated to beat or exploit the system. I believe that everyone wants to find both quality and life in work.

—Warren Bennis

The critical business of creating positive change and responding positively to change in the workplace is bringing studies of creativity and new ways of solving old problems into sharper focus throughout the business world. New ways of thinking creatively, critically, with a perception of the system and a vision of the future are being taught in educational and business settings alike. Increasingly, business interests are calling on education for increased efforts to produce a work force that can think in ways that help meet the challenges of change in dynamic, complex systems. Conferences on creativity and innovation are being marketed throughout the world; a recent example is the First International Creativity Conference in South Africa at the University of the Orange Free State, Bloemfontein, in September 1995.

The business place that recognizes the uncountable value of its creative workers and provides them with a safe environment for new ideas is capitalizing on an important resource for survival in the competitive global marketplace of the 1990s. Creative attitudes and behaviors represent real human capital in an organization in spite of the fact that they seem unmeasurable and uncountable. Clearly creativity is becoming a major management agenda item as we approach the twenty-first century. Leon Royer, executive director of organizational learning at the 3M Company in Minnesota, says that either you will learn to acquire and cultivate creative people or you will be eaten alive. Royer suggests that cultivating the most creatively talented offers an additional benefit. Companies that provide a nurturing climate for creative minds find that it stimulates better creative efforts and spirit from every employee.

Star-Tribune, *Minneapolis. Reprinted with permission.*

Considering studies of leadership and human behavior, education and business are becoming partners in providing training in the discipline of creativity. The Creative Education Foundation in Buffalo, New York, along with countless scholars in the field of educational psychology, have been providing answers to the lingering question, "Can creativity be taught?" Yes. Both quantitative and qualitative research show that the creativity quotient increases with training and practice. Professors in the field of creative studies are inclined to think of the process of "teaching creativity" more like the process of setting free a natural function of the human mind and spirit to produce innovative ideas and make original connections. A seminal theory of the structure of human intellect by J. P. Guilford (1968) identifies divergent or creative thinking as one of the five basic operations of the mind, along with the function of memory. Everyone has it. As in the case of memory, individuals differ in the degree of development.

The task of training or teaching for creative development in the workplace is largely a task of providing an environment and an open-ended structure for the free expression of new ideas. Individuals need a climate of support for new ways of thinking in order to overcome the blocks to creativity that have been accumulated through years of conforming to traditionally absolute thinking standards. Barriers imposed by standardized educational practices and expectations can destroy the creative spirit and freeze the human instinct for personal identity. The addition of arbitrarily imposed social and cultural norms and prescriptions can silence the most creative natures. The accumulated blocks to creativity give way to a greater freedom of thought when the external environmental blocks are modified.

Specific environmental blocks to creativity often cited include:

A lack of trust and cooperation among colleagues

Autocratic bosses and supervisors who value only their own ideas and have trouble recognizing those of others

A demanding schedule that leaves no time for thinking and reflection

Frantic pace of modern life as a constant norm

Lack of organizational structure and support for considering new ideas and bringing them into action

Organizations are looking for ways to better understand the highly creative person, whose style often represents a particular challenge in a traditional workplace. Studies of behavioral characteristics of the creative adult reveal qualities of complexity and contradiction. Both positive and negative characteristics define creative styles that often fail to fit into existing patterns of operation.

On the positive side, highly creative persons are inclined to be intuitive, curious and perceptive, independent in thought and action, energetic and task driven, able to deal with complexities and ambiguities, given to broad, lateral interests, open to new experiences, and motivated toward high standards and improvement. However, behavioral traits associated with the creative personality can be disruptive to established norms and perceived as negative. These can include a critical attitude, sometimes described as "divine discontent," impatience with the status quo, resistance to short-sightedness and authoritarian control policies, preference for autonomy, problems with consensus, boredom with routine, a constant need for stimulation, and an inclination for honest risk taking and unpopular opinions.

Working with the complexities of the highly creative adult in the workplace presents the paradoxical companion challenge of capitalizing on the particular and priceless human resource they represent. The competitive nature of the marketplace is moving business to find ways to better understand and "exploit" the entire array and diversity of talents present and often unrecognized in organizations.

One of the most effective ways of utilizing creative people is to become acquainted with the positive and negative factors of their nature through educational studies of creativity. In addition to understanding the creative person, the discipline of creative studies includes the creative process, the creative product, and the creative press (environment or climate).

Training in the creative process depends necessarily upon experiential learning and direct participation in creative, critical thinking, and problem-solving exercises (Kinsey Goman 1989). Such direct, purposeful experiences help to change old habits of inflexible thinking imposed on the creative mind through years of educational and social conditioning. Seminars and workshops in creative thinking and problem solving strategies help make the shift from old mental habits to the discovery of a "capacity for new capacities" in individuals and teams across any system.

For any organization dealing with the challenges of change, the general expectation is that training and development in creative thinking and problem solving skills will affect the cultural climate specifically and sometimes dramatically. That expectation is often met. In the year following a pair of seminars these observable results were reported by a local industry:

> Expanded thinking
> Freshness of approach to problems
> Personal growth
> Respect for differences
> New perceptions
> More innovative initiatives

Traditional differences within an organization erode the spirit and power necessary for concerted, positive action. A diversity of individuals working together to achieve clearly defined company goals contributes best when each person brings to the challenge a mind-set of creative attitudes—flexibility, initiative, perseverance, energy, vision, and commitment. Honoring such attitudes in the workplace can have a very real effect on the human need for job satisfaction and the sense of personal significance that follows when contributions are recognized.

The more qualitative, uncountable business of education in the "soft science" of human behavior and potential is teaming up with the quantitative business of countable profit. The old polarities between business and education are coming together in a way that accounts for the creative human spirit as a realistic factor in the competitive marketplace.

Engineering and the Creative Process: It's the Real Think

Perhaps our need is not so much for more scientists and engineers but for
more creative *scientists and engineers.*

—E. Paul Torrance

This chapter examines the relationships between the science of engineering and the role of creative education in the preparation of engineering excellence. It makes a case for adding to formal education the specific teaching of process of creative thinking. It presents an overview of the elements of creative thinking, i.e., person, process, product, and press. Finally, it discusses the relationship between engineering and intuition.

The challenge to restructure engineering education to meet world needs is a formidable one, and represents an important piece of the basic challenge of restructuring all of education. Even more fundamental than that is the challenge to education of teaching and learning a totally new way of thinking for a totally new kind of world (Bleedorn 1992), since every important thing we do is affected by our habits of mind (Ruggiero 1988).

Demands of a radically changing, interactive, chaotic world require new perceptive, creative uses of the mind across the entire spectrum of academic disciplines. A conference at Massachuesetts Institute of Technology in July 1994, had the theme, "Improving the Quality of Thinking in a Changing World." More than a thousand people from all parts of the world and representing the entire scope of specialization met as an integrated learning community to think about processes of thinking—creative, critical, paradoxical, global, futuristic, systemic, and more.

For many years American education (and, most likely, the process of education worldwide) has paid little attention to studies of the mind, its works, and its potential. Learning was delivered and practiced with a minimum of attention to individ-

Paper presented at the Fourth World Conference on Engineering Education, October 15–20, 1995, St. Paul, Minnesota.

ual differences and innate learning/thinking styles. Curricula have focused on the teaching of basic skills, facts, formulas, and "right answer" thinking. Scholastic records and rewards have favored students who showed up well in standardized tests and comparative statistics based on the bell curve. The organization of colleges and universities has supported the specialization and isolation of fields of study with little official regard for the integration of ideas and the perception of the reality of knowledge as an open-ended, self-organizing system. Development of the natural human capacity to explore, experiment, discover new patterns and create new products has been, for most students, left to chance.

For many years educational literature regarding the importance of individual differences and the integrative nature of learning has been slow to move from paper and pronouncements to realistic applications and practice. Certainly, until recent times, the polarization between schools of engineering and schools of education has been fairly fixed. The warning words of Buckminster Fuller (1977, 1983) have applied in his reminder that the current urge for specialization is causing us to lose the sense of the total system and our individual place within it. The global, intricate complexities of a new kind of world "disorder" are demanding paradigm shifts to new responsibilities of institutionalized education at all levels and fields of learning, including engineering education. Meeting world needs requires that all institutions and all players on the world stage shift their thinking into a new gear.

The good news is that separations and polarities are finding ways of coming together for mutual growth. A world conference on Engineering Education in 1995 was an opportunity to bring before an assembled group of scientists and educators a discussion of new ways of thinking across the entire spectrum of specialization.

A convincing argument can be made for the importance of the specific teaching of creative thinking processes as a vehicle for bringing into productive relationships the traditions of exact quantitative sciences with the more qualitative studies of creativity within educational psychology and the behavioral sciences. A work force of creative thinkers and inventive problem solvers adds a vital positive force to the globally competitive marketplace of products and services.

"Imagineering," the title of a panel at that world conference, represents a synthesis of differences. The term combines the scientific engineering discipline with the use of the imagination through the educational discipline of creative studies. The panel represents an integration of creative educators and creative practitioners from "the real" corporate world. Members of the panel included the director of the MBA program, University of St. Thomas; a professor of engineering from the Department of Engineering, University of St. Thomas; an engineer from 3M Company; a research scientist from General Mills; and the director of the Institute for Creative Studies at St. Thomas.

There are hopeful signs that new, creative ways of teaching and learning are finding their way into university course catalogues. From the point of view of an "educational entrepreneur" I can report that fifteen years ago when I introduced courses on creativity and problem solving in graduate education, entrepreneurship, and business communication, the University of St. Thomas was one of a very few higher educational institutions that offered academic credit for courses that specifically taught the process of creative thinking. At the undergraduate level the course has been required in the entrepreneurship program. Since that time the proliferation of courses in colleges and universities, both national and international, deliberately teaching creativity and other higher level thinking processes has been dramatic. At the same time, training and development programs in creative thinking and problem solving throughout the business community have continued to expand.

An interesting example of the global dimensions of applied creativity comes from South Africa where new ways of thinking and creative problem solving are having positive political and social effects on that country's challenge of creating a new, integrated society. *The Spirit of African Transformation Management* (Lovemore and Maree 1995) describes the African concept of "ubuntu," a creative process of thinking at a level of paradox that harmonizes differences and perceives the workplace as an integrative, interactive system. In September 1995, the first International Creativity Conference in South Africa met at the university in Bloemfontein. The theme of the conference was *Creativity by Choice, Not Chance*. The director of the conference was Dr. Kobus Neethling, whose preparation for creative leadership includes studies in this country with Dr. E. Paul Torrance, international pioneer and authority on creativity.

The South African conference theme recognized that creativity is too important to be left to chance, and that the demands of a radically changing world and marketplace require activation of the creative, innovative talents of everyone.

Enlightened educational leadership in many places is making the choice of recognizing creativity as "a new psychology" and including the specific teaching of creativity throughout the curricula (Swede 1993).

Good thinking has a direct influence on good engineering. It provides access to unbridled imaginative power as well as to the strict discipline and painstaking care of responsible science. Universities have traditionally educated engineers to retain formulas and uphold the scientific method. Technical subjects have taken full precedence over the teaching of creative and other higher level thinking processes that result in new product design, invention, product improvement, process redesign, waste reduction, and more.

An example of the relevance of creative education to inventiveness came into sharp focus when Charles Remke, a retired patent examiner from the United States Patent Office, audited the undergraduate class on Creativity and Problem Solving a few years ago at the University of St. Thomas in St. Paul. His awareness of the rapidly decreasing number of patents being issued to American inventors had become a matter of concern. When he discovered the nature of the creativity course, tools for stimulating idea production and the enthusiasm of students in practice sessions, he saw a connection. He became a tireless advocate for new ways of identifying and cultivating creative talents throughout the established system of education, taking his argument from a book by Arnold Skromme (1989), *Memorization Is Not Enough.*

Gradually, application of the concept of multiple intelligences "Way Beyond the IQ" is finding its way into the school experience. *The 7 Ability Plan* of Arnold Skromme (1989) identifies seven qualities of intelligence that education should be recognizing and developing: academic, creativity, dexterity, empathy, judgment, motivation and personality. Of the list, the factor of creativity has the most substantive academic accumulation of research, methodologies, resources, and specific classroom strategies for entire courses as well as for components of other courses.

The teaching of processes of creative thinking and problem solving in any academic content area begins with the assumption that new thinking is best taught when direct purposeful learning experiences are an essential part of the plan and when a balance is maintained between serious and playful thinking. Academically, courses in creative studies cover four interrelated factors, as mentioned earlier (Bleedorn 1995):

> The creative person
> The creative process
> The creative product
> The creative press (climate or environment)

The Creative Person

Research has shown that the cognitive domain of creativity is measurable (Torrance 1967). Included are cognitive factors of:

> Fluency (rapid production of new ideas and connections)
> Flexibility (broad-based; capacity for recognizing remote relationships
>   and changing perspectives)
> Originality (uniqueness, usefulness)
> Elaboration (attention to detail and refinement)

The basic premise that everyone is creative has been well established. However, in the case of the highly creative person, certain behavioral characteristics are found to apply: curiosity, independence, risk taking, tolerance for ambiguity, preference for complexity, intuition, sensitivity to problems, ability to visualize, and persistence. The paradoxical nature of highly creative people can contribute significantly in an engineering department or organization facing the need for new innovative ideas and action. At the same time the highly creative personality can be unsettling and threatening to highly structured "left brain" people and closed systems.

The Creative Process

Although the human brain/mind has an enduring quality of mystery, a great deal has been learned about the process by which new ideas are born and problems are solved. The Parnes Osborn Creative Problem Solving Process follows a natural progression of six steps: (1) recognizing a problem or challenge, (2) gathering relevant facts and data, (3) carefully defining the "real problem," (4) generating quantities of ideas for possible solutions, (5) making critical thinking choices of the most promising ideas based on relevant criteria, and (6) developing a plan for putting the best idea into operation.

This problem-solving system can be applied and practiced individually or in groups. Authorities suggest that creativity on demand and practiced in group settings relates to secondary creativity outcomes. The more individualized and non-directive the process, the more likely a prepared mind is to produce breakthroughs and major creative leaps of understanding and discovery that characterize primary creativity.

The Creative Product

A distinction is being made by many scholars regarding the definition of creativity. A difference is claimed between the process of "creative thinking" and the total process of "creativity." It is suggested that creative thinking to produce a new idea is the beginning of creativity; but translating the idea to a new concrete product, procedure, original communication, or some other tangible interpretation of the original thought is required to complete an act of creativity. Some authorities insist that the truly creative product also meet the criterion of usefulness. Susan Besemer (1995, 137–139) offers a list of fourteen criteria for the assessment of the relative value of a creative product. Her list includes:

> Novelty (original, transformations, germinal, does the product generate related ideas?)
> Resolution (function, does it do what it is supposed to do?)
> Value (aesthetic, monetary)
> Elaboration and Synthesis (attractive, stylized)
> Complexity
> Elegance
> Simplicity

How do you know that the product is truly "creative"? The answer is not yet final.

The Creative Press

The fourth factor in the teaching and application of creativity has recently become identified as the creative press—the environment or climate experienced by the creator. Both external and internal climates are included in the concept of press. External environmental factors that encourage creativity include empowerment and autonomy for employees, openness and flexibility in organizational structure, the use of cross-functional teams, information through open communication systems, and resources that are easy to acquire. Challenge, freedom, idea support, playfulness and risk taking have also shown up in research on the creative press. The concept of internal press is understood to involve the personal state of mind present in the individual and the current level of stress or anxiety experienced at the time of creative effort. Realities or perceptions of personal worth can negate any effort by management to provide a "climate for creativity."

There is an additional factor relevant to creativity that has had less formal attention in studies of both engineering and creativity. It is the reality of extended consciousness and the often unacknowledged higher creativity possible in the human mind. Art Plium, inventor and staff member at 3M Company in St. Paul, Minnesota, has provided the following description of the role of intuition in processes of engineering and invention.

Engineering and Intuition

It is usually a shock to engineering students to discover what a small percentage of decisions are made on the basis of calculations which involved so much study time in school (*Report on Engineering Design* 1945). As this suggests, many of the methods for discovering new ideas or creating new knowledge in the sciences are not based on calculable things. Instead, they come about through visualization, speculation, creative testing of hypotheses, sketches, verbalization, and other such acts. It is often the case that we make inventions and create things initially when we have no idea of the principles behind them.

How can this work? One of the most powerful tools of the human mind is its ability to make connections and associations even in the absence of what would appear to be adequate information. A general outline of a desired outcome is created/sketched in our thinking in a very loose way with some framework of restriction, sort of a decisive inertia. We then begin to add information to the general framework, testing its validity in many different ways. A picture begins to emerge whether it's a new bridge, a hair shampoo, or an aria. As the concept becomes clearer, we can then apply the metrics used to ultimately characterize and define the outcomes. We also intuitively know that not all the concepts conjured are going to fit our desired scenario or may not even be valid. Again, through our creativity and intuition, combined with a strong sense of intellectual integrity, we will find our way through a maze of seemingly contradictory information to provide a useful direction.

It is important to recognize and celebrate that beginning phase of the design process that favors the new concept. By resisting closure and a premature decision that often accompanies it, room to explore and understand what we are trying to accomplish is provided. From this groundwork new and useful inventions are made, both scientific and aesthetic.

Conclusion

Restructuring engineering education for meeting world needs will require bold, transforming *leadership*—flexible, open-ended, integrative, and trusting of diversity. It will be quite different from traditional top-down management (Bleedorn 1988). The much larger challenge of improving the quality of thinking across all levels of specialization and institutions is an awesome one. It is also possible.

Human Resources/
Human Capital in Organizations

Go to work, and above all cooperate and don't hold back on one another or try to gain at the expense of another. Any success in such lopsidedness will be increasingly short-lived. These are the synergetic rules that evolution is employing and trying to make clear to us. They are not man-made laws. They are the infinitely accommodative laws of the universe.

—R. Buckminster Fuller

Introduction

An *organization* is a number of individuals systematically united for some end or work. The study of organizational patterns and interactions is complicated by rapid social and scientific change to the extent that most "facts" must be perceived in process and "findings" be characterized by a quality of tentativeness. The literature abounds with reports and predictions. Gibson, Ivancevich, and Donnelly (1982) discuss organizations from perspectives of *behavior, structure,* and *processes.* A number of other authorities address themselves to specific questions of organizational power, decision-making, motivation, and management/leadership. Throughout the literature there is a marked emphasis on the human component of organizational operation and effectiveness.

The impact of rapid technological and sociological change on the human psyche and quality of life has its share of attention in psychological studies. In the case of organizations, the challenges of coping with constant and radical changes intrapersonally, interpersonally, and environmentally (in relation to economics, politics, government regulations, materials, communication, transportation, and countless other factors) are multiplied to a magnitude dependent on the size and goals of the organization.

The purpose of this chapter is to discuss a number of organizational models as presented in the literature. Particular attention will be paid to factors of *power, motivation, decision making,* and *management/leadership.* I will also make observations regarding the integration of their content. Since preparation for organizational leadership must necessarily include a projection beyond current, often traditional, practices toward more international and futuristic dimensions with which organizations and people who influence them are increasingly concerned, trends in growth and development will be considered. Central to the issue is the reality that "organizations" don't grow, decide, solve problems, take risks, produce, or make profit. It is *people* who do things. So the study of organizations becomes essentially the study of human behavior as individuals and groups are processed (or process themselves) through the interstices and indeterminacies of the structure (Wheatley and Kellner-Rogers 1996).

Macro-Organizations

According to Gibson et al. (1982) macro-organizations, or the overall characteristics of the organizational structure, can be identified basically as "universal" or "contingency." Universal theories suggest that there is one best way to design an organization. Contingency theories reflect the position that the best way is contingent upon the situation and the accompanying factors of technology and environmental differences. Universal theories include classical and bureaucratic organization theories which resemble each other in that their emphasis is on formal structures, often closed systems, organized in hierarchical patterns of authority and power, and dedicated to principles of measurable production and efficiency. System 4 organizations, another example of a universal or "one right way" system, are directly opposite from classical/bureaucratic models. Their modus operandi has its base in individual and group behavioral processes, participation, and satisfactions. Contingency design is a more current model of organizational operation, and represents the options of choice between the universal models, depending upon contingencies in the situation. It is a more open-ended design and capable of responding to changing factors by developments in technological, environmental, and informational systems.

In times of rapid and radical social change and the resulting effect on humans, it seems logical to predict that classical and bureaucratic models, which functioned satisfactorily during other periods in organizational history, would lose their effectiveness when the human components responded to the stresses of change and growth. The exertion determined by power and control, bureaucratic decision making, and authoritarian leadership and management, which serves the classical and bureaucratic design, becomes inappropriate when members of the work force change in their perceptions of quality of life and the rewards that identify their job satisfaction.

Argument for System 4 theory, and organizational systems in direct opposition to classical/bureaucratic theory, is based on the changes that have rendered classical designs ineffective. The changes, according to Likert (1967), include competition from foreign countries, American society's trend toward more individual freedom and initiative, educational levels that equip workers for more responsibility, concerns for mental and physical well-being, and complex technologies requiring teamwork across levels of authority.

The interpretation of System 4 theory builds, ideally, on high levels of trust and confidence between and among organization roles, shared decision-making, opportunity for human growth and development, well-developed communication systems "up, down, and across," open-ended interaction, and the cultivation of confidence in one's ability to contribute to the setting and to the realization of organizational goals.

Contingency design theory is based upon choice and balance. It is representative of the growing trend toward the development of a level of mentality that can integrate opposites and deal effectively with paradoxes. Even as paradoxical thinking demands a higher level of thought process than absolutism and "one right way" thinking, so also does contingency design represent a more complicated approach than the universal. Contingencies which determine in a major way the key factors upon which choice of systems are based are differences in technology, differences in environment, and information processing.

In terms of differences in technology, research has been reported showing that size of the organization affects the impact of technology on its system, with the greater impact occurring in large organizations.

Lawrence and Lorsch (1969) added the factor of environment to the variables in the success of the contingency model. Differentiation and specialization of labor resulting in departmentalization of task and behavioral types was identified as a key concept. The differences between task and person-oriented personnel, between short- and long-term goals, and between individual and systemic patterns of thought and attitude were listed as components of differentiation that influenced the degree of success in application of the contingency model.

An increasingly complex social system toward which the environment is trending requires a matching organizational complexity if a system is open-ended enough to affect and be affected by change. The classical, bureaucratic models of organizations do not demonstrate the awareness of changes in human development as described by Lawrence and Lorsch (1969). The stability of structure in their organizational models loses its value when changes in technological and human sub-environments go unacknowledged and are not integrated into their patterns of operation. An integration of strengths of universal models with System 4 concepts into a contingency model, which fuses both into a system of choice and differentiation, would seem best suited for the ambiguity of the times.

Micro-Organizations

In contrast to the functional structure of the *macro-organization design,* the *micro-organization design* models itself on client-based principles. Gibson et al. (1982) provide a conceptual framework for a system centered on job-related issues and individual differences in reactions to jobs. As is the case with any system dealing with the vagaries and vicissitudes of the human resource, design of a job-oriented micro-organization is a study in complexity.

In spite of the emphasis on quality of work, life and job satisfaction, the needs of the organization itself are equally considered. It is no surprise that "when personal needs of employees are satisfied, the performance of the organization itself is enhanced" (Gibson 1982, 318). In the interpretation of job design and redesign, basic efforts are directed to identify important needs of employees and to remove obstacles on the job which interfere with the meeting of those needs. A job preference form can provide an analysis of individual job design priorities. Ten descriptors (Gibson et al. 1982, 143) which the respondent is asked to prioritize are variety in tasks, feedback on performance from doing the job, autonomy, working as a team, responsibility, developing friendships on the job, task identity, task significance, having the resources to perform well, and feedback on performance from others, including co-workers.

With these preferences as guidelines, job design and redesign have reasonable expectations for job placement that results in job satisfaction, productivity, and organizational effectiveness. The problem of underemployment, with its accompanying problems of apathy, frustration, and stress, can be circumvented by attention to job scope with analytical attention to range and depth. *Range* refers to the number and variety of jobs performed. *Depth* refers to the level of personal discretion for altering the job. Persons for whom autonomy is a value have a greater likelihood of contributing to organizational goals and objectives if jobs are extensive in range and depth.

Environmental, situational, and managerial differences combine with individual differences to further complicate the question of job design. A factor dependent for its satisfaction on the entire interactive system is the growth need. Employees differ markedly in their motivation for new growth and development experiences on the job. Performance reviews and feedback have greater value to those with higher growth needs. Related to job performance is the issue of individual motivational patterns, according to the equation "Job performance = Ability x Satisfaction" (Gibson et al. 1982, 332).

The role of management in designing and assigning jobs has critical dependence on psychological and social principles and their interaction. Instruments for assessing individual attitudinal differences regarding scope, relationships, content, and performance outcomes of jobs are serving organizational goals through the translation of quality of employee work life into economic effectiveness.

In addition to empirical data on individual differences resulting from surveys and other identification instruments, managers are, in many cases, able to provide effective job design and placement by the exercise of their intuitive skills. In the collection of books on management is *Intuitive Management: Integrating Left and Right Brain Management Skills: How to Make the Right Decision at the Right Time* (Agor 1984). Although the title suggests a somewhat extravagant claim for decision making, the reference to the integration of "left-brain" and "right-brain" management skills is an enhancement of traditional management theory. Agor emphasizes the importance of balancing rational, logical thinking with intuitive thinking in the making of decisions. Characteristics of highly intuitive managers have a considerable relationship to characteristics which are associated with the creative personality. They include: good self-image, curiosity, independence, inner—versus outer-directedness, preference for action to inaction, risk taking, preference for informal rather than formal style, and focus on solutions rather than problems (Agor 1984).

It remains to be seen whether intuitive management and decision making will become a recognized contribution to the literature and research seeking new directions in management in the current period of intensive and extensive technological, social, and environmental change includes an instrument for the identification of personal brain dominance under the title "Test Your Management Style" (Agor 1984). Outcome of the test identifies the respondent as "left brain," "right brain," or "integrated" in dominance. As an ingredient in the *micro-organization design,* the development of the intuitive function in management has a potential value.

Organizational Design: Division and Delegation

Organization charts represent clearly the hierarchical nature of departmentalization from the top down and the suggestion of fixed relationships among jobs in the organization. Gibson et al. (1982, 289) suggest a structure represented by four components: division of labor, or *specialization of tasks;* regrouping of tasks with a common basis, or *departmentalization;* number of groups reporting to one superior, or *span of control;* distribution of authority, or *delegation.* Variations in the scale of each component's application result in diversities characterizing individual corporations. A high level of specialization, homogeneous departmentalization, few members in the group span of control, and centralized authority typify the extremely bureaucratic model of management. Low division of labor, heterogeneous departmentalization, many members reporting to one superior, and a decentralization of authority would suggest a structure with a high degree of flexibility. Although corporations could be organized around the same principles, there could be an extreme range of variation in the degree to which individual organizations respond to changes in social and psychological trends among workers.

The recurring theme of change in organizations is addressed by Peter Drucker (1982), especially as it affects the world of the executive who, in the judgment of many authorities, holds the key to climate, innovation, and response to environmental and social change. His discussion of the "Changing World of the Executive" offers a challenge to administrators and executives to perform more effectively—to do a better job and, above all, to welcome and accommodate the new and different in the rapidly changing world of organizations—changing internally with respect to the visions, aspirations, and even characteristics of employees, customers, and constituents while changing externally to new economic, social, technological, and political realities.

Peter Drucker neglected to mention radical changes in the natural environment which may be the greatest long-range threat of all. In that oversight he has been no different from most other authorities in the field of organizational theory.

Transition from an analysis of individual jobs to combinations of individuals into groups or teams reflects the process of departmentalization. Grouping may be based on functions, geographical areas, products, or customers. When functional criteria are used as the departmental basis, a problem easily arises. Specialists, unified by their common understanding and expertise, readily become focused on a single specialization and tunnel-visioned to the extent that the interrelatedness of all departments in the achieving of the organizational goals is sacrificed. This disadvantage is overcome in the larger, multi-product operation by the departmentalization of products, which allows personnel to develop "total expertise in researching, manufacturing, and distributing a product line." The need of many employees for challenge and change in their work life can be better met by a diversity of interrelated functions.

Mixed departmentalization is a current trend as managers learn to cope with changes in markets, products, services, and government regulations. Personnel who have a tolerance for ambiguity are more likely to feel comfortable with the multi-departmentalization model than those who have a natural requirement for absolute structure and repetitive processes, another reminder of the importance of the psychological factor in the success and productivity of an operation.

Inherent in the departmentalization model is the concept of delegation of authority, or the right of managers to make decisions without approval by higher managerial levels. Trends toward decentralization of authority and decision making are credited with the development of professional managers who are required to adapt and prove themselves on the basis of results rather than on personality or politics. Autonomy to solve problems and to act on the basis of one's own judgment and creative managerial skills can be an important individual contribution to organizational growth and development.

Gibson et al. (1982, 302) provide attention to some of the negative aspects of the trend from a centralized to a decentralized design of management: (1) the training required for programs in problem solving and decision making are an expense item for the organization; (2) old attitudes developed in centralized structures resist or change slowly and prove costly; and (3) alteration of accounting and performance-appraisal systems becomes necessary. It should be said that when the immediate cost of training and changes in accounting systems is compared with the subjective value of personnel who want to be involved in decisions that affect their work life, the cash outlay may be well justified. The factor of time would be significant in that the subjective value may not be immediately quantifiable.

Another design emerging on the organizational scene is the *matrix organization,* designed to maximize the strengths and minimize the weaknesses of both functional and product structures. Typically it provides a balance between functional and product organization and between departmentalization by process and by purpose, thus developing a dual authority to whom personnel report. This contribution to the avoidance of strict sequential, hierarchical patterns of authority helps to avoid duplication of processes by isolated units of operation and leads to sharing and team building through the interrelating of specializations. Another advantage of the *matrix organization* is the encouragement of constant interaction and communication among project and product units regarding manufacturing, marketing, engineering, and financial functions. Communication is current and flowing, making response to changes in environmental conditions more immediate and effective. In terms of human behavior, matrix organization serves as opportunities for personnel to develop skills and knowledge because of the diversity provided; however, a study by Argyris (1985) concludes "experience with matrix organization structures were relatively unsuccessful, but not because of defects in the structures. Rather it was due to faulty implementation resulting from managers' inability to adjust their traditional behavioral styles" (p. 31).

Systems Model of Organizations

All organizations, including business, educational, and human/health services, are tending toward a realization that "the ultimate survival of the organization depends upon its ability to adapt to the demands of its environment, and in meeting these demands, the total cycle of input-process-output must be the focus of managerial attention" (Gibson et al. 1982, 29). What evolves is an open system dealing simultaneously and systemically with internal and external aspects of the organization and their input interdependence. Resources from the external environmental system (input) are processed by the organization internally to be returned to the environment (output). In the field of business, the two major categories of inputs are human and natural resources. Output takes the form of products or services. The measure of success or survival depends upon the ratio between acceptability by the environment of the output and requirements of the business to replenish input.

Benton (1978) uses the term "systems engineering" and describes it as "a method by which one looks at a problem in its totality—objectives and alternatives, inputs and outputs, costs, benefits, sequences, and schedules—and tries to think through, early in a project before serious mistakes and big commitments are made, which approach will work best (p. 79). He suggests five features of the application of systems engineering:

identifies needs, opportunities, and limitations so overall goals can be stated and priorities assigned;

appraises alternative solutions and develops measures of their relative costs;

distinguishes between what is known and what is still to be learned;

selects and develops the most promising avenues for action; and

constantly reviews or monitors the whole process by which innovations are introduced to the public so the needs of users will be met as fully and promptly as possible. (p. 79)

These features bear a striking resemblance to the steps in the creative problem-solving process.

The concepts of subsystems and sub-environments are developed by Lawrence and Lorsch (1969) in their discussion of differentiation and integration in complex organizations. Their study examines the internal functioning of organizations in relation to the demands of the external environment and the ability of the organization to cope effectively with its demands and feedback.

Differentiation, as addressed in the Lawrence and Lorsch study (1969), is the state of segmentation of the system into subsystems, each with particular attributes in relation to requirements of the external environment, and including behavioral attributes of members of the organizational subsystem. Integration is defined as "the process of achieving unity of effort among the various subsystems in the accomplishment of the organization's task" (p. 4), with "task" referring to the complete input-process-output cycle of goods and/or services.

Major segmented subsystems are sales, production, and research and development. Subsystems of the environment are identified as market, technical—economic, and the scientific sub-environment. Relationships between subsystems are apparent. The degree of their formalized structure is said to be determined to a degree by the relative complexity and ambiguity of the task. Whereas relatively simple tasks are performed more effectively with preplanned structure, those involving the uncertainties of changing environments are more successful at coping with a low degree of formal structure, i. e., "organic" rather than "mechanistic." Listed below is a series of hypotheses which formed the basis of Lawrence and Lorsch (1969) investigations:

1. The greater the certainty of the relevant sub-environment, the more formalized the structure of the subsystem.

2. Subsystems dealing with environments of moderate certainty will have members with more social interpersonal orientations, whereas subsystems coping with either very certain environments or very uncertain environments will have members with more task—oriented interpersonal orientations.

3. The time orientations of subsystem members will vary directly with the modal time required to get definitive feedback from the relevant sub-environment.

4. Members of a subsystem will develop a primary concern with the goals of coping with their particular sub-environment.

5. The greater the degree of differentiation in subsystem attributes between pairs of subsystems, the less effective will be the integration achieved between them.

6. Overall performance in coping with the external environment will be related to there being a degree of differentiation among subsystems consistent with the requirements of their relevant sub-environments and a degree of integration consistent with requirements of the total environment subsystem.

7. When the environment requires both a high degree of differentiation and a high degree of integration, integrative devices will tend to emerge (pp. 2–6).

Behavioral factors were a prime focus of investigation in this empirical study of relationships between differentiation and integration. Findings in general led to the conclusion that "differentiation and integration are essentially antagonistic," which underscores the fact that organizations recognize and struggle with the challenges of reconciling the need for differentiation with the need for coordination of effort. As science and technology escalate and intensify dynamic changes in the environmental systems, the investigation of the influence of the behavioral factor will come to take increasing precedence, as human systems and their natural complexities are recognized as a critical subsystem in total organizational effectiveness. Further discussion of behavioral issues will be addressed later.

Participatory or Organizational Model

In broad terms participative management is a system that involves employee participation in developing and implementing decisions that directly affect their jobs. Questions of decision making, motivation, leadership, and power have a direct relationship to participatory management, and integrate in particular ways with issues of organizational development. It can be generally conceded that there is evidence of a growing trend in the direction of human relations based on "trust, respect, and supportiveness between managers and subordinates" according to Gibson et al. (1982, 129). The expressed need of informed persons to participate in a meaningful way in matters affecting their work life has a parallel on a larger social/political scale in the urgent call for participatory democracy by Toffler (1980). Observers of change in the 1980s and beyond (Ferguson 1980) identify that period as a period of personal and social transformation. A significant factor in that process is the dynamics across lines of authority in a sharing of responsibility for shared goals, in this case for the achievement of organizational objectives.

Participation follows a variety of dimensionalities. It can be forced or voluntary, formal or informal, direct or indirect. The degree of participation from none through consultative to full participation in decision making is a further variable. Application of participatory decision making is reported to be appropriate in routine personnel matters; job design, methods, goal setting; working conditions; company policies regarding layoffs, profit sharing, fringe benefits, and other areas. A major benefit to the effectiveness of organizations with the practice of participative management is the commitment to the job that can result when employees have a voice in decision making and develop a sense of "ownership" of the project. An increase in communication flow upward, downward, and laterally is a further plus.

Although evidence has been produced to show that humanistic psychology is providing practical and theoretical advancement in more positive and satisfying attitudes by its emphasis on involvement in decision making on the job, authorities remind us that individual differences in thinking and in attitudinal styles are a constant influence on effectiveness. The reminder is consistent with a statement by Gibson et al. (1982):

> Individual differences are now recognized as crucial variables to consider when designing jobs. Experience, cognitive complexity needs, values, valences, and perceptions of equity are some of the individual differences which influence the reactions of jobholders to the scope and relationships of their jobs. When individual differences are combined with environmental, situational, and managerial differences, job design decisions become increasingly complex. (p. 340)

The process of change continues to escalate and intensify in all arenas of the human experience. Organizations face challenges of constant change. The degree to which subordinates are involved with managers in meeting challenges, solving problems, and taking advantage of opportunities covers the range (Gibson et al. 1982, 539) from unilateral (with management reaching decisions), through shared (with emphasis on interaction and sharing of authority between manager and subordinates) to delegated (emphasis on subordinates reaching decisions). Any group decision-making process has the benefit of the availability of the combined knowledge and the collective judgment of the group with the capability of covering a broad range of perspectives, rather than a dependency on a single perspective and judgment.

A number of problem solving systems are in current practice throughout organizations. Among them are Quality Circles, Creative Problem Solving, and Synectics. In all cases, success of the process depends on the development of an atmosphere supportive to creative thinking. The Parnes Osborn Creative Problem Solving process provides a structure, theoretical principles, and hands-on techniques which encourage full participation in a balanced application of both major thinking modes, convergent and divergent (or "left brain" and "right brain" processing of information). The Creative Education Foundation at the University of New York, Buffalo, represents more than forty years of research, theory, practice, and growth in the understanding of the creative person, process, product, and press (climate or environment). Information and materials serve both national and international business and educational communities.

The importance of developing creative talents for leadership in a global future is underscored in the results of a survey (Bleedorn 1988) which placed the rank-ordered position of a talent for creativity in first priority from a list of thirty-three talents identified as critical to effective leadership in the emerging global age. Business leaders, educationists, and college students were included in the survey population.

The scope of the general trend toward participatory and workplace democracy is discussed by Mason (1982), who reports "widespread recognition in the managerial literature that worker participation may be a critical variable in determining the success of contemporary workplaces" (p. 178). As evidence he lists Likert (participatory group-system 4), Argyris (adult role and reality-centered), Barnes (open system), Bennis (problem solving, democratic), Blake-Mouton (concern for people), Leavitt (people solutions), MacGregor (theory), Blau (democratic), Burns-Stalker (organic), Shepard (organic), Lowin (participatory decision-making), and Bovard (group-centered).

Although the terminology differs, the implication is that authorities agree that problems of productivity, work quality, and morale in contemporary organizations can be alleviated by workplace participation.

The concept of participatory management is not limited to contemporary literature (Porter, Allan, and Angle 1985). It is suggested that participatory management can increase the amount and the accuracy of information workers have about work practices and the associated environment, as well as the degree to which group members feel they "own" and control their own work practices. According to Porter, conditions required to maximize individual work effectiveness through group participative techniques are suggested: "The topic of participation must be relevant to the work itself and the objective task and environmental contingencies in the work setting must actually be supportive of more effective performance" (p. 359). During the years since 1975, attention to participatory management has resulted in a greatly expanded understanding of the many issues contingent on its success.

Bureaucratic Organizational Systems

In addition to the earlier discussion of bureaucratic, there is further evidence of the polarities between participatory and bureaucratic systems. Among the interpretations of the term bureaucracy is one by Max Weber (in Gibson et al. 1982), who refers to it as the "sociological concept of rationalization of collective activities" (p. 353). In the bureaucratic operation the predictability of the behavior of employees in the organization is said to be assured. Many whose work involves them in large bureaucratic systems are impatient and frustrated with "red tape," information flows downward and ideas flow upward through complex communication channels, creating a feeling of powerlessness over relevant decisions in their work life. A review of strategies which are said to govern bureaucracies is suggested by Weber (in Gibson et al. 1982), and accounts for the loss of human capital and human spirit in organizations:

1. All tasks necessary for the accomplishment of goals are divided into highly specialized jobs. Jobholders could become expert in their jobs and could be held responsible for the effective performance of their duties.

2. Each task is performed according to a "consistent system of abstract rules" to assure uniformity and coordination of different tasks…so managers can eliminate uncertainty in task performance due to individual differences.

3. Each member or office of the organization is accountable to a superior. A chain of command is thereby created.

4. Each official in the organization conducts business in an impersonal formalistic manner, maintaining a social distance with subordinates and clients to assure that personalities do not interfere with the efficient accomplishment of the office's objectives and no favoritism results from personal friendships or acquaintances.

5. Employment is based on technical qualifications and promotions based on seniority and achievement, with employment viewed as a lifelong career, engendering a high degree of loyalty. (p. 353)

The constraints to the human spirit and the absolutism of inflexible authoritarian policies inherent in these bureaucratic strategies register as anathema to an employee functioning in an environment of galloping technological, sociological, environmental, economic, and political flux and motivated for personal growth and creative identity.

Self-development as a goal is discussed by Maccoby (1981). He argues for the identity of the organization as a means rather than an end, and suggests that when the individual humanism of the worker is sacrificed to the bureaucracy, people put their faith in bureaucracies rather than "the divine spirit in each other, and the self remains childish and undeveloped" (p. 234). In a further negative expectation he offers the opinion that leaders today would likely not learn about the human spirit at school, since "teachers of the humanities have lost their confidence and sense of mission in a world oriented to the career ethic…and if our society is to function, leaders cannot wait for the academics to teach them" (pp. 235–236).

An additional argument in response to the bureaucratic strategies listed earlier is for flexibility of structure in organizational design. When old belief systems are maintained beyond evidence of new environmental realities, bureaucracies are often blinded to new opportunities and dangers. Open, participatory systems, where goals are shared in a climate of trust and understanding of human differences, are in a more enviable position for positive response to change as well as a proactive capability to anticipate and prepare for new opportunities (Donaldson and Lorsch 1983).

Motivation

The collection of articles edited by Hackman, Lawler, and Porter (1985), with its emphasis on human behavior, is a significant resource in the understanding of both psychological and social forces and factors that cause persons to spend their energies in the accomplishment of a purpose. New understandings of individual differences are resulting in a new approach to the search for meaning of motivational patterns. Assumptions about the causes of behavior in organizations are presented by David Nadler (in Hackman et al. 1985) in his discussion of a new approach to human understanding:

1. Behavior is determined by a combination of forces in the individual and forces in the environment.

2. People make decisions about their own behavior in organizations.

3. Different people have different types of needs, desires, and goals.

4. People make decisions among alternative plans of behavior based on their perceptions of the degree to which a given behavior will lead to desired outcomes (pp. 67–68).

In essence, the claim is that people are inherently neither motivated nor unmotivated; motivation depends on the situation they are in, and how it fits their needs. When this theory is related to Maslow's Hierarchy of Needs, the connection to systems models of organizations becomes quite apparent. Since individuals are necessarily at different places in their pursuit of need gratification on Maslow's model, the freedom to grow, which is provided by systems models rather than by bureaucratic, highly controlled operations, serves the individual and, in turn, the organizational objectives. In addition to psychology and educational psychology, other components of the behavioral sciences (anthropology, sociology, and social psychology) are providing guidelines for more effective patterns of management of human resources. According to Lorsch (in Hackman et al. 1985), some guidelines based on behavioral theory are provided on:

> how to communicate effectively; how to give performance evaluations to employees; how to resolve conflicts between individuals or between one department and another; how to design organizational structures, measurement systems, and compensation packages; how to introduce changes in organization, procedures, and strategy. (p.29)

While motivation of employees is under scrutiny, a like attention is developing in the study of executives and their motivation to change or grow in their understanding of the farther reaches of human behavior, including their own. When Peter Drucker writes about the changing world of the executive (1982), he highlights changes in the work force and in the newer office and workplace relationships that are making increasing demands on middle and senior managers.

Organizational reward systems discussed by Galbraith (1985) include choice of various compensation plans, promotion systems, leadership styles, selection strategies, training programs, and job designs. Without attention to individual personality and situational differences, outcomes of extrinsic reward systems are marginally predictable at best. The detailed analysis of the motivational model and the development of resulting formulas seem to be giving way to an emphasis on intrinsic motivation. With the number of direct production workers dwindling and knowledge workers on the increase, traditional motivation efforts by management lose their relevance. The worker's need for achievement is marked. They are said to respond to responsibility and opportunity to contribute and appraise their own contributions, do the work that they are being paid for, and be assigned or reassigned where they can be productive (Drucker 1982). Although productivity and job satisfaction of the knowledge worker are not readily measurable, they represent a motivational force that can translate from human capital to real capital.

Decision Making

As indicated earlier, a recurring theme in the literature is the trend toward the expressed need of workers to have some involvement in the making of decisions that affect their work life. In macro/bureaucratic operation of organizations or highly structured, departmentalized, hierarchical systems of management, the privilege of participating in those decisions was essentially denied the employee. Decisions and policy making were the domain of the executive and managerial levels all along the chain of command. The development of systems and participatory models of management has institutionalized group problem solving and decision making as a component of managerial trends. Major decisions or strategic choices are reserved for executives who, in order to "accomplish corporate immortality," must make choices within two sets of objective constraints according to Donaldson and Lorsch (1983, 9)—constituency expectations and financial goals. In addition, the psychological constraints of their own belief system and the effort to develop a committed and loyal employee force have to be incorporated into their decision making.

When a high degree of group involvement in the decision-making process is practiced and promoted, effectiveness of the process is said to depend on the degree of "innovation, risk taking, flexibility, and trust in the executive system" (Argyris 1985, 337). Top management testifies to the importance of these qualities as key characteristics, but according to Argyris, the actual behavior of top executives during decision-making meetings often does not jibe with their attitudes and prescriptions about effective executive action.

The key qualities cited (innovation, risk taking, flexibility, and trust) are characteristics identified with the creative personality. The significance of creative persons and processes in response to change in organizations is uncontested. *The Journal of Creative Behavior* is a quarterly of ideas, observations, and research in the investigation and cultivation of creative potential, published by the Creative Education Foundation at the University of New York, Buffalo. Business and education are sharing a growing interest in the journal's reports and theoretical updates on creativity as the world of education and the "real world" of business discover their compatibilities and their interdependent need for new insights into the factor of human behavior.

The quality of trust that is included in the list of key qualities comes into focus in the discrepancies reported between words and behavior. The example of "groupthink" relates conversely to trust. Social conformity, which operates in a cohesive group when subtle pressures deny members the privilege of raising challenging questions or suggesting alternative solutions, results in a "deteriorization in mental efficiency, reality testing, and moral judgments" (Janis 1985, p. 378). The power of communication—verbal, tonal, and by "silent language"—has the capability of retranslating some of the best articulated intentions.

Power

Power is defined by Galbraith (1985) as the possibility of imposing one's will upon the behavior of other persons. He suggests that power has passed from the individual to the corporation or organization in modern times; power no longer resides exclusively in personality, property, great wealth, or most of the other accouterments associated with the heyday of mercantile capitalism. His identification of the conditions by which organizations wield power are power to coerce, reward, and change belief. In his opinion, bureaucracies have taken the place of great men and women whose power base derived from their charisma. The power of the individual thinker has, in modern times, been supplanted by organizational power. A reviewer of Galbraith's *The Anatomy of Power* points out the weakness in the book's argument. It fails to acknowledge the reality that fundamental power has, historically, been wielded by revolutions of the mind, those in which major idea systems are shattered, with new ones succeeding them. This concept underscores the recurring theme in the literature—the reiteration of the human bottom line and the innovative, revolutionary thought and evolving consciousness of individual minds impacting powerfully on the system.

Another simple definition of power is from Salancik and Pfeffer (1983, 417): "Power is simply the ability to get things done the way one wants them to be done." The term "influence" is used interchangeably with the concept of power. Both use and abuse of power and influence figure in the process of organizations. For those which are bureaucratic in process, power from the top down is exerted over each succeeding level of authority. In participatory systems of decision making, power and influence are more inclined to be shared and the "strategic-contingency" theory applies where those subunits most able to cope with the organization's critical problems and uncertainties acquire power. Implications for strategic-contingency power in an information-based society are clear. Those subunits with access to information most adequate for successful response to the challenge assume or are granted the power to make decisions and take action. The effectiveness of their use of power will depend to a great extent upon the openness of the organizational system to the realities of the external environment and the flexibility it expresses in dealing with the changes in those realities.

An analysis of personal power in organizations is developed by Hagberg (1984), and provides new perceptions of the complexities and levels of power as exercised by individuals in their effect on organizations. She defines personal power as

the extent to which one is able to link the outer capacity for action (external power) with the inner capacity for reflection (internal power), which develops from introspection, personal struggles, the gradual evolution of the life purpose, and from accepting and valuing yourself. (p. xxvi)

External power alone does not yield personal power, according to Hagberg. Hagberg's model of personal power includes six distinct stages arranged in a developmental order, beginning with powerlessness in stage one and moving to stage six, power by gestalt (Hagberg 1984). The stages must be experienced only in the order in which they are numbered, and although people can be in different stages of power in different areas of their lives, at different times, and with different people, each person has a "home" stage that is most representative of him or her:

Stage One: Powerlessness
Stage Two: Power by association

Stage Three: Power by symbols
Stage Four: Power by reflection
Stage Five: Power by purpose
Stage Six: Power by gestalt (p. xxvi)

It is suggested that stages two and five are perceived to be more feminine, stages three and four to be more masculine, and stages two, three, and four most often rewarded in organizations. The perception of power in terms of personal power, developed in hierarchical succession, adds another factor to the human formula evolving in the study of organizations and how they function.

Leadership/Management of Organizations

The concept of leadership is, by admission of authorities, an ambiguous one. The juxtaposition of the concepts of leadership and management in the literature and from public platforms leads to further confusion. One of the distinctions encountered in the literature is the definition of management as the process of maintaining the status quo, and the definition of leadership as moving the organization along into new directions and responses to the external environment. In the history of the studies of leadership, early emphasis was on trait theory. Empirical studies identified personal traits that represented aptitudes for getting the job done. Current attention to the study of leadership has emphasized the situational theory. As with the question of models, the final observation suggests that rather than arriving at absolutes and quantifiables, the better judgment is to acknowledge the qualitative contingencies that affect the outcome of the leadership process and assume most results to represent an integration of diverse approaches.

Maccoby (1981) argues that the social character and global environment are undergoing so radical a transformation that "a new model of leadership is needed to bring out the best, not only in a new social character, but also in the older social characters that coexist with it" (p. 17). He suggests that to determine what kind of leader we need, we must also understand how we are changing and why old models of leadership no longer serve. He identifies four types of leaders of large corporations: the craftsman, the jungle fighter, the company man, and the gamesman. Most leadership is said to have elements of all, though most leaders are dominant in a single type, each of which has both positive and negative traits. The more bureaucratic models of organizations can readily be identified with the jungle fighter and his need for power and survival at any cost. The more participatory models would relate to the gamesman style with its inclination for energetic new ideas, and enthusiasm for creative accomplishment.

Theories of Lawrence and Lorsch (1969) base the means toward productivity in its relationship to leadership on the degree of differentiation and integration expressed by major subsystems in complex organizations. Findings in their research suggest that the two states are "essentially antagonistic," but that the possibility of achieving both high differentiation and high integration is a reasonable expectation (p. 47). The task of leadership in the turbulent environment created by science and technology will have need of the ability to deal with such paradox.

The interpersonal style of the leader in the subsystems of complex organizations is a critical factor. A major difference was found to exist between persons with a primary concern for task accomplishment and those with a primary concern for social relationships (Lawrence and Lorsch 1969). Kellerman (1984) adds to the understanding of the distinction as it relates to organizational models by suggesting "task-motivated leaders are more likely to tend toward autocratic or minimally consultative styles while relationship-motivated leaders more often use group-oriented and participative styles (p. 98).

The entry of women in to managerial positions has caused an association of feminine styles with relationship-orientation and masculine styles with task-orientation. In an unpublished paper Bleedorn (1984b) reported results of her investigation of literature on the topic, "Management: Impact of Women's Values on the Future." Her annotated bibliography includes books and articles from the growing collection of resources on the subject. The concept of the androgynous manager as an integration of both masculine and feminine-related styles and values emerges as a preferred model which helps to move students of leadership away from polarized, stereotypical assumptions of masculine and feminine roles and aptitudes to more realistic, individualized expectations of talents and functioning. Sargent (1981) discusses the androgynous manager in terms of the transformation of leadership to a balanced state between task and relationships, reason and intuition, left hemisphere and right hemisphere, and strengths for planning change on frontiers of action as well as on inner frontiers of changing values and human progress.

The reality of change in the expectations of the functions of leadership/management is pervasive throughout the thinking of authorities on organizational behavior, structure, and processes. Pascarella (1981) makes a case for the changing focus on humanistic individualism:

A leader doesn't necessarily do all the things that many organizations expect of a manager. For the leader, the goal comes first; the organization is secondary. Owners, employees, and others may prefer to entrust the organization to someone who, above all else, will see to its survival, its permanence. In this sense organizations are often designed with a bias against leaders. In strict hierarchical organizations, leadership qualities among non-management employees are viewed as a threat to the system. But with the rise of individualism on the part of non-management, autocratic rule is giving way to leadership—wherever it can be found. As human management ("humanagement") extends democracy into the workplace, leaders are needed who can develop consensus amidst what might otherwise be chaos (p. 104).

A particular manifestation of independent, innovative creation is the emergence of entrepreneurship, defined by Drucker (1992) as the ability to create and direct an organization for the new. The ability to predict technological advances and future markets is a fundamental of successful entrepreneurship (Sexton and Bowman-Upton 1991). When complex organizations realize the economic loss they suffer when independent, spirited idea people leave the system to express their innovative ideas in the form of profitable products, in other places, some of the big companies fight back (DeMott 1985). Their leadership is trying to create the spirit, zest and rewards of entrepreneurship right in their corridors, shop floors and laboratories, giving employees the resources and freedom to pursue their own ideas, cutting back on traditional red tape, endless meetings and other obstacles that can slow down innovation. The code word for this kind of operation is "intrapreneurship," and business is being encouraged to use those talents inside large organizations as an alternative to "stagnation and decline" in a time of rapid change.

Developments of this kind can be compatible only with organizational models that are open-ended, tuned in to the realities of the external environment, and staffed with persons that admit to the importance of individual styles and expertise while at the same time practicing the arts of integration and team building.

Organizational Development

In 1969, Peter Drucker made organizational headlines with his discussion of "The Age of Discontinuity." Since then countless observers of the scene have reflected on the unprecedented pace of change and the difficulties of managing both personal and institutional lives productively in times of radical uncertainty. Drucker (1968) recognized four major discontinuities:

Genuinely new technologies are upon us, creating new industries and rendering others obsolete.

A world economy has been created, "cutting across national boundaries and languages and largely disregarding political ideologies as well."

A pluralistic society and polity exists, posing new political, philosophical, and spiritual challenges.

Knowledge has become the central resource of the economy, changing "labor forces and work, teaching and learning, and the meaning of knowledge and politics. (p. ix)

Discontinuities demand change and growth of organizations, not only in a reactive form, but most especially in a proactive modus operandi, which exercises the vision to look beyond the existing system and perceive the directions that current trends will take in internal and external environments.

One of the most recent and critical developments in the complexity and demands on organizational growth is the expansion to multinationalism. The problems of multinational people management were called to the attention of business by Noer (1975) with his discussion of the importance of selection criteria for personnel for overseas employment. Emphasis on special attention to the behavioral characteristics and the cultural adaptivity of persons considered for international business appointments is a reminder of the importance of understanding human behavior as a critical factor in successful management. Noer extends the responsibilities of multinational organizations to include systems that deal with the acknowledged interdependence of global economic, social, and environmental systems; since the future will dictate global allocation of resources, the prime contractors will inevitably be the multinational enterprises. At any rate, it is fair to conclude that multinational organizations will prosper relevant to the degree of human growth, development, and pluralistic sophistication they bring to the international scene.

Summary

In response to the literature on organizations, the intended focus here has been on the behavioral component. It is clear that better understanding of human nature and human behavior will need to evolve to new levels if organizations are to prosper. Hagberg (1984) suggests that we will have to expand our concept of what power and leadership mean and how they are acted out. We will learn to go beyond our own egos. Drucker (1982) talks about "business ethics" as becoming the "in" subject and replacing yesterday's attention to "social responsibilities" (p. 234). The ethics of prudence and self-development and interdependence are specifically identified expectations of organizational leadership. The ultimate ideal for the future organization is reflected in the words of Drucker: "It must expect its managers, executives, and professionals to demand of themselves that they shun behavior they would not respect in others, and instead practice behavior appropriate to the sort of person they would want to see in the mirror in the morning" (p. 256).

Hackman (Hackman et al. 1985) sees work redesign in organizational and societal contexts both optimistically and pessimistically. He suggests that the key challenge to change is "getting behavior to change, getting behavior to stay changed, and getting the changes to spread to other organizational systems and practices" (p. 256). Cause for pessimism is the reality of human behavior and attitudes that are programmed in the past. This brings the discussion full circle to the need for leadership with talents for innovation, risk taking, tolerance for ambiguity, and trust.

The challenge is on. The outcome, although uncertain, has elements of hope. Lehrer (1980) said, "We human beings do have the ability to make the right decisions for the future. But we won't unless some of us lay aside the baggage of the twentieth century. And there is a lot of baggage to be discarded. It's the baggage of self-interest and conflict, myopia and tunnel vision, among many other things" (p. 214). In a larger sense, what is required is, "creating the structures and processes that further human and economic development, that involve people in solving problems equitably, and understanding themselves and the universe in a spirit of disciplined play and informed benevolence" (Maccoby 1981, 237). In the words of the philosopher, "There we stand, ready to escape into the future with a joyful uncertainty."

Creativity and Innovation
in Bureaucracies

The farmer cannot make the germ develop and sprout from the seed. He can only supply the nurturing conditions which will permit the seed to develop its own potentialities. So it is with creativity. How can we establish the external conditions which will foster and nourish the internal conditions.

—Carl R. Rogers

Introduction

The unprecedented acceleration of change and growth in social and technological complexities is demanding a radical change in the ordering and management of institutions. One of the major challenges of business, educational, and political institutions is the need for identifying and developing talents for the productive integration of change into the existing structures of management. Literature in both education and business is providing persuasive arguments for the importance of creative and innovative thinking and behavior as a crucial factor in institutional effectiveness and productivity.

Given here is the theoretical background of creativity and innovation in relation to bureaucratic functioning and speculates on their integration with other current issues closely related to management and leadership. In addition to theoretical considerations, attention is given to specific strategies for the development of creative potential, both individual and collective.

Five major topics are addressed.

1. Creativity and innovation in changing times
2. Sense of systems: technological and human
3. Paradox and balance: new levels of thinking
4. The question of power
5. Theory into practice

Creativity and Innovation in Changing Times

Anyone who is involved with an organization can testify to the evidence of changes in the recent past. The pluralistic nature of society, communication, information retrieval systems, and the decline of plenty are basic external changes that influence and demand internal change. Growing complexities in social, technological, political, environmental, and economic systems impact dynamically on organizational patterns of operation and demand response. In 1982, John Naisbitt described ten megatrends that were moving into national institutions at a penetrating level, reshaping in major ways the nature of their operation. Naisbitt cited evidence that with quick and easy access to information through technological advances, options for learning and working are making employees more entrepreneurial and open to choice. Long-established managerial patterns are in need of being replaced to reflect a continuing attempt to maintain a balance between technological developments and human/personal contact and relationships.

With a major change of attitude in the workplace, it becomes incumbent on institutions to "relax their traditional bureaucratic structure to encourage autonomy throughout the company (Kanter 1984). Acting as change masters requires specific skills, according to Kanter:

> Change masters thrive on novelty; they know how to "twist and shake up" their habitual mind-sets to create new patterns of thought.
>
> They inspire co-workers with clear vision and a sense of direction, knowing instinctively how to articulate change with faith and conviction.
>
> They build coalitions of support within the organization and form alliances to shape their visitors into working realities.
>
> They work through teams, encouraging democratic decision making on projects and discourage segmentalism (guarding turf against incursions).
>
> They promote self-esteem among employees by praising employees and encouraging open communication. (p. 44)

In Kanter's (1977) opinion, bureaucracies which are rigid and mechanistic, will be as obsolete as dinosaurs.

The focus of change on the human environment in the corporate setting is discussed from the perspective of resistance to change by Silber and Sherman (1983). Of a list of reasons for resisting change, one relates in a particular way to the creative person in a bureaucratic setting when it suggests that a supervisor can generate and intensify resistance if people feel they are serf-like beings who are forced to comply in a feudal managerial climate. Being somebody else's peon is not conducive to motivation, especially when it results from management behavior. When people are forced to change, with no control about the changes that will affect them, they are likely to lose their sense of importance.

In the discussions regarding the human factor in the process of change, a connection between change and innovation in bureaucracies and new understandings of the creative person in the creative process becomes readily apparent. Characteristics of curiosity, risk taking, tolerance for ambiguity, sense of humor, a spirit of independence, problem sensitivity, to name only a few, are consistently cited as descriptive of the creative personality. The literature on leadership and management continues to call for managerial qualities of a similar description.

The concept of "participation management" discussed by Kanter encourages and rewards the full use of ideas that are constantly being developed by creative minds throughout and across all levels of operation within the corporation. The free flow of ideas and problem solving skills is said to be a key to American corporate renaissance. Development of a worker's ability to function as part of a participation management team has failed to keep pace with the development of the technology which serves the flow and integration of information for solving organizational problems and making organizational decisions. There continues to be a slippage between the language, which the need for creativity generates, and the actual communication and use of innovative ideas for meeting and anticipating the challenges of change.

Traditional preparation and social conditioning of managers has established perceptions quite different from those required for the successful interpretation of innovative management. Bradford and Cohen (1984) report responses by managers who were asked what made them feel validated as competent (translating to their model of the ideal manager). Their perceptions are that good managers know at all times what is going on in the department, have more technical expertise than any subordinate, are able to solve any problem that comes up (single-handed, or at least ahead of any subordinate's input), and have the major responsibility for the success of the department. Models of the "good manager" so incompatible with the concept of participation management can set up almost insurmountable roadblocks for creative innovative thinking and behavior across levels and upward through bureaucratic hierarchies.

Whereas traditional systems of "ideal" management may have been efficient and even effective in earlier times, frustrations and stress mount in seasons of radical change when the unwieldy organizational structure lags behind the individual in its response to change. Men and women in the workplace are looking for new qualities in their work. There are countless testimonials to their need to have a feeling of achievement from their work, see long-range opportunities for growth and advancement, feel that they are in the kind of work where their abilities are used best, and most of all, to know that their ideas are welcomed. When the quality of work denies workers access to these personal satisfactions, underemployment, frustration, and stress take their toll. Programs and treatment for stress management and chemical dependency drain funds and energy from the organization.

It would be too simplistic to claim that the development and integration of creativity in individuals and organizations provide immediate and complete relief from the impact of radical change. It is reasonable, however, to suggest that an emphasis on the recognition and reward for creative, productive ideas and their implementation is a major clue to motivation, communication (up, down, and sideways), shared problem solving, and decision making. Creative behavior that expresses itself in an attitude of sensitivity to problems (challenges and opportunities) and a visionary, holistic sense of the system, is recognized in corporate literature as one of the most valuable and least exploited of human talents. The irony is that the age of explosive technological development has upended traditional procedures in institutions. Machines, however complex, adapt and function (and multiply) passively and on command. The human "machine," the ultimate in complexity, has to deal with the amorphous nature of its humanness in the processing of change. When executives and persons in positions of power are faced with the challenge of change, the threat of having to share power or acknowledge ideas or expertise from other sources can confound and impede progress.

Facilitating creative ideas upward is caught in a double bind when management operates on the illusion that "managers welcome change; it's only workers who resist" and "good managers plan change down to the last detail—in advance" (Sayles 1979, 175). When, on the other hand, inventive, creative workers in a new products division complain—as they have been heard to do—that they have no problem initiating and developing new ideas for product development, it's getting an audience or approval for their implementation that presents a problem.

More flexible, open-ended systems and a conditioning for the creative mentality of "deferred judgment" across levels and categories would help to dissolve the rationalizing by both ends of the polarity.

Sense of the System: Technological and Human

The realities of a "shrinking world," intensified by the immediacy and intimacy of global communication systems, require new ways of perceiving and functioning. The natural growth and evolution of consciousness for which the human organism is programmed, according to Land, (1973) is in need of support. Buckminster Fuller, in the course of his extensive writing and lecturing, made repeated references to one of the basic problems in society. His claim was that the system had so regimented, labeled, categorized, and specialized learning and services that it had become almost impossible for specialists to perceive at a level that recognized the interconnectedness of all forms and functions of any living system (Fuller and Dil 1983). "Project managing" is the term used by Sayles (1979) in his discussion of the facilitation of change.

To implement change, managers must be able to tie together elements of the organization often not closely interrelated:

1. Handling subordinate reactions and suggestions
2. Moving back and forth from early plans and designs through the final use stages
3. Facilitating trade-offs between and among groups when their coordination patterns have been changed or when cooperation is required. (p. 164)

Since so much of the educational preparation for careers in business is structured categorically and sequentially, the talents for systemic, lateral thinking in the art of change agentry have only a limited availability in many business settings. Edward de Bono (1970) has argued for a balance between vertical, analytical thinking (digging the same hole deeper) and lateral, broadly inclusive systems thinking (digging a lot of holes).

Agor (1984) defined three management styles as "left brain," "right brain" and "integrated," the latter being a parallel to De Bono's concept of vertical and lateral thinking balance. According to Agor, left-brain types of management employ analytical and quantitative techniques to make management decisions.

So called rational and logical methods of reasoning are primary in the process. The preference is to break down problems into manageable parts and rely on data, technology, and logical sequential methods for decision making. Right-brain skills place primary reliance on feelings, intuition, and inductive techniques. Problems are solved by looking first at the whole, and decisions are reached through "intuitive insights or flashes of awareness that are received." In right-brain processing, the setting or climate is inclined to be more informal. In Agor's words, "participatory and horizontal authority structures are employed, and decisions tend to be made in a somewhat more unstructured fluid, and spontaneous manner" (p. 2). The balancing of the two alternatives results in what is described as the "integrated" style—using both left and right-brain skills interchangeably as the situation requires. Managers adept at integrating both logical and intuitive skills are "switch hitters" in decision making. Agor's seminal publication on intuitive management is an early sign that the doors of perception are opening on the management scene to invite more extensive use of human intellect and creative potential in the service of the systemic nature of organizations and human intellectual evolution.

The creative, innovative spirit is alive and well throughout bureaucracies, even when constraints of the system inhibit demonstrations of its existence. The discussion of "leaders as the 'first birds off the telephone wire' " (Cleveland 1984) is a reminder of the essential quality of effective leadership that takes responsibility for positive change. "People are beginning to sense that they are going to have to lead their leaders out of the wilderness" (p. 4). The analogy to the leader as first bird off the telephone wire includes some advice for the faint of heart who have no appetite for the complex dynamics of change and who stay on the telephone wire to see where the other birds are going next before moving on. The vision and spirit indispensable to leadership at all levels serves the "get-it-all-together function in a complex system—the breadth, the capacity to relate disparate 'facts' to a coherent theory, to fashion tactics that are part of a strategy, and to act in ways that are consistent with a studied view of the future" (Cleveland 1984, 4).

The concept of systems in technological terms with its input-output cycles and cybernetic feedback and feedforward has its share of familiarity in most bureaucracies. Elements of the system which may include production, efficiency, satisfaction, and adaptability have traditionally been based on the measurable or countable components. The more qualitative factors, which must include the diversity and attitudinal flux of the human condition, have been elusive to the degree of being almost entirely unacknowledged. Changes in attitudes and developments in the understanding of differences in individual thinking and learning styles (Gregorc 1983) are adding the human system to the technological system as the more realistic general system governing the future of organizations.

Gregorc (1983) says that different people need different styles of management. Better understanding of differences in thinking and attitudinal styles are illuminating the processes of individual functioning and of interpersonal relationships in work and society. He describes four basic preferred learning and thinking patterns which determine to a considerable extent how individuals are inclined to process information and to behave. His classifications can have major implications for business and management. According to Gregorc (1983), thinking styles are identifiable in both perception and ordering, perception being the means through which people gain information, and ordering the ways in which people arrange and systematize information. Perceptions may be concrete or abstract, through reason, emotion and intuition or through the physical senses. Ordering abilities may be sequential or random, step-by-step or non-linear. The combinations result in four major styles of thought:

> Concrete sequential (seeing is believing)
> Abstract sequential (eternal student)
> Abstract random (idealistic)
> Concrete random (trouble shooters, change agents). (p. 1, 4)

A more thorough acquaintance of the differences in thinking styles can stimulate greater rapport, compassion, and a sense of respect for the diversity and value of the human design.

In addition to the four thinking styles, Gregorc (1983) provides new ways of identifying relationship abilities and styles in the way people function in groups and leadership roles. He describes six ways in which people relate, with possibilities of evolving from dependence through independence to interdependence. His identifying terminology is descriptive:

"Groupies" have an unthinking association with the group, need to feel safety in belonging; and can be swayed by charismatic leaders and peer pressure.

"Super-subs" are either superordinate (boss) or subordinate (underling). They function through doctrines and specific procedures, each in his prescribed mode.

"Separatives" prefer to work on their own; may work with a mentor or go to extremes, rejecting all rules and forms of dependence; they may become self-centered.

"Symbiotics" form loose associations with others of like mind or interests; learn to negotiate and compromise; for them, the whole equals the sum of its parts and each does his part.

"Synergists" believe that the whole is more than the sum of its parts, feel empathy with others and attunement with the group; go beyond specialization to deeper connections.

"Hologroupists" see through "outer differences to a conscious oneness with the total environment." They are the world servers and world citizens, are not judgmental or righteous; they have access to other relationship abilities when appropriate for a given situation (p. 4).

The recognition of differences in relationship abilities and the evolution to the eclecticism of "hologroupists" could have a powerful influence on the effectiveness of all social and business organizations.

Paradox and Balance: New Levels of Thinking

One of the challenges of organizations in the complexities of external and internal change is the design and function of a communication system that sends information down and ideas up through the organizational structure. Perceptions from opposite ends of the continuum fall readily into conflict when simplistic thinking styles are limited in their ability to perceive, let alone empathize, with an opposing point of view.

Considerable interest has developed among both educators and business leaders in the concept of "right brain" and "left brain" differences and dominances as discussed in foregoing articles. Research by Roger Sperry (In Ornstein 1977) for which he was awarded the Nobel Prize in Medicine, reported evidence that the two symmetrical parts of the human brain have distinctive spheres of consciousness and function in somewhat specialized ways. The "left brain" function is associated with rational, objective, quantitative, analytical, and verbal specializations. It is the verbal, talking brain that perceives and communicates in logical, linear thought processes. In contrast, the "right brain" perceives and expresses itself non-verbally and multi-dimensionally in imagery and feelings. This is the intuitive, creative, and innovative side of our head which associates with the internal nervous system (Feather 1979). With Sperry's research as a basis, a better understanding and validity of differences is making its way into the operation of organizations in business, education, and human services. A number of instruments and surveys for determining individual styles of thinking, learning, and managing are described by Agor (1984) in a discussion of the use of brain skill assessments to increase organizational productivity. A survey developed by E. Paul Torrance (1979) at the University of Georgia identifies three broad thinking and management styles of individuals and organizations—left, right, and integrative. A major value of the data resulting from his survey is the reminder of the transcendence of individual styles over labels. The inclination to categorize persons in a bureaucracy according to their title or level of authority raises expectations according to a label, negative or positive, and influences interpersonal realities.

These observations bring this discussion to its central argument. Persons in bureaucracies at all levels of authority or influence, if they are attuned to social change and the transforming nature of institutions, will aspire to develop thought and behavior at higher levels of mentality and maturity than were demanded during less complicated, more static periods of history. The need for this kind of Renaissance is articulated by Rosabeth Moss Kanter (1984). She says that American companies "must go further than making piecemeal responses to problems treated in isolation. They must begin at the top to build more integrative responses to problems, as well as more flexible, integrative organizations to support this" (p. 44).

The brain style termed "integrative" is one which employs both right and left-brain styles interchangeably as the management situation demands. Traditionally, the emphasis in training and development has focused on the left-brain styles as opposed to right-brain functioning. In a typical "left-brain" organization all tasks are highly specialized; all tasks follow a consistent pattern of rules to assure uniformity and to eliminate uncertainty due to individual differences; every person is accountable to a superior whose authority is based on the fact that he is authorized from the top of the hierarchy; officials conduct business in a formal, impersonal manner and maintain distance with subordinates; promotions are based on seniority and achievement.

In contrast to the framework for bureaucratic "left-brain" structures, Bradford and Cohen (1984) identify seven steps in developing a high-performing system and their interaction. The relationship of his seven steps to "right-brain" thinking and managing is unmistakable:

1. Assessing appropriateness for change (problem sensitivity and fact finding).
2. Preparing the turf with your boss and peers (relationships, up, down, and across).
3. Sending initial signals to subordinates (building awareness).
4. Building mutual-influence relationships with difficult subordinates (harmonizing differences).
5. Developing a shared-responsibility team (synthesis rather than analysis).
6. Developing individual subordinates (optimistic expectations).
7. Identifying and gaining commitment to an overarching goal (interaction and networking). (p. 208)

In an article in *Harvard Business Review* as far back as 1976, Henry Mintzberg suggested that top managers should have well developed right-hemispheric processes, and that planners should have well developed left-hemispheric processes. His early attention to application of hemispheric brain theory has been described as a profound breakthrough in management literature. In more recent interpretations, it becomes increasingly clear that the separation and independence of hemispheric functioning is neither so specific nor so absolute. Rather, the argument is for a harmonic, "whole-brained" approach in individual and group development.

When organizations reward employees more for following pre-established rules and operating procedures than for creative thinking and decision making, the working environment breeds bureaucracy and resistance to change, stifles workers and strangles productivity. In addition, the employees who are innately "wired" for "right-brain" thinking and behaving become easy victims of inhibited creative energies, frustration, and stress. Then the task of stress management takes over the time and other resources of an organization in a reactive effort to correct organizational problems, many of which could have been avoided with an organizational climate and pattern of operation more compatible with the realities of human differences in thinking styles.

It may be apparent that persons with a "right-brain" dominance (thinking in patterns, systems, intuition, qualitatives, and creativity) would be more inclined to take a broader, more humanistic and futuristic look at an organizational system, including the "left-brain" component so critical to structure and order. That leads to the general impression that "right-brain" programming could be more inclined to support closed, directed, logically ordered and often unchangeable systems than would left-brain attitudes be open to right-brain change. The effort to bring two opposite, often polarized perspectives, together into an integrated harmony is a proper challenge for persons of both brain dominances. The harmonizing of dichotomies is a task of overwhelming magnitude. What is required is a speeding up of the evolution of the brain/mind to a level of mentality that is able to deal with perceived paradoxes, to acknowledge the value of both "right-brain" and "left-brain" specializations, and to harmonize and integrate the polarities that extract such a price in economic, social, and human resources in bureaucracies. The need for individual minds and attitudes to have a healthy respect for differing opinions and a level of mentality that perceives and works together for the shared organizational vision is a major requirement for success in any system.

The Question of Power

Any discussion of bureaucracies and change has to include a reference to the question of power. Reason suggests that traditionally the rewards, promotion, status, and position in an organization went to those who had a well-developed bank of knowledge, certification, logical, sequential thinking and planning skills, communication talents, and the ability to fit into the existing system without challenge to familiar operating routines. The inclination was for success predicated on "left-brain" specializations. It follows that in many organizations the power structure was, in a major way, based on "left-brain" values. The transformations in society, resulting in a need for new ways of achieving productivity and success in business operations, find roadblocks and bottlenecks impeding efforts for change appropriate to external forces. The exercise of power over innovative ideas and procedures has much of its base in "left-brain" conditioning; "right-brain" oriented persons in an organization have often met with resistance, misunderstanding, silencing, or rejection by superiors in positions of power. The natural urge to protect personal turf and to avoid the discomfort of challenge to the comfortable status quo places power in a position that can impede positive change.

The concept of power is itself coming under enlightening investigation. A major resource for the understanding of power as it expresses itself in a series of stages in organizations is a seminal work by Hagberg (1984). The consideration of power as an evolution from lower to higher stages provides a measure of expectation that new ideas and innovative practices can find better audiences and more support for their efforts from the powers that be. According to Hagberg (1984), the growth of sophistication in the concept of power is hierarchical. She describes the evolution of personal power in six stages, as they relate to "individuals who live and work in the United States of America in the last half of the twentieth century":

1. Stage One: Powerlessness. People in this stage are those who feel almost totally dependent on other people or organizations. They have little access to information, and value the security that routine tasks and routine rewards bring to their work. They are inclined to suffer from low self-esteem.

2. Stage Two: Power by association. People can move from the stage of powerlessness to the stage of power by association, by learning more about the organization and its way of functioning, by developing confidence to be more comfortable with new situations, and by an increased self-awareness. The person depends for validation and support on someone at a higher status and/or authority—a supervisor, the leader, a teacher or public figure.

3. Stage Three: Power by symbols. People in stage three are identified by characteristics that are ego-centric, realistic and competitive, ambitious, sometimes charismatic. They are inclined to move in the fast lane, express behavior of egocentrism and ambition for new challenges and victories.

4. Stage Four: Power by reflection. In this stage, true leadership is expressed in characteristics of competence, reflection, strength, a comfort with their personal style, and mentorship skills. They have the capacity to depart from emphasis on personal ego as in stage three, and are rewarded by a sense of influence.

5. Stage five: Power by purpose. In this stage people have advanced to value and display characteristics that are calm, self-accepting, humble, confident

of life purpose, generous in empowering others, visionary, and spiritual; this seems to be the stage of power that would provide optimal support for new ideas and innovative systems of operation, since their own self-acceptance protects against behaviors of protectionism and defensiveness.

6. Stage Six: Power by gestalt. It is at this stage that the ability to be comfortable with paradox makes its entry, according to Hagberg. Functioning on the universal plane, quiet in service, ethical and wise in judgment, persons in stage six have no reason to struggle for control, since they have voluntarily given up control to others. They see the whole picture and think systemically. (p. 147)

Theory into Practice: Creativity and Innovation

After all the pronouncements of theory and references to authorities and arguments for creative development of individuals, groups, and societies, a question remains. What of the tools and strategies necessary for bringing about creative change in individuals and how they relate to each other in the workplace? Certainly there are no guaranteed formulas for achieving the creative potential of the work force. A multitude of factors can influence creativity and the dynamic nature of such factors. Latent creative potential is often hampered by perceptual, cultural, and emotional factors. In addition, organizational factors and climate have an overwhelming influence on the expression of creative ideas and behavior.

There is, however, a considerable catalogue of operational techniques that can serve as a starting point for involvement in direct experiences that open the doors of perception to creative, innovative thinking, release the imaginative powers of the mind, and overcome the inhibitions that a conforming society and a standardized, competitive educational system have fostered in many employees and officers of corporations. Sander and Ziegler (1977) prepared a review of twenty techniques designed to release the imaginative power of the mind and overcome the inhibitions that a conforming society and a standardized, competitive educational system have fostered in many employees and officers of corporations. The list includes a number of familiar techniques:

Brainstorming, when properly practiced with disciplined attention to the principle of deferred judgment, can be productive of highly original, often ingenious creations. It is especially effective in groups when individual energies combine synergistically and the diversity of knowledge and experience within the group membership stimulates remote connection-making.

Synectics, a level of ideation that uses analogy to spark new connections and insights in problem solving. The mental discipline of "making the familiar strange and the strange familiar" can be, with effective training, an alternative activation of fantasy "right brain" and practical "left brain" which results in highly imaginative, workable solutions to problems.

The Parnes Osborn method of Creative Problem Solving (1981), a method of sequential procedures that begins with the awareness of a problem or challenge and cycles through five specific steps: (a) fact finding, (b) problem finding, (c) idea finding, (d) solution finding, and (e) acceptance finding. Again, as is the case with synectics, there is an emphasis on alternating the different brain functions, in this case the balance separately between convergent, evaluative thinking and divergent, creative thinking.

Free association, forced relationships, morphological analysis, checklisting, attribute listing, are a few of the strategies within the large problem solving system that can, through practice, activate the natural but often dormant properties of the mind that lead to creativity and innovation.

The traditional emphasis in education on content, basic skills, quantitative achievement scores based on limited curricula, standardized testing, and competitive grading does little to recognize and reward creatively talented students. The art and practice of creative, innovative visionary problem definition and problem solving has, in many cases, been left to the practitioners in industry through consultants and training programs. Unless college programs in the field of business begin to include in their degree requirements a preparation in the application of creative thinking and problem solving, graduates will be sent out into the world limited to the analytical, rational reactive approach to solving problems rather than the full spectrum of mental processes that includes skills in creative, innovative thinking and behavior.

Research and observation have shown that it is possible to teach creativity and problem solving to individuals and groups—"teaching" in the sense that the natural creative process can be set free for more imaginative contributions to organizational goals and an increased sense of personal uniqueness and significance.

Effective teaching of creativity demands direct, experiential involvement of the learner in new ways of thinking. The availability of training in specific techniques and strategies for creative thinking and problem solving, coupled with the new realities of the force of the human factor on business, places managers all the way up the corporate ladder to the CEO and chairman of the board in an open position for supporting creative, productive change in their organization. The combination of creative know-how and power at any of the stages described earlier has the potential for valuable contributions in growth and development. The sharing of problem-solving skills in groups representing a cross section of perspectives, a level of trust and respect for differences, and a commitment to the system's goals is critical to any operation with an appetite for creativity and innovation.

Creative development is not the only answer to the problems and challenges of organizations, but it is a major ingredient in the solution. Those in positions of power and influence have a responsibility to improve their skills as catalysts for the creativity of others if new and innovative ideas are to make their way into application. All individuals need to be helped to understand and appreciate their own style of creativity as well as that of others, and to have the freedom to expand upon their creative predispositions in service to the organization.

Summary

A review of the literature on the subjects of creativity and innovation (and how to get information down and ideas up in organizational management) produces, along with the theoretical argument for long-term change agentry, some short-term directives for immediate application. The following are excerpted from a variety of sources and offered here as a summary of the discussion.

Guidelines for creativity and innovation in bureaucracies:

1. Encourage creativity by providing a measure of freedom for workers and making them responsible for results.

2. Be a "Rock Roller." What "rocks" can you roll out of the way so performers can perform (Silber and Sherman 1983)?

3. Cultivate "change agentry"—affecting others through example.

4. Practice mental flexibility: "I don't know." "I made a mistake." "I changed my mind" (I redecided).

5. Treatment for rigid thinking in organizations:
   • bring in consultants
   • bring in new personnel
   • bring in greater call for and sense of responsibility
   • move jobs and structure around
   • organizational flexibility

6. Realize that creativity is there waiting to be tapped—many novel and brilliant ideas. Pay attention to how new ideas are treated. Are they knocked out in their infancy? (Note: There are limits to deviancy; be aware of a level of weirdness.)

7. Check into ideas that fall between "worthless" and "perfect," and develop them to meet criteria: Is there an element of newness? Is the idea feasible? Is there some commitment to its implementation?

8. Practice effectiveness rather than efficiency. "What is the best use of my time right now?" (Lakein 1973)

9. Have the courage to be yourself. Have the courage to be imperfect.

10. Try for diversity of perspectives in problem-solving group membership; then practice astutely the principle of deferred judgment. Apply rigorously the rules for brainstorming.

11. Develop the mechanics for cross fertilization of people and ideas; look carefully at reward and recognition systems in the organization.

12. Understand that creativity is a skill all can develop. All work is creative. Provide conditions for its expression. Cultivate a level of confidence between superior and subordinate necessary for creative functioning.

13. Move from a chain-of-command system to a more collegial system.

14. To bring innovation into large organizations:
    • Accept the right of people to be wrong.
    • Don't give up easily.
    • Follow through on good ideas.
    • Take small steps. Don't wait for the big ones.

• Discriminate between good and bad change.

15. Recognize that a critical and evaluative attitude can stifle creativity in others; people will submit ideas with increasing reluctance if they are pounced upon immediately and subjected to critical evaluations. They soon refrain from suggesting anything at all or resort to second guessing in an attempt to suggest something that will be accepted.

16. Respect and trust intuition, balance intuition with reason in decision making.

17. Be less category conscious.

18. Internalize the fact that organizations don't do anything, people do.

19. Be reminded that every thinker puts some part of the established system in peril.

20. Operate on the observation by Kanter (1984):

If education is balanced by a general education giving a broader view and an ability to make intellectual and interpersonal connections with people in other fields, then the potential innovative capacity of the organizations that employ them is expanded.... Individuals can make a difference, but they need the tools and the opportunity to use them. They need to work in settings where they are valued and supported, their intelligence given a chance to blossom. They need to have the power to be able to take the initiative to innovate.... The promise of this corporate Renaissance depends on how fully corporate leaders understand this need and decide to act on it. (p. 19)

Thinking Together Creatively: The Level of Paradox

Conflicting beliefs divide us within and without. If we could see through them to the level of paradox, we would understand more and fight less.

—Author Unknown

Years of study and investigation have made it clear that everyone has the capacity to be creative, everyone can increase his/her creativity quotient, and creative thinking can be taught. Throughout society and throughout the world, wherever people come together to work for a common purpose, there is a growing awareness that meeting the challenges of life and work as we approach the twenty-first century requires all people to learn to improve the quality of their thinking—to think smart.

In radically changing times, business depends for its success upon the capacity to respond positively to constant shifts and challenges of a dynamic marketplace. Creative, innovative thinkers in any organization represent a most valuable human asset with their capacity for imaginative ideas, flexibility, risk taking, and a tolerance for ambiguity. The creative spirit in the workplace and everywhere else is a primary source of energy and motivation to get the job done.

In an address at the University of Minnesota by the distinguished South African educator and current Ambassador to the United States, Franklin Sonn emphasized the importance of thinking together. The specific teaching of the process of creative thinking is distinctly different from the teaching of skills and content. Whether in a classroom or in a training session in a business setting, methods for the teaching of creative thinking and problem solving depend upon the active participation of everyone involved. Learning is experiential. Strategies for thinking in new ways are presented and practiced individually and in groups. An open-ended climate encourages freedom to be both playful and serious when practicing the art of thinking in new ways—creatively, critically, and paradoxically.

The Parnes Osborn Creative Problem Solving Process as it is taught at the annual Institute in Buffalo, New York, requires the exercise of creative thinking for the production of ideas and critical thinking for decisions on choices and priorities. Thinking at the level of paradox requires the integration of these two opposites at a level that can be creatively critical as well as critically creative. It has been said that the test of a superior intelligence is the ability to keep two opposed ideas in the mind at the same time and still maintain the ability to function. Differences between people, groups, religions, nations, cultures, and ideologies can be resolved when we can see through them to the level of paradox—the level of thought that leads to greater understanding and mutuality (Handy 1994).

Figure 1 presents an argument for the value of the creative process as a mutualistic force for dealing with paradoxical situations requiring a harmonizing of differences. The framework for representing the issue of paradoxical thinking is fish bone, a familiar visual for describing a system. The application in this example is in business where management and employees differ in their perceptions of the workplace. Valuable energy is lost when misunderstanding and conflict between groups or organizational levels interfere with a company's productivity, efficiency, service and revenue. The argument made by the fish-bone graphic suggests that if all members of an organization, regardless of job or label or status, learned the art of creative thinking and problem solving, that shared process of thinking together would be a strong force in eliminating needless conflict and moving the company toward collective goals and objectives. In spite of differences in organizational position, the commonalities of thinking and problem-solving strategies would cause a shift from old, habit-bound, polarized thinking to the more enlightened level of paradoxical thinking that creates a unity of differences. More creative, harmonious work attitudes characterized by flexibility, cooperation, and risk taking are "money in the bank" for any business or institution.

It is not an exaggeration to suggest that the traditional system of categorizing, labeling, and subsequently polarizing people and groups has resulted in a "crisis of perception." Instead of perceiving each part as an essential piece of the total interactive system and each person as an interconnected player in the evolution to new patterns of leadership, limitations of labels and categories inhibit the best in all of us. Separateness is itself a crisis. In spite of the literature of enlightenment, there remains a strong inclination to perceive management and employee as polarized and unable to bring the best of differing talents together. Sharing the creative process and its applications provide a common meeting ground for the integration and promotion of diversity wherever people share a common goal.

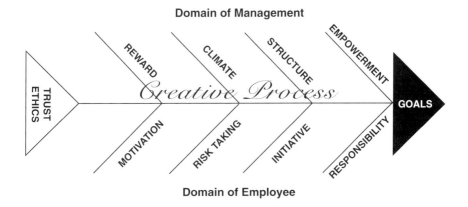

Figure 1—The Creativity Fish Bone: Process for Mutuality

The creativity fish-bone concept applies to any group or organization. The application of the model is to the world of business. The interpretation is as follows:

1. The goals are the driving force and direction of the organization, and are represented as spearheading the system.

2. Behind the goals are pairs of forces, one operating from the domain of management, the other from the domain of employee, in direct relationship with each other, but not always so perceived. The first pair (empowerment and responsibility) represents efforts by management to empower employees; employees respond by recognizing the genuine invitation to assume more responsibility. If management is prepared to relinquish power, and employees are prepared to be empowered and to be responsible for results, new levels of mutuality are achieved.

3. The second pair of perceived opposites (structure and initiatives) suggests that a major role of management is to provide a structure of operation that is open-ended and flexible enough to support employee initiatives for new product development, quality improvement, procedural and money-saving changes, worker satisfaction, and more. Employees who value the freedom to express their ideas and to initiate positive change take advantage of the system structure and exercise the privileges of shared leadership and followership.

4. The organizational climate or work environment is largely determined by management. The third pair of opposites (climate and risk taking) suggests that a creative environment is central to creative thinking and innovation on the part of employees throughout the workplace. A creative work environment that encourages creative factors of awareness, curiosity, experimentation, and risk taking on the part of employees cultivates enthusiasm and spirit, cooperation, and a sense of personal significance.

5. The fourth pair of opposing perceptions (rewards and motivation) recognizes that rewards originate in the domain of management, whether individual worker motivation is for extrinsic or intrinsic rewards. Extrinsic rewards in the form of salary, promotion, and perks are joined by the intrinsic rewards of job satisfaction and a quality of work life that encourages full individual participation and teamwork. An important asset in any organization is a fully functioning work force, where personal rewards include a place of work that provides each person a place to shine, grow, and be recognized by peers and by management.

6. The subtle and sensitive factors of trust and ethics represented by the fishtail serve as a stabilizing and energizing force for the entire operation. It may be that these uncountable, qualitative factors of trust and ethics do as much as the more traditional quantifiable features of a business to affect the profit line.

7. In the fish-bone metaphor, the creative spirit and process of thinking together at a level of paradox are the spine and central nervous system in the life of any organization, and could even apply in the hope for a more just and peaceful world. The creativity fish-bone framework is a helpful system for identifying and addressing paradoxes and polarities that impede progress and interfere with harmony, not only in the business world but throughout the personal, political, and social arenas of human affairs.

The natural human inclination is to perceive a situation from the perspective of one's own experiences and personal advantages. The capability of perceiving beyond or in addition to one's own life and personal paradigm requires a deliberate major shift in the understanding and practice of new ways of thinking together—imaginatively, critically, and paradoxically. In addition, the dynamic and uncertain nature of our time in history as we approach the twenty-first century demands the highest possible orders of thinking—futuristically, systemically, and globally.

An Open and Shut Case for Business

Innovation requires a trust in the future that is difficult to arouse or sustain in organizations constantly looking to the past. Living with change need not imply insecurity but, rather, developing new forms of security.

—Rosabeth Moss Kanter

There was a time in history when it made some sense for business operations to be organized in closed systems with well established guidelines and policies spelled out in detail and firmly fixed, with the expectation of a long, dependable life. The accelerated rate of change in society and the global marketplace has changed all of that. A business that adheres to yesterday's closed system of leadership built around traditional absolutes of inflexible hierarchical power and influence predicts its own ruin.

The observation that "minds are like parachutes, they don't function unless they're open," is more than appropriate when applied to modern business systems. The impact of technological and other radical changes on the workplace and the work force demands a more open, flexible style of operation. Meeting the challenges of change simply by a redistribution of tangibles like funds, space, equipment, personnel, and power misses a critical component of any system. The missing component is the unlimited factor of human intellectual capital present and under-utilized in most organizations, especially in those where size, growth, and complexity complicate the flow of communication.

A more modern and effective systems for success in business suggests three necessary factors:

Information. Communication of facts and developments up, down, and sideways throughout the organization

Interrelationships. Recognizing and integrating the interrelationships, separate parts and procedures within the total system

Vision. A sense of agreement regarding the direction, purpose, and values of the shared business mission.

The successful practice of all three factors in a business adapting to the demands of radical change would be powerful groundwork for the ultimate evolution to a self-organizing system of operation. Already evidence grows that traditional management patterns of control are giving way to more integrative leadership styles as business comes face to face with new work-related realities. Unconsciously the trend is moving in the direction of the conscious acknowledgment that when organizations face constant demands for change, every player in the system needs to have a conscious awareness of the individual's capacity to contribute to the challenge of self-organizing the system.

The accomplishment of major changes in a business operation depends upon the prevailing attitudes that help to make up the culture of any workplace. An article by Albert Wight in the *Journal of Creative Behavior* as far back as fall 1970, predicted changes in the attitudes and social creativity of the world of work. He drew a distinction between attitudes and behaviors that help to move organizations from exclusive, regimented, closed systems of management to more inclusive, dynamic, open systems of leadership.

Capitalizing on Human Capital

The twenty-seven years since the publication of Wight's article have witnessed increasing attention to the need for balance between growth in the development of technological know-how and growth in the understanding of human capital and its contribution to the "bottom line" (Beuys 1998). To some degree his predictions are proving valid. Greater efforts are being made to provide leadership that capitalizes on the unlimited human power and spirit of work life in an open system rather than the outmoded closed system. Some of the following distinctions apply:

Open System

Attitudes of self-confidence and self-esteem which allow for more flexibility and the capacity to entertain new ideas and abandon the irrelevant.

Individual behavioral tendencies toward initiative, creativity, innovation, and curiosity.

Climate for shared power, participatory decision-making, and group problem-solving that invites and supports genuine trust and cooperative teamwork.

Emphasis on free interplay of differences without personal conflict or polarization of opposing, competitive forces.

Work environment supportive of honesty, integrity, responsibility, involvement, and mutual appreciation.

Closed System

Attitudes of excessive caution, inflexibility; inability to relinquish the old and explore the new.

Behavioral tendencies toward conformity and submissiveness, fear, and distrust.

Climate of conflict, competitiveness, power over others, negativism, withdrawal.

Emphasis on either/or mentality rather than both/and mutuality.

Work environment reflecting lack of concern, cynicism, priority on protection of personal power and status.

How does an organization, business, or institution go about the task of converting from an essentially closed system of stagnation to one of vitality, openness, and growth? The question has particular importance now, when evidence of success in businesses characterized by trust and openness are being joined by appeals from the business community for an improved work force with skills and qualities equal to the demands of a society in transition. Answers to the question come in a variety of packages and programs from books and professional literature to research, surveys, and analyses, conferences and seminars, and training and development programs of many kinds. Search for a fundamental focus of reform leads ultimately to a reality that subsumes the entire collection of resources. Sooner or later it becomes evident that the years spent in schooling where habits of thinking and reasoning are developed can make the difference. Recent understanding of different levels of brain/mind functioning is resulting in trends to add the deliberate teaching of quality thinking to the curriculum. Teaching strategies and training programs that identify and encourage creative and critical thinking, problem solving and decision making, all integrate well with the successful teaching of reading, math, and other important basic skills throughout the schooling experience.

Polarities and Paradox

Business and education are not separate camps in the professional world in spite of testimonials to the contrary. Academicians limited to theoretical pursuits and business practitioners who disdain theoretical education as impractical in the "real world" miss the familiar lesson that "both/and" thinking is far more productive for everyone than the "either/or" trap. In addition it exercises the paradoxical level of intellect which helps humans to "understand more and fight less." It is increasingly important to acknowledge the fact that the more business and education discover the reality of their necessary integration, the more they enhance themselves and support each other. That discovery is a major step in the evolution from a closed to an open system.

The sequence in that evolution is as powerful as it is natural. It begins with an attitude of trust in the sharing of information within an organization and across specializations. What follows, when every player at every level in the organization practices quality thinking, is a recognition of the interconnectedness of all the separate parts into a whole interactive, conscious or unconscious self-organizing system. To complete the formula for success in business, add the factor of vision, where everyone, regardless of rank or label, shares in a common perception of the purpose and genuine value of the company's work and their own individual purpose and value within the open, fully functioning system.

Attitudes of self-interest and commitment to group goals need not be incompatible. Creating a unity of differences is the work of the paradoxical mind. We can be logical and visionary at the same time.

For Lesson in Creative Teamwork, Try Listening to Some Jazz

Music is the archetypal ordering of sound. It patterns and reinforces the powers of listening, attention, and memory for people of every culture. Music is not only art and a refined form of beauty's expression, but it is also the subtle and dynamic power that unifies breath, rhythm, and tone of the human body. Every thought, feeling, and movement has its own musical qualities.

—Don Campbell

I had a real "light bulb" experience not long ago while enjoying the relaxation of musical listening.

A jazz trio—saxophonist, guitarist, and bassist—was entertaining at a Sunday brunch, playing requests for easy listening that were popular during the era of the Big Bands. After the trio established the melody or theme of the song, each member would play a solo that improvised and elaborated the melody while the other two members played support.

It was not difficult to see their performance as a significant metaphor for effective, natural, harmonious, and productive teamwork that is so vital to business and other organizations (Campbell 1991). I began to wonder whether the trio members were even aware of the remarkable process of thinking in which they were engaged.

Except for an expression of focused pleasure and an occasional glance or nod of appreciation for some particularly creative interpretation, there seemed to be no visible communication among the artists, yet the outcome of their teamwork was a model for the unity of differences.

Somehow in the integration of brain/mind/body/spirit each instrumentalist managed to fit his own separate piece into a pleasing unity with two other separate pieces. Three totally different instruments played with totally different kinesthetic skills by three different personalities and aesthetics with three different sets

Minneapolis Star-Tribune. *Reprinted with permission.*

of feelings about the song's melody and lyrics and evoked memories were creating a human harmony spontaneously and unrehearsed.

A Lesson Here

I was quite stunned at this demonstration of the marvels of the human brain/mind.

I wondered whether the demonstration of the process of teamwork by a jazz trio could be analyzed as it applied to the search for team building strategies in other places. Could the same principles be translated from sound to words in an articulation of guidelines for teamwork anywhere? The question was worth pursuing.

The trio was invited to a demonstration of their musical art and an invitation to discuss the process by which the separate parts integrated themselves into a positive team product. Applications of the process of improvisational professional jazz to team building in business are especially appropriate, since the dynamics of any team of individuals are complex and unpredictable. Musical performances that follow a rehearsed score would not apply.

After a few introductory tunes, the trio discussed the process of their art and answered questions from the listeners.

There were specific answers to the question, "Just how do you do it?"

Pay Attention

"Above all, you listen carefully to the other players and are responsive; you share the leadership; i.e., when another member takes a solo, you support and encourage him. You have to be aware of your own mood and the mood of the other players. It helps to be able to interpret and even anticipate subtle communications during the performance. It is important to continue to practice and improve the skills of your particular musical art."

If teams in the workplace could relate their task to the jazz process as described by a group of thoughtful, articulate musicians, their guidelines would probably go something like this:

Listen carefully to everyone else. Be supportive.
Balance the leadership and followership; Give everyone a chance to "solo."

Be sensitive to the moods (internal environments) of the others.

Trust your intuitions.

Risk expressing your ideas, even when you are not totally sure of them.

Be "playful." Lighten up, and think smart simultaneously.

Be open to new, experimental patterns and directions outside of the "square."

Bring the outside world into the picture. Think systemically.

Maybe the best way to harmonize and motivate a team is to listen to a live improvisational jazz performance of relaxing, mellow music, everyone a separate artist. Experimentation and innovation stimulate and energize a jazz offering. Communication and empathy with the audience enriches the performance. Mutual respect and love for each other and for the shared musical soul of the group is the ultimate feature in the fabric of the team.

Creativity Connections and Extensions

An Expanding Revelation

Everything is in evolution, including the discipline of creativity. It would be quite impossible to become involved in the creativity explosion without having intimations of the broad expansion of its influence. Jonas Salk (1983) called attention to a sense of an evolving society and universe of "shifting patterns" and "something strong and powerful that is acting with interior as well as exterior force." Both reason and intuition suggest that one of the powerful forces affecting individual, interior patterns of thought is the growing realization that within each of us is a creative being which needs to be understood and given expression. The exterior force is the reality that all of humanity is intimately linked with each individual member. New discoveries and dynamic events in the world force the creative, inquiring mind to wonder and reflect on the nature of human development and the meaning of the changing relationships making an impact on life everywhere (Csikszentmihalyi 1993).

Although the basic purpose of this publication is to argue for the specific teaching for understanding and practice in the art of creative and other specific thinking processes, it is important to add to the realities of the discipline a measure of intuitive, speculative insight. We can all know without knowing how we know. New connections and perceptions occur unbidden to the mind without benefit of substantiating research. The articles in the section on creative connections claim only that a relationship exists between creativity as we know it and the events that make up our shared human history.

Reflections regarding the expanded applications of creativity included in the section on connections are in order here:

Unlike most of the population, the creative genius of thinkers like William Blake and Albert Einstein needed no formal lessons for its emergence and preservation.

The failure of school and society to provide for legitimate, positive expression of the creative force is reflected in the report on observations from creative problem solving classes in a state prison.

The human expression of laughter and humor is explored as it relates to the creative capacity of the mind to recognize remote connections of thought.

The issue of thinking at a creative level of paradox requires the mind to hold two opposing thoughts simultaneously and still continue to function. The familiar challenge to the role of media is the traditional polarization between the right to know and the right to privacy. An extension of the challenge is to find the balance that makes harmony of differences applies especially to the role of international media. Their position of influence in the creation of a global family depends upon the paradoxical level of thinking that interprets world news without bias and that assigns relevance and value to human diversity in its search for common ground.

Intuitive leadership as an accompanying feature of radical, unpredictable change is finding a place of merit in human affairs. Unexpected developments are forcing leaders and decision makers to depend not only on the time consuming "truth" of research and trend extrapolation, but more and more on unexplainable, intuitive perceptions of systems and their future developments.

Scholars from disciplines of both science and studies of human behavior have been sharing their thinking regarding the pervasive nature of the creative force, its influence on the evolving self, and a sensitivity for where humans are in the universe and in the world in both time and space. In times past Iqbal, a Persian writer and philosopher, expressed his perceptions of those vast mysteries in the narrative poem, "The Javid Nama." An exploration of the poem's Eastern thought by a Western thinker is included as a reminder of the common human urge to understand the mystery of human life and its changing patterns, its spiritual meanings, and its vast possibilities.

The reader is invited to consider the subjects of these readings as a beginning network of connections to creativity beyond the focus of existing labels and familiar applications. Study and speculations of a universal trend toward an evolving change in habits of mind make possible the dream of a world of peace and justice. The realization of such a dream can be created through the understanding of the individual and the collective forces inherent in the human mind awaiting expression in human affairs.

The Contraries in Science and
the Arts of William Blake:
A Growing Mutuality

There is a feature of the contemporary world that is of unparalleled relevance to the future of humanity; it is the creative interplay of diversification and integration. It applies with equal force in nature and to history. There is nothing that would grow and evolve in the world that would not have in some measure both unity and diversity.

—Ervin Laszlo

Introduction

There is growing evidence that William Blake and his work are becoming a cynosure of inquiry into the nature of imagination and discovery. Certainly there is much about Blake and his work that demands attention. Scientists and general systems theoreticians are expressing a particular interest and excitement regarding the interrelationships between science, the arts, and their unifying principles (von Bertalanffy 1968). Distinguished writers from the scientific community (Bronowski 1943) have, for a long time, been preoccupied with the personhood, creative processes, and uncommon works of William Blake as an illumination in their own search for understanding and discovery of the mysteries of the universe and man's place in it. As society moves into new dimensions and a growth of human consciousness, attention to Blake's work increases. The Tate Gallery in London recognizes Blake's creative exceptionality with an extensive special gallery of his works. His art and poetry hold a somewhat mysterious, provocative psychic fascination for many. An exploration into his life and the intuitive genius of his work can provide clues to reasons for the preoccupation, especially among members of the disparate discipline of science, with the man without a mask (Bronowski 1943). An effort is made here to begin to answer the question: What is there about William Blake—poet, artist, social dissenter—that excites growing attention from the scientific community?

The Background

To begin with, it is important to look into the personal life and characteristics of the man toward whom scientists gravitate as a symbol of their own creative processes. Ironically, William Blake's biographical data reflect little of the exceptionality of his genius. The events of his life, and the times in which they were set, assigned little significance to his art, writing, or his concern for social justice. He has been described as:

> A little man, with much of the eighteenth century John Bull about him, pugnacious, stubborn, prejudiced, insular with the insularity of one who never left his native island, and one who would give a good account of himself in a fight and would never be beaten, more of a "Christian bulldog."…He could bear poverty cheerfully, though he did not attach to it the mystical virtue which those who were better off may have imagined, and was quite clear about the preferable advantages of some measure of appreciation and material reward. His life was an open book, and what was called his madness was often more an index to the foolishness of those he met with than anything else. (Gaunt 1956, 195)

Charges of madness were as paradoxical as the "contraries" of his work: "His madness was too evident, too fearful. It gave his eyes an expression such as you would expect to see in one who was possessed" (Klonsky 1977, 13), and, in contradiction,

> in the sweetness of his countenance and gentility of his manner he added an indescribable grace to the conversation. And that, apart from his visions and references to the spiritual world, his observations were sensitive and acute. (p. 13)

> There is evidence that he recognized honesty and valued his own unlimited perception and visionary imagination in contrast with the level of those qualities in ordinary men. He wrote: "If the doors of perception were cleansed, everything would appear to man as it is, infinite. For man has closed himself up, till he sees all things through narrow chinks of his cavern." (Klonsky 1977, 7)

Scientific interest in these limitless dimensions is understandable, since Blake expressed a sense of limitation in scientific practice, insisting that mathematical abstractions and metaphysical generalities were incapable of perceiving the infinite. As science urges itself toward universal understandings, the puzzlements that accompany insights into links between science and the visionary poetics of Blake take on new meaning. When he suggests that only "in minute particulars" can the infinite be observed and that "whatever the seer sees—whether envisioned in a religious trance or in a poetic or prophetic rapture—has to be seen by himself alone, no other witness" (Klonsky 1977, 7), the mystery and provocation grow. Blake's prophetics of scientific theory, moving beyond Newtonian physics to quantum mechanics, are materializing long after his death (Zukav 1979). After two hundred years, he is becoming recognized more as an age than an individual (Bronowski 1943).

Blake's struggles for a life of imagination and his spirit of freedom and brotherhood during years of political and social suppression distinguish him historically. He seemed to see and hear what others failed to observe:

In every cry of every Man
In every infant's cry of fear
In every voice, in every ban
The mind-forged manacles I hear. (Kazin 1976, 12)

He was an example of the creative, energetic personality who looks on the world as fit for change, and on himself as an instrument for change—the world a canvas and himself a divine agent of change (Bronowski 1965).

It is possible that the political and social constraints of his time in history—England during the American War for Independence, the war with France, and the Industrial Revolution—disruptive challenges to human dignity and security, provided materials and energies for his dissenting spirit, resulting in art and poetry of a creative dynamic not likely in less troubled times. Although his writing attacked social and governmental institutions and their leadership, he practiced the diplomatic obscurities and subtleties of a "…mystic with a harsh understanding of the world in which he was forced to live, in which he knew himself to be a rebel, and in which he felt himself a prisoner" (Bronowski 1943, 56). The law he believed in he described as "…a state in Eternity, composed of the innocent civilized heathen and the uncivilized savage who, having not the law, do by nature the things contained in the law" (Klonsky 1977, 8).

For his dedication to freedom and his literary efforts against war, injustice, and the hypocrisy of the times, he was brought to trial on charges of seditious writing. In his own defense he wrote: "Everyone here is my evidence for peace and good neighborhood; and yet, such is the present state of things this foolish accusation must be tried in public" (Bronowski 1943, 74). Although he was acquitted, he became baffled and hopeless, as do many radicals. However, Blake never lost his social conscience. As Bronowski suggests "The end which he sought was more than a social righting. It was the right. He believed that this end is found in no society, but must be found by man himself" (Bronowski 1943, 94).

In an interpretation of that concept, Bachalard (1969) could be speaking of a Blake:

It would seem, then, that it is through their 'immensity' that these two kinds of space—the space of intimacy and world space—blend. When human solitude deepens, then the two immensities touch and become identical, toward unlimited solitude that makes a lifetime of each day, toward a communion with the universe, in a word, space, the invisible space that man can live in nevertheless, and which surrounds him with countless presences. (p. 203)

Works of art always spring from those who have faced the danger, gone to the very end of an experience, to the point beyond which no human being can go. The further one dares to go, the more decent, the more personal, the more unique a life becomes. (p. 220)

If the intense human solitude, which seems so pervasive a quality in Blake's life, is necessary to enter the universal dimensionalities of the creative mind, members of a scientific community may be deprived of those limits beyond limits, since, according to Bronowski (1965), the scientists, unlike the artist/poet who works within the "intimate immensities," often function collectively, building brick on brick and idea upon idea sequentially.

The Common Ground: Bisociation

Whether the content of the operation of discovery and imagination is of a scientific or an artistic nature, the process by which the original product is arrived at has many commonalties. Arthur Koestler (1964) has identified the essence of creativity, that creative acrobatics of the mind by which two mutually incompatible contexts are brought into meaningful relationships as "bisociation." The product may take the form of a new product, an original art work, a scientific principle, a procedure, or a total paradigm shift. Recognizing subtle relationships, imaging "irrationalities," and making them rational depend upon the creative mental spark that is shared by those of creative talent for whom the shared process provides a kind of bond of understanding and brotherhood.

What makes a great scientist? He is made as every creative person is made, painter or novelist, musician, poet, or scientist. A person can only create something of which he has a vision—and that has already been said by the poet, William Blake as if he were speaking about science, "What is now proved was once only imagined" (Bronowski 1943, 1965; Deutsch, Priestly, Brown, and Hawkins 1958).

The Common Ground: Paradox and Contraries

The value of bisociation reveals itself in another of the levels of intellect common to the act of creation. Recognition of the unity of differences, the androgynous blendings into harmony of polarities and contradictions are familiar mind functionings to both scientists and artists. Blake's use of the term contraries to describe paradoxes is apt. He wrote:

Without contraries is no progression. Attraction and repulsion, reason and energy, love and hate, are necessary to human existence. From these contraries spring what the religious call good and evil. Good is the passive that obeys reason. Evil is the active springing from energy. Good is heaven. Evil is hell (Bronowski 1943, p. 92).

The philosophical questions that arise from some of Blake's contraries take the mind beyond its limits of perception. Blake dealt in a system of concrete metaphysics, an unpopular and suspect dimensionality for his times. Coupled with his reports of conversations with spirits and angels, he gave the people of his time reasons for accusations of madness. A friend wrote in his defense:

> I never in all my conversations with him could feel the least justice in calling him insane; he could always explain his paradoxes when he pleased, but to many he spoke so "that hearing they might not hear." (Klonsky 1977, 14)

There is enigmatic significance in that statement, which provides a clue to the interest that scientists have in Blake's visionary, enduring genius, especially in our era of parapsychological interests and cosmic connectedness.

Common Ground: Observation and Coincidence

Another common quality contributing to the spirit which is growing between disciplines is the quality of creative curiosity. In discussing the procedures of the research scientist, Blade (1963) describes the related process of observation:

> By observe, I mean a great deal more than just "taking a look." I have in mind an intense concentration on the subject of inquiry, coupled with a singleness of purpose and the persistence to overcome difficulties. This requires a high degree of "inner direction." We are so constituted that, although we have eyes that see, they often see not. Perception takes a lot of looking which is likely to be very tedious. Often only a consummate curiosity can carry one through. The best word I have ever heard for it is passion. (p. 202)

Relating Blake to this description of the scientific process causes the impression that he compounded and compressed the process in his approach to his work, and became the essence of "entrances into the infinite." His concept of "minute particularity" raises observation to new heights:

> As poetry admits not a letter that is insignificant, so painting admits not a grain of sand or a blade of grass insignificant, much less an insignificant blur or mark. To him any picture or picture-poem, if inspired by the Divine Imagination was "as holy as holy writ." (Klonsky 1977, 12)

Common Ground: Serendipity

From the shared value of observation is derived the creative commonality of chance coincidence or serendipity. Alertness to the system beyond immediate investigation opens a multiplicity of options for new connections and hence new discoveries. Major breakthroughs in science have occurred by "chance," arriving unbidden during moments of complete relaxation or incubation. Capitalizing on the synchronicity of time and space adds a productive resource to creative connections. In *The Ghost in the Machine,* Arthur Koestler (1967) reminds the reader of the realities of phenomena for which there is no present scientific explanation. Koestler's book is said to be essential reading for all those who feel that the sciences of man in the contemporary form fail to address the real problems of human existence. Science could do well to search Blake for entry into new scientific/humanistic dimensionalities. Those searches may be in process.

The Uncommon Ground

Although scientists identify with many processes in William Blake's creative genius, they may recognize, along with the likenesses, some uncommon, contributing exceptionalities in his nature.

The aim of science is to seek the simplest explanations to complex facts. The poet's aim is to overcome the tendency of language to reduce complex experiences to a succession of simple elements (Deutsch et al. 1958). The subjective nature of Blake's concept of universal systems contrasts with the scientific, mathematically calculable nature of reality:

To see a World in a Grain of Sand
And Heaven in a Wild Flower,
Hold Infinity in the palm of your hand
And Eternity in an hour. (Kazin 1976, 150)

The title of this famous poem, "Auguries of Innocence," with its poetic reference to time and space, is in sharp contrast to the traditional concept of scientific objectivity which rests upon the assumption of an external world which is "out there" as opposed to an "I" which is "in here" (Zukav 1979, 55).

Although the science of physics deals normally with the "invariants of physical reality," the theory of relativity began the scientific effort to understand and quantify the poetic concepts of time and space, accommodating Blake's familiar subjective insights with scientific objectivity. Zukav (1979) writes: "Wu Li Masters perceive in both ways, the rational and the irrational, the assertive and the receptive, the masculine and the feminine. They reject neither one nor the other. They only dance" (p. 65).

To visualize a fourth dimension requires a particular act of imagination which "is never wrong, since it does not have to confront an image with an objective reality," according to Bachalard (1969, 152). Blake provided countless clues to his concepts of visionary thought and its limitations, especially in respect to Newtonian physics:

> Now I a fourfold vision see,
> And a fourfold vision is given to me.
> 'Tis fourfold in my supreme delight
> And threefold in soft Beulah's night
> And twofold always.
> May God us keep
> From Single vision and Newton's sleep. (Klonsky 1977, 10)

In Blake's words, the "single vision" occurs when we see with, not through our eyes. But fourfold vision, his "supreme delight," is attained only when the phenomenal world has been transcended by the Divine Imagination and reunited with Spirit, "liberating imagination that has no connection with organic incitements" (Klonsky 1977, p. 11). Bachalard (1969) says that

> …in the exercise of a pure, free imagination, the poet does not shrink before reversals or dovetailings. Without even thinking that he is scandalizing reasonable men, contrary to the most ordinary common sense, he actually experiences reversal of dimensions or inversion of the perspective of inside and outside. (p. 225)

Newton's mechanical universe was familiar to Blake through his experiences in the "Satanic Wheels" of the Industrial Revolution, making known the price of uncontrolled scientific progress in human disruption and displacement. In Blake's words:

> The Villages lament; they faint, outstretched upon the plain.
> Wailing runs round the Valleys from the Mill and from the Barn.
> The Horse is of more value than the Man. (Bronowski 1943, 64)

In Bronowski's (1943) explanation:

> The Industrial Revolution moved forward by the skill of its mechanics. It moved from what the engineer asked to what the mechanic could make, from what the mechanic made to what the engineer might plan. Its horror was that the mechanic's skill commonly threw him out of work. (p. 64)

Blake's empathic sensibilities are given expression in much of his writing during the periods of war and social agony in England. He sensed not only the griefs of the present, but also the greater dimension of their implications for political and human futures:

> A Robin Redbreast in a cage
> Puts all heav'n in a rage.
> A dog starved at the master's gate
> Predicts the ruin of the state. (Kazin 1976, 150)

And "On Another's Sorrow" from *Songs of Innocence*:

> Can I see another's woe,
> And not be in sorrow too?
> Can I see another's grief,
> And not seek for kind relief?
> Can I see a falling tear,
> And not feel my sorrow's share? (Kazin 1976, p. 97)

Rapid advances in science, technology, genetic engineering, atomic weaponry, and countless mechanizations are again raising challenging questions for the scientific community. Who speaks for the human condition, the quality of life in the global village, and the long-range future of planet earth? Blake's metaphysical and prophetic vision may provide insights into the art of accountability for the uncountable.

The multidimensionality of Blake's personhood included a factor not commonly associated with the serious, scientific manipulation, quantification, rearranging, and combining of data, looking for a spark of an idea which will make harmony of chaos. Blake added a sense of humor to his life and writing. Klonsky (1977) refers to his style of humor as "raunchy and subversive wit." Examples of satiricism abound in his political and social/artistic criticisms. Puns were also a part of his playful/serious observations: "Spirits are lawful, but not ghosts; especially Royal Gin is lawful spirit" (Bronowski 1943, 26).

His sense of humor derived from the general spontaneous joy and lighthearted, sensuous response to the world of nature and its events. For example:

He who binds to himself a Joy
Doth the wing'd life destroy
But he who catches joy as it flies
Lives in eternity's sunrise. (Kazin 1976, 135)

and in "Laughing Song"

When the green woods laugh with the voice of joy,
And the dimpling stream runs laughing by;
When the air does laugh with our merry wit,
And the green hill laughs with the noise of it;
When the meadows laugh with lively green
And the grasshopper laughs in the merry scene,
When Mary and Susan and Emily
With their sweet round mouths sing "Ha, Ha, He!"
When the painted birds laugh in the shade,
Where our table with cherries and nuts is spread,
Come live & be merry, and Join with me,
To sing the sweet chorus of "Ha, Ha, He!" (Kazin 1976, 89)

Bronowski (1978) makes an important and specific point to add to the uncommon ground between science and the arts in his book, *The Origins of Knowledge and Imagination*. Excerpts from his discussion of the subject follow:

> …what has made science successful as a social leaven over the last three hundred years is its change from the practice of individual, however great their ingenuity, to a communal enterprise.… I do want you to see that even that tremendous mind of Leonardo da Vinci could not work in isolation…a particularly crucial point because, in a way, everything that I have been saying about the maverick personality so far is really true of all creative minds.… It is rather puzzling why, on the whole, science took off about three hundred years ago and has been so very successful in expanding its kind of knowledge while, on the whole, the same cannot be said of the arts.… Now, this is because science is and can be practiced as a communal activity. The community of scientists has a special strength; it has to do with the fact that in the practice of science everybody knows what everybody else's work is. It is very simple; in the end you cannot propose a scientific theory unless it conforms to a certain sanction of fact. (pp. 122–124)

Bronowski's pronouncement that man is a double creature who needs to be sustained by his fellows, yet think alone, may not apply to Blake's pattern of needs. The lack of support from his fellows and society during his lifetime may account for his "fourfold vision." The spirits with whom he reported constant companionship would seem to have served him better in special ways than a support system from a literary community or the patterns of scientific systems. The imaginative products of his singular vision may account for the excitement of the scientific collective in his imaginative genius and cosmic realities, those waves of world consciousness that emanated from his "dreaming self."

The Meeting Ground

Beyond considerations of the common and uncommon grounds, the natural direction toward which humans strive for meaning and understanding is onward, upward, and in constant systemic expansion. Whatever the differences, the unities are there waiting to be discovered. Edgar Mitchell, scientifically trained in engineering, aeronautics, and astronautics for piloting the Apollo 14 moon landing, represents a mental meeting ground between traditional science and psychic phenomena associated with the work of Blake (Mitchell 1979). The sight of the entire earth at once from space was, for Mitchell, a peak experience that resulted in a more holistic, integrated perception of the natural universe as distinguished from the traditional scientific perception of the material universe. Hence, his leadership is bringing a new validity to the investigation of the extraordinary mental functions apparent in Blake's poetry and art. It remains to be seen whether the miraculous, paranormal, supernatural, spiritual, and other-worldly can be scrutinized and researched by persons highly skilled in such disciplines as theoretical physics, mathematics, neurophysiology, and psychology, to the satisfaction of entrenched scientific traditionalism. The establishment of the Institute of Noetic Sciences in Menlo Park by Edgar Mitchell is one beginning of a trend to discover the processes of Blake's imagination and the sense of his communications with the universe (Gell-Mann, 1994).

Jacob Bronowski saw the natural flow and blend that connects the scientist to the poet when "the doors of perception are opened." He describes the processes that move from visionary, subjective, qualitative thought to the precision of quantitatives. This is a direct reflection of the concepts of balance between right and left-brain hemispheric differences from the work of Robert Ornstein (1977). In the words of Bronowski (1978):

> Now we begin to see where the path from metaphor to algorithm always goes. When Newton saw the moon as a ball that had been thrown round the earth, he was initiating a gigantic metaphor. And when it finished up, it was in calculable form, it was an algorithm (a formula with which you can calculate). And that is the path from metaphor to algorithm—from Blake phrase to the Newton formula—that every scientific theory has to follow because it is a human section of the totality of experience which excludes some of the connections which are there. (p. 61)

It is questionable whether the scientific theory of holography could have been advanced and articulated without the perceptions of "the world in a grain of sand." It suddenly occurs that it is time for a new term, "metaphormula" to describe the integrative process suggested in Bronowski's foregoing statement.

If science looks to understand and/or emulate Blake's art of imagination and discovery, the value of the mysterious, complex, unfathomable individual mind and the products of that mind, whether rational or irrational, far out or scientifically connected, need consideration even before being empirically tested and authenticated. The main tenet, according to von Bertalanffy (1968), in his discussion of General Systems Theory follows:

> Man is, before and above all, an individual. The real values of humanity are not those which it shares with biological entities, the function of an organism or a community of animals, but those which stem from the individual mind.... Human society is based upon the achievements of the individual, and is doomed if the individual is made a cog in the social machine. This, I believe, is the ultimate precept a theory of organization can give; not a manual for dictators of any denomination more efficiently to subjugate human beings by the scientific application of Iron Laws, but a warning that the Leviathan of organization must not swallow the individual without sealing its own inevitable doom. (pp. 52–53)

The rapid advances of science and technology have placed on an elite scientific community the responsibilities of choice in invention and scientific capabilities that directly affect the moral and ethical values of humankind, even as they may affect their basic value of survival. Sensitive professionals are concerned with the priorities of their imaginative and inventive efforts. What is scientifically and materially possible today may have disastrous results in the long-term projected history of the human family. Science may have to accept the fact that coupling between science and its social environment in modern times may mean the disappearance of that degree of autonomy which scientific research has hitherto enjoyed. In writing of science and the creative spirit, Harcourt Brown suggests that the ethics of science, which had been a celebration and defense of autonomy, has to become an ethics in which science seeks the freedom of society rather than freedom from society (Deutsch et al. 1958).

Ethical and moral values will be needing more subjective, visionary, prophetic qualities with futuristic time realities after the style of William Blake's perceptive genius. His works can provide a pathway to the meeting ground between science and the arts for people of mutuality, good will, and global concerns. By opening the doors of perception they can find a way to "see visions, dream dreams, and converse with spirits" in the manner of Blake, who wrote: "He who does not imagine in stronger and better lineaments and in stronger and better light than his perishing and mortal eye can see, does not imagine at all" (Klonsky 1977, 13).

Blake's case for the concept of shared consciousness is suggested in his writing:

As all of us on earth are united in thought, it is impossible to think without images of somewhat on earth; as it is impossible to know God or heavenly things without conjunction with those who know God in heavenly things; therefore all who converse in the spirit converse with spirits. (Klonsky 1977, 13–14)

Apologists for General Systems Theory are tuned in to the meeting ground of science and humanities. General Systems is defined by von Bertalanffy (1968) as:

...the formulation of principles that are valid for "systems" in general whatever the nature of their component elements and the relations or forces between them...a general science of whole-nests, which up till now was considered a vague, hazy and semi-metaphysical concept—an open system of dynamic equilibrium. (p. 37)

He says further that:

Scientific control of society is no highway to Utopia. If we would have a well-developed science of human society and a corresponding technology, it would be a way out of the chaos and impending destruction of our present world. (p. 52)

Teilhard de Chardin (1964) was an early proponent and delineator of systems which are at the same time scientific and poetic. His vision of an unfolding, enfolding universe "scandalized reasonable men" in the same manner as did Blake. Long after his death, his reasonableness is registering in the marketplace and is making persons of serious thought aware of our place and responsibilities in the universe.

Marilyn Ferguson (1980), prominent general systems activist and author of *The Aquarian Conspiracy,* has provided dynamic leadership in the paradigm shift from a materialistic, technocratic, competitive, egocentric value system to one of more humanistic, mutualistic values for the future of the human family and its planetary home.

Summary

What more can be said? Time runs out. Visions of the future are often put on "hold" until their evaluation on the basis of present rationality is complete. Man-made values, sacrosanct and often limited to quantifiables, are in lag with those of social and universal growth toward humanization and the extension of human consciousness and potential. Blake had some didactic and symbolic words for scientists and all who are trying to understand:

There Is No Natural Religion
(Selected Propositions)
I. Man's perceptions are not bounded by organs of perception; he perceives more than sense (tho' ever so acute) can discover.
II. Reason, or the ratio of all we have already known, it not the same that it shall be when we know more.
IV. The bounded is loathed by its possessor. The same dull round, even of a universe, would soon become a mill with complicated wheels.
VII. The desire of Man being Infinite, the possession is as himself Infinite.
Application: He who sees the Infinite in all things sees God. He who sees the Ratio only, sees himself only. Therefore God becomes as we are, that we may be as he is. (Kazin 1976, 78)

Transformation theory says that it is the mandate of all living things to grow or die (Land 1973). Things take time, but the promise of growth and change is inherent in universal systems. Bachelard (1969) said that all values must remain vulnerable, and those that do not are dead. The excitement of the scientific community in the art and imagination of William Blake is prophetic of growth and change in their system of values.

The Not Quite Comprehensible Genius Of Albert Einstein

Systems thinking about outcomes may be found in dispositions: enhancing one's capacity to direct and control persistence, impulsivity, creativity, metacognition, precision and accuracy, listening with empathy, risk taking and wonderment.

—Bob Swartz

Introduction

Fascination with the genius of Albert Einstein has produced great quantities of literature—biographical, scientific, and analytical—all given to the particular qualities of his mind and manner. Isaac Asimov wonders about the analysis of genius (Lerner 1973):

> Certainly, it would seem that in many fields genius is a law unto itself and cannot be restrained and confined by any limits drawn by words or logic…The final test of genius in a scientist is how deeply and powerfully he peers into the laws governing the universe as decided, not by ourselves and our feelings or by a few experts and their feelings, but by the universe itself. (p. ii)

Thus, the final test of genius in Einstein-the-scientist is better left to the universe to judge. Here the concern is with Einstein-the-human-thinker and will speculate, on the basis of evidence in the literature, regarding the factors and forces that combined themselves into the creative person, the creative process, and the creative genius of Albert Einstein.

Life Environments: Early Shaping Factors

Lerner (1973, 22) provides a sketch of Einstein's family life. He was born in Ulm, Bavaria, in 1879, the son and first child of Hermann and Pauline Einstein. Albert was a "much-wanted" baby, and was blessed with affectionate parents, who were said to be "always on a honeymoon." His father was a "happy, optimistic man, not ridden by goals." His mother was an accomplished pianist who read the classics to Albert and initiated his studies of music. At the age of six he began the study of the violin. Later he taught himself to play the piano, and music became a necessary part of his life; also, it may be assumed, of his thought process. On one occasion (Lerner 1973) he was asked after a performance, "Do you count the beats?" Einstein laughed, "Heavens, No! It's in my blood" (p. 95). There was little shyness when it came to music. It has been said that he was not a very good technical performer, but that few could exceed him in fervor and sensibility.

The records show another significant family force. When Einstein was four or five years old, he was given a compass by his Uncle Jacob. His delight and curiosity with the mysterious magnetic needle absorbed the naturally inquiring nature of his mind and could be said to have helped to lead him to the preoccupation with the mysteries of the universal forces which he later helped to unravel. His uncle emerges also as a relative of some significance in Einstein's family circle. His sensitivity to and recognition of the uncommon qualities of young Einstein's mind must have been extremely satisfying and encouraging to a student whose record in school had left some doubts as to his mental qualifications. A letter to young Albert from a friend (Hoffman 1972) is quoted:

> Your uncle told me that he had had great difficulty with calculations for the construction of some machine. Some days later he said, "You know, it is really fabulous with my nephew. After I and my assistant-engineer had been racking our brains for days, that young sprig had got the whole thing in scarcely fifteen minutes." You will hear of him yet. (p. 27)

Einstein's inclination to reject and, as a result, to fail in the institutionalized, prescriptive process of education prompted a physics teacher in college to say (Lerner 1973): "You are a very clever boy, Einstein, an extremely clever boy, but you have one great fault. You never let yourself be told anything" (frontispiece). Einstein had no argument with that pronouncement. He is quoted as saying of himself, "I have no particular talent—I am merely inquisitive" (Lerner 1973, frontispiece).

"Merely inquisitive" was a companion quality to independence. He spoke in later years in *Mein Weltbild* (My View of the World) of his lack of need for direct contact with other human beings and communities (Einstein 1954):

I am truly a lone traveler, and have never belonged to my country, my home, my friends, or even my immediate family, with my whole heart; in the fact, of all these ties I have never lost a sense of distance and a need for solitude— feelings which increase with the years. (p. 9)

There is evidence to the contrary. He is said to have had numerous loyal friends, and those who knew him were always impressed by his bright and simple qualities. That he was very close to his immediate family is a matter of record. Others in Einstein's family included two sons (who remained with his first wife, Melvinia, at the time of their divorce), a younger sister, and the two daughters of his second wife Elsa. The literature testifies to the genuine affection Einstein felt for them all. However, it was Elsa who figured in a most essential way in his life and work. Antonia Vallentin (1954) provides one of the most intimate encounters with the person and lifestyle of Einstein. Qualities that consistently reveal themselves in her accounts are modesty and the need for privacy, both of which came into serious challenge as he continued to emerge as an international public figure. The fact that he managed to maintain the postures of his innate sensibilities is testimony to his genuineness and his persistence. Vallentin (1954) says:

Albert Einstein's life has been a constant struggle between his love of anonymity and the burdens of his fame, and at times only his sense of humor has saved him from complete exasperation. He has never let himself be carried away by the enthusiasm he provokes. He bows without embarrassment to the frenzied applause which greets him, but there is a conspiratorial twinkle in his eye for his relations and friends as if calling them to witness that these strange proceedings have nothing to do with him. His smile of amusement is always tinged with the same faint surprise, as though he recognizes that the crowd has to have an idol, but still cannot imagine why they should have picked on him to fill the role. (p. 9)

In one of his letters (Lerner 1973) he said of himself:

I must confess that the exaggerated esteem in which my life work is held makes me feel very ill at ease. I feel compelled to think of myself as an involuntary swindler. If one attempts to do anything about this, one succeeds only in making matters worse. (p. 102)

The qualities of generosity and altruism also have major attention in Vallentin's discussion of "The Drama of Albert Einstein" (Vallentin 1954):

> Fame brought material comforts. It might have brought a fortune, but Einstein refused all fabulous offers—astronomical fees, for example to appear for ten minutes on the screen. One got the impression that Albert and Elsa were eager to get rid of all the surplus money left over from their modest way of life. They were besieged by beggars as well as by celebrity hunters. They found they had hordes of relations who confidently expected to be helped, and complete strangers asked for their help with the same confidence. (p. 91)

Friendships

Because Einstein did not speak fluently until he was nine years old, but thought much and kept to himself, he was referred to as "Pater Langweil" (Father Bore) and "Biedermeier" (Square) according to Lerner (1973, 23). He had no interest in sports; he preferred, as activities, gadgets and how they worked and music. Such personal qualities exercised a natural limitation on the numbers of friends in his early environment. Two brothers, however, Max and Bernard Talmud, entered his life and had a marked influence. Max took a particular interest in young Albert during his tenth to fifteenth years, and did much to guide and nourish his learning, since the two shared an unlimited love of learning and a talent for self-instruction. Max's description of Albert is consistent with other sources. He spoke of his friend as: "The pretty, dark-haired, brown-eyed boy with exceptional intelligence which enabled him to discuss with college graduates, subjects far above the comprehension of children of his age" (Lerner 1979, 24). The two discussed physics, geometry, calculus, and philosophy. He was not seen with boys his own age and remained aloof and absorbed in books and music.

Einstein's excitement and success in independent learning added to his dislike for the rigidity of formal education, and he refused to conform. In answer to a question he is reported to have said: "I don't know. I don't crowd my memory with facts that I can easily find in an encyclopedia" (Vallentin 1954, 31). His work in science and mathematics was superior, but his Latin teacher told him he would never amount to anything. School officials were happy when Einstein left at fifteen to join his parents in Milan. They had been trying to find a way to drop him because of the poor effect they thought he had on student morale.

He seemed to understand well the influences that shaped his life and style. He could be speaking for humankind (Einstein 1950):

> Man is, at one and the same time, a solitary being and a social being. As a solitary being, he attempts to protect his own existence and that of those who are closest to him, to satisfy his personal desires, and to develop his innate abilities. As a social being, he seeks to gain the recognition and affection of his fellow human beings, to share in their pleasures, to comfort them in their sorrows, and to improve their conditions of life. It is quite possible that the relative strength of these two drives is, in the main, fixed by inheritance. But the personality that finally emerges is largely formed by the environment in which a man happens to find himself during his development. (p. 125)

Educational Environment

The influence of the educational environment as a shaping force in the life of Einstein is best recognized in his own observations from Mein Weltbild (My view of the world) (Einstein 1954):

> To me the worst thing seems to be for a school principally to work with methods of fear, force, and artificial authority. Such treatment destroys the sound sentiments, the sincerity, and the self-confidence of the pupil. It produces the submissive subject. Give into the power of the teacher the fewest possible coercive measures so that the only source of the pupil's respect for the teacher is the human and intellectual qualities of the latter. (p. 61)

In a response to a letter from a young girl (Einstein 1954) he has a more personal statement to make:

> I suffered at the hands of my teachers a similar treatment; they disliked me for my independence and passed me over when they wanted assistants. (I must admit, though that I was somewhat less of a model student than you). (p. 56)

In *Out of My Later Years* (Einstein 1950), the statement on independent thinking could be a standard for educational reform in schools throughout the globe in efforts to develop global leadership equipped with thinking processes equal to the complex task of thinking globally and acting locally. Early school experiences against which Einstein rebelled stand out in sharp contrast with his description of educational priorities:

> The development of general ability for independent thinking and judgment should always be placed foremost, not the acquisition of special knowledge. If a person masters the fundamentals of his subject and has learned to think and work independently, he will surely find his way and besides will better be able to adapt himself to progress and changes than the person whose training principally consists in the acquiring of detailed knowledge. (p. 36)

In another section of *Mein Weltbild* he adds this emphasis:

> I wish to emphasize once more that what has been said here in a somewhat categorical form does not claim to mean more than the personal opinion of a man, which is founded upon nothing but his own personal experience which he has gathered as a student and as a teacher. (p. 64)

This total and genuine respect for independent learning and individual differences permeated his own teaching style. Reiser (1930) writes of the success of Einstein's genuineness with students in his first teaching job:

The young men who attended this school were without academic training, and the twenty-one-year-old instructor at first found it difficult to get along with his scholars, for the most part older than he. Feeling superior to the young academician in age and in numbers, they enjoyed showing what they felt. Albert's first practical activity was thus hardly pleasant. He once more perceived how harsh and cruel the world could be to the individual, especially to one as dreamy and unarmed as he. After a short while, however, Albert showed a definite talent for teaching. The students saw how much they could learn from his courage and forgot the youth of their teacher. They respected him and no longer interrupted his lessons (p. 61).

The same fundamental philosophy of learning reveals itself in a biographical portrait published during the height of Einstein's career and popularity (Reiser 1930):

Today Albert Einstein still advises young scientists to work at a 'shoemaker's job.' It seems to him the only possible way of escaping a one-sided intellectual life which may too easily lead to an empty business without depth or content, as well as to forced scientific over-production, as a result of which the truly valuable contribution can only suffer. Every talent, every creative genius, is a blessing, a divine gift, which must be guarded against the dangers of the daily commonplace and the world interested in profits. A practical profession, however, is an excellent means of furthering the quiet and free development of the creative mind. (p. 65)

Another reference from Reiser's highly personal biographical portrait merits attention, since the rejection of formalities and academic posturing typified Einstein's teaching style; this trait is described consistently throughout the literature.

He showed a definite timidity, which even to-day he has not overcome, toward speaking in public. He always called his lectures "performances on the trapeze." His nature, which above all enjoyed being alone, or with his work in the silence of his own room, found his professorial activity hardly pleasant. (p. 75)

The understanding and protection of Einstein's necessary privacy was provided by his family environment in the person of his second wife Elsa, a cousin, to whom the Reiser biography is dedicated. It is said that she was the only real and true companion to the great scholar during the difficult and often painful periods of his life (De Broglie, Arnold, and Simon 1979). She is described as:

…an infinitely discreet and self-effacing woman. She never dreamed of interfering in any of the research which Einstein pursued; she knew how to take perfectly good care of Einstein, and God knows how difficult this was when he truly became a figure of international stature and renown. (p. 15)

Genius Ideas: What of the Process?

Where do ideas come from? Sometimes from looking at one thing and seeing something else. Where, especially, did Einstein's ideas come? Anwar Dil (Fuller and Dil 1983) quotes some most enlightening ideas on thinking from Einstein himself:

When at the reception of sense-impressions, memory pictures emerge, this is not yet thinking. And when such pictures form series, each member of which calls forth another, this too is not yet thinking. When, however, a certain picture turns up in many such series, then.… precisely through such return.… it becomes an ordering element for such series, in that it connects series which in themselves are unconnected. Such an element becomes an instrument, a concept, I think that the transition from free association of dreaming to thinking is characterized by the more or less dominating role which the concept plays in it. (p. 60)

After the benefit of the description by the master himself, it may be redundant to explore further efforts to determine the process of ideational genius. For further elaboration on the subject Einstein remains, naturally, the best resource. He refers often (Einstein 1950) to intuition as the means of rational scientific illuminations and argues for a broad and lateral examination of concepts outside of one's own specific field for the process of critical thinking in the work of the physicist. He speaks often of the connections and coordinations that are fundamental to the mature thinking process: "Operations with concepts, and the creation and use of definite functional relations between them, and the coordination of sense experiences to these concepts…a fact which leaves us in awe but which we shall never understand" (p. 60).

The genius mind was at the same time simple and complex; discrete and unified; intimate and immense. It never gave up in the search and the prospect for understanding yet another universal dimension. A well-recognized statement of Einstein's faith in further disclosures of the vast immensities is quoted repeatedly in the literature (Einstein 1950): "The eternal mystery of the world is its comprehensibility; the setting up of a real external world would be senseless without this comprehensibility" (p. 61).

Some of the most interesting observations on Einstein and the processes of genius are to be found in a comparison between the processes of the scientist and the processes of the artist in, "Einstein's Space and Van Gogh's Sky" (LeShan 1982). A statement on alternate realities is quoted from Arthur Koestler, early authority on the act of creation (Koestler 1964):

Einstein's space is no closer to reality than Van Gogh's sky. The glory of science is not in the truth more absolute than the truth of Bach or Tolstoy, but in the act of creation itself. The scientific discoveries impose their own order on chaos, as the composer or painter imposes his; an order that always refers to limited aspect of reality, and is based on the observer's frame of reference, which differs from period to period as a Rembrandt nude differs from a nude by Monet. (p. 3)

So the scientific genius seeks meaning of the universe and its operations as the artist seeks meaning of life's realities and within the same limited aspect of "reality." In a sense, science becomes an art and art a science. The process may be the reality. Einstein is said to have observed that without the illumination of consciousness the universe would be "a mere rubbish heap." LeShan (1982) adds: "We invent and discover its continuities and discontinuities, its coherences and its 'spots and jumps.' It [reality] is somehow there, but we alloy it into being with our consciousness" (p. 26).

One of the most poignant revelations of the thinking patterning of Einstein is the report of Einstein's version of a story from his childhood (Holton 1982):

He said that when he was between two and three years old, he formed the ambition to talk in whole sentences. If somebody asked him a question and he had to answer, he would form a sentence in his mind and then try it out on himself, thinking that he was whispering it to himself. But, as you know, a child is not very good at whispering, so he said it softly. Then, if it sounded all right, he would say it again to the person who had questioned him. Therefore, it sounded, at least to his nursemaid, as if he said everything twice, once softly and once loudly, and she called him "der Depperte" which is Bavarian for "the dopey one." The nickname stuck and that, at least in Einstein's mind, was the cause of all the stories about his slow development. (p. 419)

A significant event to add to perceptions Einstein had regarding thinking is the surprise he expressed when he and a co-worker had been trying to solve a problem without success. Returning to work the next morning, they found that each had made some progress on it, and after batting it around together, they arrived at the solution. As reported by Holton (1982):

Einstein's reaction was strange. He said, "This has never happened to me—we thought together. Two people being able to think! I never thought this was possible. I was always convinced that thinking was a singular occupation." He seemed to have considered the event some kind of miracle. (p. 420)

A comparison between Einstein and Newton elevates Einstein to a lofty place in the total scheme of the search for universal genius qualities (Lerner 1973). Of Einstein and Newton it is said that the

...two men were the most intelligent people who ever lived. Using only pencil and paper, they formulated laws of nature and displayed a capacity for abstract thought combined with creativity that was unique among men. Although they shared some personal and intellectual characteristics, totally different lifestyles emerged in their later years. Unlike Einstein, Newton sought honors and recognition. Einstein, in contrast to Newton, had little use for the dogma of organized religion, but was considered a deeply religious man by those who knew him. (p. 11)

Einstein's own modesty and respect for the power of ideas has importance to our topic:

The man who has discovered an idea which allows us to penetrate, to whatever slight degree, a little more deeply, the eternal arcanum of nature, has been granted a great favor; if, in addition, he experiences the best help, sympathy, and recognition of his time, he attains almost more happiness than one man can bear. (Reiser 1930, frontispiece)

The "great truth" which, according to Reiser (1930), has raised Einstein, since early youth, above the scientific commonplace into the rarer atmosphere of investigation and discovery is "that great scientific intuition which relates pole and pole; the given problem and the suspected solution; the traditional enigma and the current postulate. All these extremes together must contribute to a single work" (p. xiv).

Reiser's recognition of the process of the creative union of opposites applies to the seminal theory of creativity from Koestler's *Act of Creation* (1964), in which he describes the process of bisociation or the process of bringing seemingly unrelated polarities into meaningful association. Koestler's basis of the bisociative principle on the process of humor makes Einstein's predilection for humor, as well as for scientific discovery, quite understandable. Einstein credited intuitive artistics and deductive physics for his thinking process, again an integration of what might seem, on the surface, opposing forces (Reiser 1930). In Einstein's view:

> The greatest task of the physicist is the search for those general elementary laws, out of which by pure deduction his picture of the world is formed. There is no logical road to these elementary laws other than intuition, applied by the understanding of experience. (p. 77)

His working procedure was said to be analogous to that of the artist, whereby once he had come upon a problem, he had a definite vision of a possible solution, and moved "not only by the sum of new scientific truth, but by aesthetic pleasure" toward the answer, at which times Einstein had been known to say, "What a beautiful solution!"

Einstein's Humor: Pervasive Power

The persistent power of "Einsteinian" humor in his life system for thinking and coping is a revelation and one of the most enlightening discoveries in this investigation of "the greatest scientific mind of the century." With all of the attention to his remarkable scientific achievement, the genius of the phenomenon of laughter has been, in many cases all but forgotten. Lerner (1973) chronicles Einstein's sense of humor:

> The gift of laughter has been given him in full measure. There is nothing preternaturally solemn professor about him. He can laugh heartily and he does. He enjoys a joke, and he can often see the funny side of situations most people would regard as utterly tragic and I don't mean utterly tragic for other people but for himself. I have known him to laugh even when a mishap or misfortune has really moved him…he never loses his sense of humor no matter what the situation. He greatly appreciates mother wit and is as delighted as a child with his own witticism, even when sometimes a biting remark slips from his lips amongst friends. His company is easeful. (p. 96)

Throughout biographical writings on Einstein, incidental references continue to remind the reader of the unique quality of humor that is such an addition to the appreciation of his humanness. A poignant observation by Lerner (1973) tells about Einstein's love of recounting jokes and of the poor job he did of it because before he came to the punch line he would anticipate the joke's climax, begin to smile, eyes twinkling, and break into uncontrollable laughter, amused by his own story, including the risqué ones, before his listeners had the advantage of the punch line, the whole performance quite delighting his audience.

Einstein's own personal style of original humor can be categorized as philosophical; he is quoted as saying that "whoever undertakes to set himself up as judge in the field of Truth and Knowledge is shipwrecked by the laughter of the gods" (Einstein 1954, 27).

Other examples of his natural style of humor appear as gems of empathy in the reader's encounter with the Einstein genius. As Reiser (1930) records:

> The parting from Europe was not very hard for him. He took it with humor and, in his diary, entered this monumental event as his last on his native continent: "Lost my wife at the border, but she recovered immediately." As the most vivid memory of the city of Marseilles he entered, "Bugs in the morning's coffee." (p. 172)

His humor seems to have served as a defense against social and political cruelties and misunderstandings. Reiser (1930) reports:

> Einstein himself bears such hostility with a sense of humor. He can not be angry with anybody. He has a sympathetic understanding for everything and a hearty laugh. He finds a too-obtrusive friendship much more unbearable than hostility. (p. 169)

The eldest daughter of Elsa, Einstein's second wife, had a particular appreciation for his special kind of humor, according to De Broglie et al. (1979): "He saw everyday facts in a rather comical light; his humor was quickly apparent; his laughter was a source of joy, a lively stimulant for those who were around him" (p. 207).

Whitrow (1967) is another biographer who saw humor as an important identifying quality. He quotes a classmate's description:

Unhampered by convention, his attitude towards the world was that of a laughing philosopher, and his witty mockery pitilessly lashed any conceit or pose. In
conversation he always had something to give. He is said to have "loathed any
display of sentimentality" and to be "one of those split personalities who know
how to protect with mocking wit an intense emotional life." (p. 3)

A close examination of the literature discovers, somewhat buried under other
headlines, pervasive and various descriptives—his impishness and mock solem-
nity, his inclination to "laugh uproariously," the robust quality of his humor—all
have their share of attention.

That his sense of humor endured throughout his life is testified to in an
interview with a professor Bernard Cohen of Harvard who had interviewed
Einstein a fortnight before he died (Whitrow 1967). His picture of the aged
genius is bittersweet:

…a beautiful and extraordinary face, contemplatively tragic, deeply lined,
and yet his sparkling eyes gave him a quality of agelessness. While we spoke
his eyes watered continuously and in moments of laughter he would have to
wipe away the tears with the back of his hand; the contrast between the soft
speech and ringing laughter was enormous. He enjoyed making jokes and
every time he made a point he liked, or heard something that appealed to him,
he would burst into booming laughter that would just echo from wall to wall.
It was most extraordinary. (p. 82)

There apparently never was an interruption in the treasure of humor that Einstein
brought to his life and times. In his last hours, according to Hoffman (1972):

He faced death unafraid, and even with a jest. He was serene, untroubled in
spirit, and ready for the last great adventure. He spoke calmly and with his
customary humor of personal matters and of science, and more sadly of
America and of the dimming hope of world peace. (p. 261)

The Process: A Continuation

Einstein was often asked to describe the process of his thinking. His effort to do so presented the problem of transferring his "right brain" imagery to "left brain" articulation. His description said things about the essential part being "rather vague," with the non-logical mentality playing with visual and muscular signs before explanatory words could be laboriously sought for. By means of his peculiar gift for analogy, his description of his mental processes took on more definitive form. An Einstein quotation reported by Hoffman (1972) says:

> I do not know what I may appear to the world; but to myself, I seem to have been only like a boy playing on the sea-shore, and diverting myself now and then finding a smoother pebble or a prettier shell than ordinary, whilst the great ocean of truth lay all undiscovered before me. (p. 257)

His thought and action in science and life are said to have been interrelated in a way no dramatist would dare to conceive (Clark 1971). It is a matter of record that Einstein never got used to being treated like a genius and so tried to avoid talking about his method and process of thinking. There is one particularly revealing and personal piece of direct testimony. Schwartz (1979) quotes Einstein:

> I must confess that at the very beginning when the Special Theory of Relativity began to germinate in me, I was visited by all sorts of nervous conflicts. When young I used to go away for weeks in a state of confusion, as one who at the time had yet to overcome the state of stupefaction in his first encounter with such questions. (p. 82)

Einstein's basic interpretation of the scientific process is reflected in his observation that in science the work of the individual is so bound up with that of his scientific contemporaries that it appears almost as an impersonal product of his generation. Newton, according to his biographers (Lerner 1973) would have made a quite different and much less generous observation. An on-the-spot description by a fellow scientist of his behavior in the process of a breakthrough idea provides a graphic picture (Whitrow 1967):

When, in pursuit of an idea, he would say in his German pattern, 'I will a little tink,' followed by a dreamy, far-away and yet a sort of inward look on his face, there was no appearance at all of intense concentration. Another minute would pass and another, and then all of a sudden Einstein would visibly relax and a smile would light up his face; he seemed to come back to his surroundings and to notice us once more, and then he would tell us the solution to the problem and almost always the solution worked. (p. 75)

In summary, it could be said that Einstein's success in physics was his irrepressible curiosity and his unsurpassed ability to think clearly. Of himself, Einstein said modestly, "God gave me the stubbornness of a mule and a fairly keen scent" (Whitrow 1967, 91).

The Universal Connection

From the beginning and throughout his life, Einstein's curiosity and his genius for making sense of the wonders and vast mysteries of nature found their integration and satisfaction in his intellectual energies. His preoccupation with the pocket compass at the age of five moved his inquiring mind, and although there was nothing visible to make the needle move, he concluded that something that attracts and turns bodies in a particular direction must exist in space that is considered empty. This, no doubt, was one of the impressions which later led Einstein to pursue the mysterious properties of empty space. Imprinting from his early readings in *Naturwissenschaftliche Volksbucher* (Popular Books on Natural Science) introduced him to a full range of scientific topics: animals, plants, their mutual interdependence, and the hypotheses concerning their origin: they dealt with stars, meteors, volcanoes, earthquakes, climate, and many other topics, never leaving out of sight the greater interrelation of nature (Frank 1947).

Roland Barthes (1980) writes profoundly about "The Brain of Einstein," and points out the quality of his genius so often overlooked in the emphasis on scientific and mathematical formulations and quantitatives. He says:

Paradoxically, the more the genius of the man was materialized under the guise of his brain, the more the product of his inventiveness came to acquire a magical dimension and gave a new incarnation to the old esoteric image of a science entirely contained in a few letters. There is a single secret to the world, and this secret is held in one word; the universe is a safe of which humanity seeks the combination; Einstein almost found it, this is the myth of Einstein. (pp. 94–95)

Einstein's very appearance seems to have suggested his access to the secrets of the world. Charles Rapport's description (De Broglie et al. 1979) has a particular level of intensity: "Oh, those eyes…. Those who have seen them will never forget them. They have such depth that one might say that the habit of scrutinizing the secrets of the universe leave indelible traces" (p. 97).

The world view that dominated Einstein's life and work has one of its best and most dramatic descriptions in Einstein's own words, quoted by Anwar Dil (Fuller and Dil 1983):

Out yonder there was this huge world, which exists independently of us human beings and which stands before us like a great eternal riddle, at least partially accessible to our inspection and thinking. The contemplation of this world beckoned like a liberation, and I soon noticed that many a man whom I had learned to esteem and to admire had found inner freedom and security in devoted occupation with it. (p. 57)

The response of Buckminster Fuller (1983) to the Einstein observation during his conversation with Anwar Dil is most interesting in that he makes a spontaneous association between the idea of the great eternal riddle of the huge world and the quality of childlike wonder when he says, "I think Einstein was fortunate in that he probably never lost his childhood" (p. 57). In the sense that childhood is a time of creative wonder, there is plenty of evidence that Fuller was quite right.

Einstein's early introduction to and intellectual conditioning for perceiving the synthesis and symbiosis of the natural forces of the universe had a continuation in the style of his genius. Reiser (1930) makes an astute observation:

Einstein is certainly the complete human being, and, as such, a rarity in contemporary intellectual life. His completeness does not lie in his ability or in his learning, but in his interests and in his inclinations. A genuine creative power always sees beyond its province of specialization, and finds it necessary to attach itself to the collective human mind, that is to humanity itself.

One must be aware that each work is organized in the time and space of creative reason, and that everything created belongs to the great fellowship of creations. He is interested in all values and occurrences that touch the intellect. (p. xviii)

The chronicler who described Einstein's "surprised questioning look that always gave one the impression that he was only a visitor on Earth" (De Broglie et al. 1979, 20) probably came as close to capturing his cosmic essence as any of the lengthy efforts at analysis.

Einstein's Personal Time and Space

In his discussion of *Intellectual Leadership: Ideas as Moral Power,* Burns (1978) reflects on the confusion that arises over the definitions and roles of intellectuals beyond reducing their identity to that of "the scribbling set." He says: "The ambiguity rises in part from a failure to distinguish between the intellectual as a relatively autonomous and detached figure and the intellectual as a person hovering in a particular cultural milieu or social class" (p. 141).

There can be little doubt that Einstein hovered in a particular milieu of scientific and political turmoil. That the Theories of Special Relativity derived, as suggested by Hart (1978), not rationally on the basis of careful experiments, but rather on grounds of symmetry and mathematical elegance, ran counter to the basically empirical outlook of modern science, but "continues to be generally acknowledged to be the most beautiful, elegant, powerful, and intellectually satisfying of all scientific theories" (p. 85). In addition, his contribution to the quantum theory and development of the atom bomb placed him well in the center of a great deal of scientific controversy. The contradictions and paradoxical nature of Einstein's hypotheses as they related to existing scientific paradigms required a genius of faith. Hart (1978) says:

It was part of Einstein's genius that at the beginning when his ideas were still the untested hypothesis of an unknown teenager, he did not let these apparent contradictions cause him to discard his theories. Rather, he carefully thought them through until he could show that these contradictions were apparent only, and that in each case there was a subtle but correct way of resolving the paradox. (p. 89)

Einstein's emphasis on the simplicity of science could have been disconcerting to colleagues struggling to understand his belief that "The whole of science is nothing more than a refinement of everyday thinking" (Einstein 1954, 290). For him the concept of simplicity was

> …intimately connected with the concepts of harmony, beauty, and symmetry. There must be one, generalized, simple concept of field or law; these three concepts are organizing principles for intuition, and phenomena will behave accordingly. Asymmetry is disruptive, unnatural, misleading." (in Holton 1982, 224)

The one generalized, simple concept, the unified field theory, the synthesis that would embrace the universe, for which Einstein continued to search throughout his life, eluded him. Vallentin (1954) provides a discussion of the scientific factors that constituted his theory and the observation that the scientific world of his time thought of his thesis as a revolution.

Besides the tumult of the scientific period of his time, which, indeed, he helped to create, the world political climate became a constant presence of uncertainty and disruption for Einstein. His Jewish heritage was the cause of continued threat during the Hitler regime in Germany, and the fact that he was able to maintain his composure, convictions, his incorruptible judgment, and unceasing search after scientific truth is a testament to his compelling, philosophical integrity. There emerges through the literature the impression that it was his depth of cosmic spirituality that sustained him during the countless disruptions and tensions of family, flight, and political and scientific tumult. He wrote with fervor on the "Religious Spirit of Science" (Einstein 1950), an essay which leaves little doubt concerning the universal quality of his spirituality:

> But the scientist is possessed by the sense of universal causation. His religious feeling takes the form of a rapturous amazement at the harmony of natural law, which reveals an intelligence of such superiority that, compared with it, all the systematic thinking and acting of human beings is an utterly insignificant reflection. This feeling is the guiding principle of his life and work, in so far as he succeeds in keeping himself from the shackles of selfish desire. It is

beyond the question closely akin to that which has possessed the religious geniuses of all ages. (p. 40)

Added to his cosmic spirituality as a psychological strength was his indestructible, amusedly ironic humor in the face of difficulty.

Einstein was tragically saddened by the question of the morality of the A-bomb and the responsibilities of the scientific community, including his own part, in creating so gruesome a method of annihilation preoccupied his mind in his later years. He gave a wealth of energy to work in the cause of peace.

At the Intellectuals' Conference for Peace his address was as courageous as it was humane (Einstein 1950):

> A Message to Intellectuals
>
> By painful experience we have learned that rational thinking does not suffice to solve the problems of our social life. Penetrating research and keen scientific work have often had tragic implications for mankind, producing, on the one hand, inventions which liberated man from exhausting physical labor, making his life easier and richer; but on the other hand, introducing a grave restlessness into his life, making him a slave to his technological environment, and…most catastrophic of all…creating the means for his own mass destruction. This, indeed, is a tragedy of overwhelming poignancy! (p. 152)

Summary

So we add the genius of humanity to the popular concept of the scientific genius in our thoughts of Einstein. The literature will continue to add to the ever richer tapestry of this intellectual leader who was at the same time a celebrity, exile, pacifist, philosopher, humanitarian, and much more; who had been variously described as a "backward child," and "academic outcast in a reluctant world," whose "aureole of white hair and luminous eyes" marked him so thoroughly in the eyes of his world for all time.

The final word must be a salute to his simple, cosmic understating of his ultimate place in the natural universe of matter and energy, waves, particles, humans, and much more (Bateson 1994). Albert Einstein's rules of work, if consistently and sensitively applied, would solve most of the human challenges in every human enterprise:

One: Out of clutter, find simplicity.

Two: From discord, find harmony.

Three: In the middle of difficulty lies opportunity.

Roland Barthes makes a final profound assessment of the unfinished enduring puzzlement of Einstein and his universe:

Einstein fulfills all the conditions of myth which could not care less about contradictions so long as it establishes a euphoric security, at once magician and machine, eternal researcher and unfulfilled discoverer, unleashing the best and the worst, brain and conscience, Einstein embodies the most contradictory dreams, and mythically reconciles the infinite power of man over nature with the 'fatality' of the sacrosanct which man cannot yet do without" (in Goldsmith 1980, 95).

Humor and Creativity:
Clues to Human Behavior

Humor is the only domain of creative activity where a stimulus on a high level of complexity produces a massive and sharply defined response on the level of physiological reflexes. This paradox enables us to use the response as an indicator for the presence of that elusive quality, the comic, which we are seeking to define.

—Arthur Koestler

The time has come to look seriously at the importance of laughter in life and in human organizations. Even the bible reminds us that "A cheerful heart doeth good like medicine, but a depressed spirit drieth the bones" (Prov. 17:22). It would seem quite incomplete for organizations to discuss the new, more qualitative, humanistic perceptions of management and leadership without taking a serious look at humor, probably the most eccentric fact of human existence.

This, then, is a discussion of humor. Contrary to possible expectations, its purpose is not to provoke laughter, but to make a case for laughter as a serious business. Education has paid little attention to the serious study of humor-what laughter is, why it is, what a sense of humor is all about and how to recognize and value it across its many forms of expression. With all of the attention to the discovery and analysis of "inner space" and behavioral psychology, humor has remained a relatively unknown quantity in efforts toward self-knowledge and the unraveling of the mysteries of social interaction. Since the process of humor is so intimately connected to the creative process in the "mind machine," the purpose of this chapter will be to:

- Discuss the emergence of recognized connections between humor and creativity;
- Discover the place of humor in human expression and the relationships between the processes of "getting the joke" and solving the problem; and
- Explore the value of good humor as a contributing force in the form and function of creative human enterprise.

163

An argument for the specific link between humor and creativity was made in the seminal work of Arthur Koestler (1964). Their natural connection was delineated in his introduction of the concept of "bisociation," which he defined as the capability of the mind to bring two or more seemingly unrelated planes of thought into meaningful association. He showed, by means of a triptych (p. 25) the commonality of the creative processes for getting the joke, for solving the problem, and for having a high aesthetic experience. The flow of the process from a bathos emotional set (humor) through a neutral emotional set (problem solving) through a pathos emotional set (aesthetic) all represented in their various interrelated forms, covers the full sweep of emotions from aggressive to sympathetic or, as is sometimes suggested, the Ha-Ha experience, the Ah-Ha experience, and the Ahhh experience.

The introductory chapter in his seminal work, *The Act of Creation* (Koestler 1964, 27–97), is titled "The Jester," and makes a convincing argument for the basic nature of creativity as expressed in the processes of humor. For Koestler, the studies of the processes of humor, scientific discovery, and the aesthetic experience are inseparable. The dialectical tension assumed in the process of bisociation has a parallel in the concept of "paradoxical intention" as a technique for distancing patients in psychotherapy from anxieties. The concept of paradox and its relation to humor is a further example of the recognition of mental processes of bisociation, described by Koestler in one of his discussions as "a process that causes the mind to turn a somersault."

Zussman (1983) uses a quotation from the writing of Gregory Bateson to relate humor to paradox:

The therapy situation is a place where the freedom to admit paradox has been cultivated as a technique, but on the whole, this flexibility exists between two people when they succeed in giving each other freedom of discussion. That freedom, the freedom to entertain illogical alternatives…is probably essential to comfortable human relations. In sum, I am arguing that there is an important ingredient common to comfortable human relations, humor, and therapeutic change, and that this ingredient is the implicit presence and acceptance of paradox. (p. 48)

The issue of flexibility so basic to the intellectual level of paradoxical think-ing has a dominant place in the connections between creativity and humor. Through the work of Dr. E. Paul Torrance (1966a, 1966b), international authority and pioneer in the development of the discipline of creativity, tests have been designed that measure four cognitive factors of the creative process: fluency-the ability of the mind to produce quantities of ideas; flexibility-the degree of ten-dency for the mind to make shifts from one direction of thought to another and to range through a broad, general background of experiences in making creative connections; originality-the ability to produce unique, relevant ideas for new solu-tions to problems and challenges; and elaboration-the inclination of the mind to associate ideas freely to produce rich detail and elaboration to ideas and their implementation. As an example of the recognized connection between humor and the expression of creative thought, in the scoring of the Torrance Tests of Creative Thinking, bonus points are assigned for evidence of humor in the creative response to thinking tasks.

The work of Paul McGhee (1979, 77) adds the position that "cognitive salience" rather than "affective salience" may be the important factor in deter-mining humor potential. These observations add to the assertion that there exists a mental process, recognized as available throughout the human species as a cat-alyst for flexibility, for a paradoxical appreciation of opposites, and for the com-fort of freedom of exchange and discussion between people. An assumption can be made that the factor of humor is identifiable and of distinctive value, and that it is cultivatable in groups. The specific identification is somewhat a matter of intuitive sense with the help of the formal definition provided by Webster (1968): "Humor: The mental faculty of discovery; expressing or appreciating ludicrous or absurdly incongruous elements in ideas, situations, happenings, or acts."

Koestler's introduction of the term, "bisociation" and its applications accord-ing to his triptych (1964, 25) provides an understanding of the variety of forms possible in the production of and response to humor. The following definitions are from a resource for teachers: "Humor: Lessons in Laughter for Learning and Living" (Bleedorn 1984):

Comic simile: Comparison of two very different things or ideas with some
    common reference—a surprising, funny image.

Witticism: A remark or response associating ideas in a new or ingenuous way—spontaneous wisecracks.

Satire: Clever observations that criticize, expose, and possibly reform through amusement—aimed at social practices, persons, or institutions.

Impersonation: Talking and expressing the personality and behavior of someone else in an amusing way.

Caricature: Exaggerating personalities or distinguishing characteristics of a person in words or pictures. Cartoons of famous political and entertainment personalities are effective (often belittling) examples.

Debunking: Calling attention to a weakness in lofty, superficial, pretentious behavior in an amusing way.

Pun: A play on words that are similar in sound but different in meaning.

Riddle: A puzzling question present in obscure terms and leading to a surprise right answer. Learned and recited rather than produced spontaneously.

Coincidence: Recognizing an unexpected coming together in time or space of persons or events, producing surprise and spontaneous laughter. (p. 9)

Creating and responding to positive humor in any of its various forms contributes to a healthy climate in the workplace and everywhere else where people gather. Expressions of wit and humor can lighten up a stressful environment and boost morale. Carl Rogers said (in Rosenbaum and Sandowsky 1976): "Being oneself, being real can have expression in spontaneous humor, a process in which it is difficult to maintain facades" (p. 88). Another perception of the value of humor has been described by Freud: "A healthy, developmentally advanced mechanism which enables the individual to cope with the vicissitudes of life, as well as providing a release for surplus amounts of psychic energy"(in Zussman 1983, 57).

Cultivating a talent for personal humor can have a "trickle-down" effect on groups and entire organizations. As is the case with creativity, the development of a talent for humor is often neglected and undiscovered. As life becomes more complex and more perplexing, there is increasing need for moments of laughter and relaxation. During uncertain times and radical change humor has a more important value than ever. Tension and anxiety are no strangers to the business climate. Good humor helps to keep it light. A joyless workplace gives up some of its productivity. Business need not be grim. Deliberate attention to the nurturing of positive, creative humor can translate to morale and good will, higher standards of excellence, and increased productivity in human operations. Instead of rewards for being serious and solemn, rewards could go to creative thinkers who, through their talents for humor, help to make the working environment a place to get more "smileage" out of life.

Creativity, Criminality, and Crossovers: A Report and a Speculation

When man is deprived of the power of expression, he will express himself in a drive for power.

—Jose Arguelles

Certainly, the idea of creative talent among criminals and law breakers has been a subject of discussion and speculation over the years. Ingenious breakers of rules and laws have often appealed to the imagination of the people and become heroes in the public eye. Adventurous exploits outside of the letter of the law may inspire admiration. There are many examples of the vagaries of public sentiment regarding guilt in the case of the clever criminal. The challenge of outwitting the law and its enforcement, it must be agreed, can require some high level creative thinking and action. If the level of criminality determines punishment, might it be that the level of creativity in public offenders deserves investigation?

These speculative questions came about as a result of a teaching experience with a group of prisoners. When I began a series of visits concerned with the teaching of creative thinking and problem solving for inmates of a state prison, I entered the experience with the expectation of finding creative thinking talent among the prisoners. What I wasn't prepared for was the very impressive level and variety of creative talent in some of the men, and the motivation to exercise it even within the psychological constraints of the prison environment.

In literature, media, and public platforms, growing attention to creativity in the development of human potential is a recurring theme. Its relation to criminality raises questions for those people concerned with education, criminal justice, prison reform and rehabilitation, human potential, quality of life, and global survival. Some obvious questions are:

Bleedorn, B. D. (1983) Creativity, Criminality and Crossovers: A Report and a Speculation. The Journal of Creative Behavior 17(4):268. Reprinted with permission from the copyright holder, The Creative Education Foundation, 1050 Union Road, Buffalo, NY 14224.

- How did so many intellectual, creative men end up in a state prison?
- What is the loss in productivity and service to society?
- What is the ratio of society's reward and punishment for original, innovative, creative behavior?
- What pressures require a denial of positive creative energies in schools and society?
- Who decides when rules are to be broken?
- What causes crossovers to criminality?
- Can creative crime be prevented?

Answers, if existent, would be merely speculative. The purpose of this writing is to report a direct experience relevant to the questions and to pay attention to some of the connections between that experience and a number of variations on the theme of breakthroughs in the understanding of human thought and action. The multi-dimensionality of the questions and their implications grew from what seemed a trifling beginning. It happened in this way.

An inmate at a state prison, enrolled as a degree candidate in a state university, registered for a creative problem solving course. Since inmates are restricted from attending regular classes, arrangements were made for me to meet with the student at the prison. With the help of a student workbook, a course in independent study, including a series of meetings with the instructor, was arranged. Our first meeting established the fact that Mr. X was bright, soft-spoken, well-read, an intellectual thinker, and highly motivated. He went well beyond the course requirements in his exploration of the literature provided, and developed a special interest in J. P. Guilford's (1977) model of the structure of intellect. It seemed paradoxical that no educator had ever, in my experience, expressed the same degree of understanding and excitement upon introduction to this fundamental theory of intellectual differences.

Mention of the independent study with Mr. X would be incomplete without reference to our final meeting and the interruption imposed by an institutional practice on Mr. X's work. Shortly before our final meeting, there had been a "shake-down" at the prison. That procedure resulted in the loss of his typewriter, his papers, his workbook, and some personal items. Fortunately, most of the work had already been reviewed for evaluation. It can only be assumed that officials who had examined his cell for contraband had redefined the term and "shaken down" a student's tools for learning and his record of accomplishment.

In the process of the creative problem solving course, Mr. X had introduced other inmates to some of the principles of creative thinking. One inmate, who had been influential in the organizing of Asklepieion Northwest was present during one of our sessions and was drawn into a practice brainstorming session. He became interested in the concept of creative thinking, and invited me to provide, on a volunteer basis, some creative thinking and problem-solving sessions for the Asklepieions. The Asklepieions are a group of prisoners organized for interpersonal experiences for self-improvement, group dynamics, and other concepts related to the study of human behavior. They place an emphasis on analysis of feelings, interpersonal communication, and proactive attitudes. they have acquaintance with the concept of T. A. (Transactional Analysis) from the book *I'm OK, You're OK.*

Our arrangements and the schedule for my visits to the prison were made by telephone with the inmate member/leader. Before the date of my first visit, I was surprised by a paradigm-altering card in the mail. It was delicate blue in color, with the handwritten message: "Big fuzzies for you from all of us at Asklepieions Northwest. Love and BIG fuzzies." The signature was a stylized heart with the proverbial arrow. The card and message dissolved any hesitancy I might otherwise have had at the prospect of presenting creative thinking sessions for twenty-five inmates in a state prison.

Security routines for prison education visits are methodical. Purses are left in an outer office in individual lockers. Briefcases with instructional materials are searched. When the guard has established the visitor's, an escort is assigned. He takes the visitor through three successive locked and barred enclosures. Signature in a "guest book" is required before being escorted down the long, empty corridors. It is strange conditioning for a creative thinking set of mind.

The twenty-five inmates who gathered in the meeting space outside of their cell block were quite prepared. It was a somewhat hesitant beginning for all of us, but the men were extremely attentive and aware. My needs for setting up the overhead projector, improvising a screen, distributing handouts, taping up newsprint on the room dividers, etc. were all noted and acted upon with the greatest demonstration of support and concern I have ever experienced upon first meeting a class. Affectively, the situation left nothing to be desired.

Two specific individual cognitive exercises were provided as part of the sessions, and resulted in data of considerable interest. The first was a ten-minute figural task of creative thinking adapted from the *Torrance Tests of Creative Thinking* (The Incomplete Figures Task). The purpose, in addition to determining creative thinking strengths within the class, was to offer a thinking experience as a basis for describing the four measurable factors of creativity: fluency, flexibility, originality, and elaboration. Sixteen of the participants responded to my request for their copies. Those copies have been reviewed. Compared with responses by participants in other problem-solving classes they suggested, with a few exceptions, a general quality of constraint. For most respondents, qualities of originality and elaboration were quite unimpressive. There were more abstractions than appear with classes in more familiar settings.

The second individual specific creative thinking exercise, presented at a subsequent meeting, produced a much higher quality of creative response. It used the recording, *Sounds and Images,* developed by Cunningham and Torrance (1965). The record is designed to stimulate creative responses to a series of electronically-produced sounds. The sounds are repeated three times with narration encouraging a stretch of the imagination into descriptions of more creative dimensionality at each successive sound repetition. It is possible that the extremely creative, productive results with inmates in this activity was due to the fact that it was used during our second meeting after the climate for open-ended, relaxed thinking had been established and a sense of mutual trust achieved. It is also possible that the dependence of the task on acoustical rather than visual stimulation was more appropriate for the development of responses in this particular group of subjects.

Sixteen inmates handed in their Sounds and Images responses. A review of the relative creative strength of the three successive descriptions shows strong gains in imagery and its expression. Qualities of originality and elaboration especially were revealed to a marked degree in contrast to results of the creative thinking exercise based on visual stimuli. Many of the responses were well in advance of the quality of responses to the same exercise gathered in standard populations with more time and experience in planned creative thinking activities. Examples of some of the analogies produced are:

Sound 1

A ship going through the light barrier

Starting a flame thrower

Roller skating off a cliff onto a track

One-hundred-foot bowling ball breaking down a forest

The earth's crust breaking and heaving up

Unloading a train full of sheet metal

Being buried alive underground in a really small box

The sounds you would hear while riding inside a boxcar

The welling up of primitive emotion in response to a comfortingly familiar
    sound

Sound 2

Psychedelic sounds being made by a sound lover

Testing memory tape

Factory whistle not working properly

1999 Wankel engine with fuel injection

Sound a fly hears when you miss

A person's screams in a slow motion picture

Late at night when you can't find a radio station

Air raid in Germany

Spinning top

A fly buzzing around and taking a dive to a person's nose

A police car in a small southern town

A deer that has been wounded and crying out for help

Air flowing on a ball bearing

Being in the chair of a crazy dentist

Apprehension, fear, and excitement

Sound 3

Men working, pounding with sledgehammers, breaking up concrete, in a cel-
    lar with pipes rattling

Being in a gopher hole with a farmer going overhead planting corn

Listening to the action of a sling shot slowed down

Cavity trying to pound its way through your tooth

Dropping marbles in a man hole

A person's ears popping in a vacuum chamber

Playing a tune on a handsaw

Walking in a Louisiana bayou in the middle of the night with leg chains on

Dungeon in a small castle where an old man is being held prisoner

Reverb on an electric amp

Underwater sonar in an atomic sub deep in the Indian Ocean

The everyday sounds if you lived in a sewer

Pressure applied to solid object ricocheting

Sound 4

Pipes leaking water, with Phantom of the Opera playing monsterish music in
the background

Walking on the ceiling and having the change fall out of your pocket and
slide down a long brass alley

Sounds made in a cheese factory on the moon

The mating call of the hydra

A big man walking through the doorway of a little store

A high school corridor

Music in a bottle

The sounds an insane person is hearing in the basement corridor of a mental
hospital

Sitting near a construction site in a city, and just daydreaming about nothing
in particular

It must be said that the ability to produce rich, original imagery had, in this
data, no positive correlation with the ability to spell. The fact that some of the
responses were spelled so poorly that they were almost indecipherable adds to the
speculation that possible learning disabilities and the lack of opportunity to reveal
imaginative thinking strengths in a climate of acceptance and reinforcement without regard for high standards of written verbal skills had brought already difficult
learning experiences to a high frustration level for many of the subjects in their
schooling history.

In the brief time available at our last session, the most we could accomplish
of the Parnes Osborn Problem Solving method was an overview and some limited
experience with the five steps. The problem statement selected for the practice
session on problem-solving was: "In what ways might schools be designed to
help prevent delinquency and crime?" Two separate groups brainstormed for

ideas and produced significant quantities. See tables 1 and 2. Time ran out before the plan of action for solving the problem was completed. (When the escort comes to walk the visitor back down the long halls and outside, there are no extensions of time for unfinished business.)

It was a brief encounter. I would like to go back and continue where we left off. There are some things I cannot forget. I can never forget the quiet question, almost an aside, from a participant during a period of heightened group ideation: "How come we never did this kind of stuff in school?" and something of a chorused "Yeah, how come?" from nearby members.

Also, I cannot forget the men who, in some cases, may be paying the high price for failure of schools and society to recognize and value a multiple of thinking and behaving talents. Publications by authorities like Robert Ornstein (1977) are describing neuro-physiological evidence that the two hemispheres of the brain perform different thinking functions: the left brain functions logically, sequentially, and quantitatively. The right brain processes information intuitively, simultaneously, and qualitatively. With current attention to the need for greater balance in their development and expression, clues and connections toward greater understanding of the human condition are being discussed from public platforms in educational and social settings in many places, and have relevance to this writing.

George Prince, author of *The Practice of Creativity,* discussed the duality of selfhood in an address at the Lawrence II Workshop on Creativity at Lawrence Academy, Groton, Massachusetts in April 1977. He described the "safekeeping, protective self" as cautious, analytical, evaluative, logical, serious, practical, organized, and comfortable with the familiar. The other self, the "idea-getting, adventurous self," he suggested, is experimental, intuitive, playful, curious, wishful, inclined to laughter, maker of connections, and appreciator of surprises. Both of the dualities are present in our interpersonal and intrapersonal processes. Prince suggested that the majority of communications to kids are the kinds that discourage learning and that those kids who are of an idea-getting, adventurous, risk taking nature are most likely to have their thinking operations repressed, since their thinking strengths are of the kind which tend to be misunderstood, ignored, or punished.

In an address on "Twin Hemispheres and the Media" at State University College at Buffalo in April 1977, Marshall McLuhan's emphasis on the distinctive thinking operations of the right and left hemispheres of the brain related significantly to the imbalance between social, educational, and institutional rewards for "left brain" linear, logical, sequential operations and "right brain" spontaneous, holistic, simultaneous pattern-related thinking. He said that "left brain" logical thinkers adopt a straight ahead, sequential direction like a freight train full speed ahead, without recognition of the totality of the problem or the hidden ground. McLuhan suggested that "the great brain robbery" occurred when we sold out our entire society to the left hemisphere. From his observation that right hemisphere auditory imagination is simultaneous recognition with the past, present, or future, we might interpret a link with the evidence of rich auditory imagination among the prison inmates with whom this report is concerned.

A search of literature has failed to discover much evidence of research on the subject of creative thinking power among inmates of prisons. This writing offers no empirical evidence upon which to base the claim that creative thinking, problem-solving potentially important to a complex, changing world has, in many cases, unnecessarily been seriously subtracted and/or forever lost to society. It is a reminder of the newly developed knowledge and insight into the need for balance in the valuing and developing of "whole brain" talents. Educators concerned about deviant behavior or apathetic attitudes in students may find partial answers in an examination of their reward and punishment ratio for different thinking processes. More attention, support, and encouragement of imaginative, intuitive minds could lead to stronger self-concept, a more positive sense of identity, a greater inclination for involvement, and higher expectations of personal achievement. The freedom to express individualistic, spontaneous ideas in appropriate, planned activities and in a supportive climate for some part of the school day could satisfy creative energies positively rather than relegating them to experimentation with negative behavior.

Curiosity about the influence of school experiences on the conditioning of thought and attitudes that could lead to delinquency caused me to look to the inmates for clues. What better place? For one of the creative thinking sessions I presented them with the brainstorm topic: "How Might Schools be Designed to Help Prevent Delinquency and Crime?" In a very short time, two separate groups produced a multitude of alternatives as presented in tables 1 and 2.

Summary

Ideas from the lists signal the need for many of the educational reforms that have been waiting a long time for serious attention. The usual quantitative reforms like spending more money and reducing the class size in an effort to improve schooling outcomes could be better balanced with attention to qualitative factors that strengthen and support students in their urge for a more positive self-concept and a genuine sense of significance. Practice with creative and critical thinking during the formal school experience could prepare students for dealing realistically and effectively with real life challenges. Creative problem-solving and decision-making skills can and should be learned as a deterrent to crime prevention. Dealing with problems and challenges in ways that will have positive results contributes to a better quality of life personally, interpersonally, and socially.

In addition, this brief but satisfying experience in creative studies with prison inmates suggests a vital need for the inclusion of creative-thinking, problem-solving, and decision-making classes in rehabilitation programs for prison life and for reentry into society after sentences are served. Justice, punishment, and crime prevention have natural connections to creativity, individuality, and personhood. Techniques and methods for recognizing and rewarding creative behavior are available and ready to be incorporated into programs to meet the urgent need for better balance in rewards for different thinking talents. Beyond serving individual needs in a prison setting, a strong program could result in problem-solving teams for contributing imaginative ideas toward the solution of problems both inside and outside the walls. An abundance of learning experiences and high level information are stored in the minds of inmates, and available for processing in constructive ways through creative programs.

Potential and actual prison populations are fertile and critical places for action.

A final word from Mary Richards (1964) is a reminder that "We have to realize that a creative being lives within ourselves, whether we like it or not, and that we must get out of its way, for it will give us no peace until we do" (p. 4).

Table 1

List of Brainstormed Ideas by Inmates—Group 1

Topic: How Might Schools Be Designed to
Help Prevent Delinquency and Crime?

Trained teacher in therapy

Smaller classes

Role models

Floor Plans

T. A. classes

Flexible schedule

More variety in classes

Encourage creativity

Revise grading system

Dump labels

Stop making comparisons

Allow spontaneity

More community activity participation

More family participation

Dump dress codes

More student feedback

Let kids teach some classes

More responsibility given to kids

Dump traditional modes of education

Individual pace of learning

Teachers trained in observation

Change in traditional school year
    structure

More rap sessions in classes

Allow kids to share what they learn
    other than through tests

Cut down competitive learning

Let students choose teachers

Role play in classes

Smaller more classrooms

Better qualified teachers

Allow kids to study at their own speed

Building complex (stores, shops)

Reinforce strong points

Supervise kids and not teach them

Reinforce new ideas

Let kids design own tools for classes

More attention

Special workshops for teachers

Let kids come when they want

Six hours for study

Influence individuality

Allow for feelings!!!!

Cut competition

Less structure

More men teachers

Redefine delinquency

More creative art expression

School year stretch out

More nature programs

One on one

Inner role modeling

Integrated more with sex

More selection in innovative problems

More reassurance in individual feel-
    ings

More parent involvement

More about cultural backgrounds

Explain parents problems

More fun in eating

More field trips

More teacher caring

Teachers being more aware of the
    child's environment

Table 1—*cont'd.*

More exercises	Let them win at what they do
More financial funding	Ideas selected in solution finding
Stress autonomy	process for most promising:
Treatment	More student input in classes
Strokes	Teachers to be more knowledgeable
Love	of students
Set goals	More creative expression
Let them solve their own problems	Students solve their own problems
Stroke 'em down	(with the teacher)
Candy for positive	Flexibility of schedule
Kids teach	More sharing of outside learning
Kids design own classroom	No comparing in grading system
More hobby craft	More nature programs

Table 2

List of Brainstormed Ideas by Inmates—Group 2

Topic: How Might Schools Be Designed to
Help Prevent Delinquency and Crime?

Comfortable chairs	Sell school stock to students
Prison tours	More freedom of expression
Breaks between classes	Better breakfast program
Drug awareness classes (ex-abusers)	Own choice of what to learn
Closer communication between par-	More learning projects outside school
ents and teachers	(nature,; work, etc.)
Equal opportunity	Teachers in touch with student wants
Open hour classes between 7:00 and	and abilities
10:00	Teach problem solving to teachers
Start at early age	Teach problem solving to students
Less time on basics	]Teach problem solving to parents
Ban non-up-to-date textbooks	Have More parent involvement
More time spent on health	Have more creative time to vent feel-
Field trips for everyone	ings

More diverse educational rewards

Permission to think for selves

Prayer meetings

More learner than authoritarian teachers

Sex education

Moral support

Responsible positions for students

Allow children to be more expressive

Better qualified teachers

Permit child to think more for himself; what works for him/her is important

Human concern; not being there for the money; taking a genuine interest in what they are doing

More humanistic

Improve teaching

Recognize student talent

Increase instruction of teachers

Decrease emphasis of unimportant facts

Control children

Increase communication

More language skills

More family ties

Teachers more together with kids

Give kids more information about life

Ask kids what they are going through

Help kids solve problems

More advanced skill structure

Teachers be straight with student

Not look at teaching just as a job

Get involved with student's life

Global Journalism and the Creative Integration of Differences

The global press wields tremendous power today as a purveyor of vital information. It has the potential to help erase erroneous impressions and stereotypes and to ease tensions; it can also create fears and needlessly perpetuate anxieties. It can shake people from their complacency or it can lull them into an unthinking and dangerous sleep.

—John Merrill

Although this review of ideas of international communications was current in the 1980s, its relevance continues to apply with equal sensitivity in the 1990s. This is a reminder that the thinking patterns of reporters for global affairs continues to be fundamental to the quality of their influence on global futures.

The study of international communications features reviews, reruns, and replays of a familiar theme. It is the theme of the conflict of opposites. The question addressed in this discussion centers around the proposition quoted here from an unidentified source: "Conflicting beliefs divide us within and without. If we could see through them to the level of paradox, we would understand more and fight less." The purpose here is to:

1. Examine a number of polarities attendant on the increasingly vital question of mass media's role in an advancing global society with an uncertain future, and
2. Explore the possibility of "bridging the gap" between the challenging state in which technological developments in communication have placed human society and the level of consciousness required for meeting the challenge.

The effort is an experiment in force-fitting the current realities of international communication as presented in a cross-section of the literature with current expectations in the study of individual and social evolutionary change (Bushrui, Ayman, and Laszlo, 1993).

Polarities and Paradoxes

Examples of polarities, sometimes implied and sometimes stated, permeate the media literature. Berdes (1969) called attention to the melancholy paradox that demands further study in that the Washington news reporters he interviewed on the subject of press/government relations and the right to know and the right to privacy reflected an obsession with conflict and discord, sometimes "amplifying the echoes of battle long after it has been fought." His description of "news management" raised the issues of specialization in government and in news coverage with the result that the integration of specializations and a sense of the total interactive system were lost. In addition, the management of news in complex bureaucracies was said to foster suppression of news by government, since operating in public requires constant justification of its practices. The paradox is stated by Berdes (1969):

> To safeguard the American public it became necessary not to inform it of certain facts which in the hands of the enemy would be lethal "weapons" and lose a tactical advantage, ultimately jeopardizing American public interests...but censorship is a matter of judgment exercised by fallible human beings and therefore open to questions. (p. 17)

Bausinger (1984) discusses the polarizations of technology and the "consciousness of the everyday, knowledge of the everyday, culture of the everyday, behavior of the everyday" (p. 343). In his observations on media as agencies of the everyday he sees empirical investigations in contrast with what he calls "essentialist perspective" which he describes as "an attempt to grasp complex processes more precisely by encircling them with meanings.... It is more important to understand something than to measure it." However, he adds a warning: "The obvious danger is that the playful encircling of the object becomes infatuated with its own motion, and so loses sight of it" (p. 347).

Wiseman (1984) in his discussion of the perceived polarities of quantitative and qualitative research provides an example of a position that searches for the creative integration of the opposites. In a direct application to the state of the art of researching, the author goes beyond the Bausinger position in his assertion that the competent researcher ought to be able to understand both quantitative and qualitative research methods that might be perceived as an exploitation of the paradox.

A perusal of *The Adversaries* (Rivers 1971) contributes to the paradoxical nature of the politics and press dichotomy and enlarges upon it by including, along with political institutions, institutions of religion and others as representing contrary perspectives. A collection of reports of incidents of freedom and control, power and privilege, integrity and distortion, and divided loyalties in the Rivers' publication underscores the realities of news reporting. The basic adversarial relationship between press and politics is said, in the final analysis, to be essential to the survival of democracy. Rather than attempt an absolute analysis, an effort at a synthesis of different realities provides the paradoxical challenge. The quotation from Mark Twain is provocative as a prescription for the press (in Rivers 1971, 237) "First get your facts, then you can distort 'em as much as you like."

In Golding's discussion of the transfer of media management to Third World countries (1977), he discusses "helplessness which comes from not knowing enough about the country and the people to truly understand the people and their culture, and from teaching through an interpreter" (p. 298). Knowledge of the people and their culture is an important step in the achievement of empathic understanding and the unity of differences. Developments since Golding (1977) suggest efforts toward the awareness of the trans-national, trans-cultural, and trans-ideological nature of a balanced flow of information.

In an earlier writing, Golding (1974) takes to task the promotion of the exogenous concept of "modernization" of Third world countries whereby developing countries emerge from static isolation requiring an external stimulus to shake them into the twentieth century. He characterizes the thinking of the exogenous view as ahistorical and ethnocentric, implying the limitations of a "them" and "us" polarization. Professional methods of journalism were examined by Tuchman (1978) who suggested that those methods so limit access to the media that they have become a means not to know. She identifies a number of standard journalistic practices which contribute to the limitation: (1) time and space assignments result in coverage of legitimized institutions; (2) inclination for facts by association with the absolutism of labels; (3) trend toward reactionism rather than a balance with proactionism; (4) emphasis on events rather than on issues which call for paradoxical levels of analysis; and (5) facts and impartiality emphasize quantifiable realities at the expense of the qualitatives. Efforts to strengthen the profession of journalism through continued research and cooperative efforts between researchers and news-workers even though friction will inevitably occur from this marriage of efforts suggests progress in the possibility of a greater unity of different perspectives.

The Imbalancing Act

The publication of the *Global Futures Digest,* which began in 1983 with the initiative of members of the World Future Society, provides an example of the reality of the interrelatedness and interdependence of the nations of the world environmentally, socially, economically, politically, and technologically. The dominance of Western media over Third World countries, although understandable from a technological sense, is a denial of the awareness of interactiveness of the global system and the need for balance.

In a discussion of the human environment (*Global Futures Digest* 1983, 22) the leaders of the world are accused of "lacking in competence and the will to face long-range global issues." Especially in the area of environmental quality, established institutions have failed to recognize the catastrophic implications of continuing the trends of today, and the responsibility would seem to fall to the world's nongovernmental organizations to play an important role. The imbalance of the media with its focus on formally legitimized operations (Tuchman 1978) stands in need of correction if global concerns for future generations are to be met.

Practices in the development of international communication are identified in four phases (Hellman 1980): (1) idealistic phase between the World Wars with relative control of content and journalistic ethics; (2) aggressive phase of psychological warfare; (3) apologetic phase with its consideration of "who says what to whom with what effect"; and (4) critical phase of cultural or media imperialism and capitalism with multinations operating as a military-industrial complex. Criticism from outside of the United States is proliferating, and an acknowledgment of the imbalance in the flow and analysis of information is accumulating from within the country, including the charge that empirical and quantitative methods in behavioristic tradition started to serve whatever ends its bureaucratic clients had in view, governmentally organized and ideologically loaded.

Advertising as a corollary to the communications imbalance is discussed by Janus and Roneagliolo (1977). In their review of the growth of industry and the pressures on the mass media which "serve as the critical link between the manufacturers and the eyes and ears of the consumer," the authors observe that the function of the nation's media system, instead of being one of education and community progress, has increasingly become one of persuading the masses to join the "consumer life style," with the whole complex of cultural values and images being transferred along with the transnational product. (pp. 81–85)

In a reflection of the vision of *Global Futures Digest,* Richstad and Anderson (1981) look ahead at prospects for the future of international news. The challenge of predicting the future of the crisis as recognized and described in 1981 was a difficult one. A summary statement held a considerable degree of optimism:

that the world is moving forward in some promising policy directions and that the spirit of the 1980s and beyond could be one of pluralism, harmony, and positive cooperation. The risks, however, are great, and the times will place a premium on not only innovative ideas but also patience and public diplomacy." (Richstad and Anderson 1981, 402)

In a further acknowledgment of trends and predictable future realities the Garnham and Collins editorial (1985) is a reminder of the shift in creating, manipulating, and in receiving information from print to electronic media. According to the writers, profound consequences in the matter of work and power in publications business can be expected. Polarization and conflict between telecommunication and strategies are forecast and include the involvement of cultural policy in the conflict of systems. It is said that "developments stemming from the field of telecommunications are impinging with force and urgency upon the traditional mass cultural consequences as yet to be adequately assessed" (Garnham and Collins 1985, 3).

The interval between 1972, when Allen Wells edited a collection of essays by authorities in the field of media and the present time has added the dimensions of future time and global space. Contributions by Shramm, Nixon, Schiller, McLuhan, Novak, and Bagdikian, along with less familiar names, provide little evidence that international communications was of major significance. The reference to intranational conflict and polarization is contained in a section on racism, sexism, and the mass media, with essays pointing out the place of media in the interpretation of culturally and racially different populations and issues.

Imbalance of resources and power leads easily to exploitation when competition based on economics drives the system with quantification out of balance with qualitative, human, uncountable values. Alpes (1984) offers a value-loaded and optimistic prediction of the improvement of technology and decreasing costs of global commercial satellite communication systems and their effect on business opportunities. He is triumphant over the prospect of the opening of enormous markets for equipment manufacturers and predicts a massive expansion of profits.

A similar technological and economic motivation dominated the presentations at a conference on Living and Working in Outer Space (1985). Ex-astronauts focused their excitement on possibilities of moon mining, satellite solar energy, space settlements, space agriculture and other technological developments. Gerard O'Neill, chairman of the board of Geostar Corporation, argued for resources and effort that would keep the United States ahead of the world in technology and economics. More subtle evidence of the limited understanding of the global claim to space and the respect for differences came in the reference to the Soviet space efforts as the "sledgehammer" technique and their inability to innovate and initiate breakthrough ideas. Another speaker demonstrated a like insensitivity when he made a visual joke of the only way the Chinese could ever get into space. As a member of the audience I made note of the imbalance of sophisticated thinking. The spectacular technological and scientific know-how was poorly matched by the level of humanistic thought. Schiller (1985) sees the less developed countries facing the most serious and intense economic and social crisis of this century with transnational corporations in position to manipulate an "unparalleled series of combinations, mergers, and buyouts…making previous bursts of takeover activity pale."

His prediction is that these powerful systems will increasingly control the economy and make poorer nations "hostage to strategic crucial foreign information" (p. 105).

Bridging the Gap

The accelerated rate of change is more compatible with technological development than with development in the ability of human consciousness to deal with the complexities and ambiguities resulting from scientific advances of their own making. Botkin et al. (1979) define the human gap as "the distance between growing complexity and our capacity to cope with it.…a lagging development of our own capacities" (pp. 6–7).

One of the human capacities critical to the process of change is the talent for leadership. In the study of leadership as it relates to contemporary society, it becomes clear that a rapidly changing, expanding world awareness is bringing into focus a changed concept of the process of leadership. The impact of media and the Information Age has made a wealth of knowledge and expertise available to cross-sections of the world's population. The need for action in response to change and in preparation for predicted possibilities makes necessary the development of talents for leadership appropriate to a complex society with a wide range of intellect and readiness to serve group purposes. The concept of leadership has, accordingly, undergone a substantial change. Burns (1978), a foremost authority on the question of leadership, distinguishes between transactional leadership and transforming leadership. Transactional leadership is of the traditional pattern whereby "leaders approach followers with an eye to exchanging one thing for another." Of the new form of leadership he has this to say:

> Transforming leadership, while more complex, is more potent. The transforming leader recognizes and exploits an existing need or demand of the potential follower. But, beyond that, the transforming leader looks for potential motives in followers, seeks to satisfy higher needs, and engages the full person of the follower. The result of transforming leadership is a relationship of mutual stimulation and elevation that converts followers into leaders and may convert leaders into moral agents." (p. 4)

Leadership patterns that de-emphasize labels and hierarchies are in the nature of human growth in the process of evolution toward a level of mentality with the capability of avoiding strictly imposed formulas and categorizations in human affairs, and acting with the understanding of a blend of differences for the accomplishment of a shared purpose.

The distinction made by Janowitz (1975) between the journalist as "gatekeeper" and journalist as "advocate" has relevance to the concept of transforming leadership. In his perception, the gatekeeper follows the scientific method of objectivity, fact, and professional orientation. The advocate, on the other hand, is more sensitively integrated with his sources and clients. He is dedicated to the representation of multi-perspectives and alternative definitions of reality in an example of lateral and empathic insights into complex issues.

In the discussion by Nixon (1965) of the Lerner concept of empathy, he suggests the need for basic communication skills required by modern man for the spreading of curiosity and imagination leading to social growth and economic development. Such an interpretation of the purposes of communication skills would separate leadership and followership roles, making media the force which leads Third World countries toward modernization after Western models rather than an effort at mutuality between leadership and followership identities which would integrate exogenous with indigenous forces.

Lee (1982) recognizes gaps in another context—that of international communication research; he identifies the following:

1. Relationship between multinational manufacturing corporations and mass media
2. Relationship between the First Amendment and the free flow of information principle
3. Comparative structure of organizations
4. Historical parallelism between the cartel of news agencies and international colonialism and imperialism
5. Codified definition of "development news" and its concomitant theoretical and practical problems
6. Role of national news agencies and dissemination of international news
7. Threats to the legitimacy of international news agencies
8. Policy alternatives. (p. 636)

All of the identified "gaps" have a degree of relevance to the paradoxical level of thought. The quantification of polarities and relationships can illuminate the issues. It will depend upon an exercise of the transforming nature of the role of leadership and a tolerance for the ambiguities inherent in the paradoxes of "contraries" for media to function in an advocacy style.

A thoroughly balanced analysis of the perceived polarity between media imperialism and the free flow of information arrives at a middle-ground perception in the work of Lee (1980). It is significant that the preface quotes the wisdom of Confucius on the changing and constant nature of the system: "Being without inclinations to either side is called CHUNG; admitting of no change is called

YUNG. By CHUNG is denoted the correct course to be pursued by all under heaven; by Yung is denoted the fixed principle regulating all under heaven" (p. 11). Such a principle internalized by representatives of media would contribute positively to the solution problems of polarities.

Opening the Doors of Perception

A listing of more than a hundred participants from all over the world gives an international validity to their Learning Report to the Club of Rome, published under the title *No Limits to Learning: Bridging the Human Gap* (Botkin et al. 1979). Unlike the first report, which sounded a note of despair over the recognized limits to growth in global resources, this second report is based on an optimistic assumption. It is the belief that the potential of human thought and perception is infinite and available for creating a future compatible with a positive human destiny. The report advances two intertwined questions:

> whether what we call progress is perhaps so hectic and haphazard that world populations are utterly confused and out of step with the waves of change…and whether present trends can be controlled and the gap bridged before a tragic fate overtakes homo sapiens. (p. xiii)

The positiveness of their position derives from the assumption that the human family has untapped resources of perception, vision, creativity, and moral energies that can be realized and activated. A discussion of cultural identity calls attention to the threat of global homogenization and local disintegration as a source of international and social conflict. The problem of polarization—i.e., the assumption that cultural identity precludes global interdependence—is said to be the result of training that sees diversity at the expense of unity. Prospects of new learning on transforming leadership are an encouraging expectation. Training and educational institutions in all areas of the globe have a responsibility to help open the doors of perception for all of the world's citizens, especially for journalists and other members of the media. Persons of influence and power, if functioning with full intellectual and perceptual potential could do much to effect planetary cultural understanding. Botkin et al. (1979) believe that what is vital in the process of enhancing cultural identity is the perception of global issues and their complexity. Every person should be able to see these issues from at least two perspectives: from a global view as well as from a culturally specific view, be it national or local. This implies a "full respect for the values of others, a consensus on a minimal set of universal values as well as a greater role for international exchanges, carried out on multi-lateral bases, for people of all ages to see the globality of the heritage of humanity from perspectives outside their own culture. (p. 117)

In addition to the foregoing appeal for the extension of human perceptions, Willis Harman (1984) discusses higher levels of creativity and their deliberate cultivation as an aid in the evolution of human consciousness. As a regent of the University of California and professor at Stanford University, as well as staff member of the Institute of Noetic Sciences, Harman provides a level of authenticity to his predictions for "opening the mind's gates" to breakthrough insights in the unifying of differences.

Images of the possible human, sometimes labeled "New Age Man" or "Renaissance Man" are based on a person of diverse talents suitable for complex change and leadership in the field of ideas. COMSTAT (1984) featured the genius of Arthur C. Clarke, "novelist, physicist, mathematician, diver, essayist, futurist, film-maker, and authority on the human uses of space." (Saft 1984, 27–36). It is significant that Clark, as an example of a "renaissance man" was credited with accomplishments of technological development rather than development of the human intellect and spirit. The implications of the "human gap" give credibility to the charge that "both the organization and content of mass-mediated culture reflect that orientation away from humanism, creativity, spontaneity, and pluralism, and toward efficiently designed and measured ledger-book results" (Real 1977, 246).

Trends and Possibilities

Media are helping to bring public awareness to the need for "psychic mobility" in all members of the global population. Figure 2 demonstrates the interrelatedness of all on planet earth.

Ringham (1985) reported the articulation by Chinese spokespersons of the reality of deep cultural and ideological differences and the importance of understanding between individuals and nations. An official of the Chinese People's

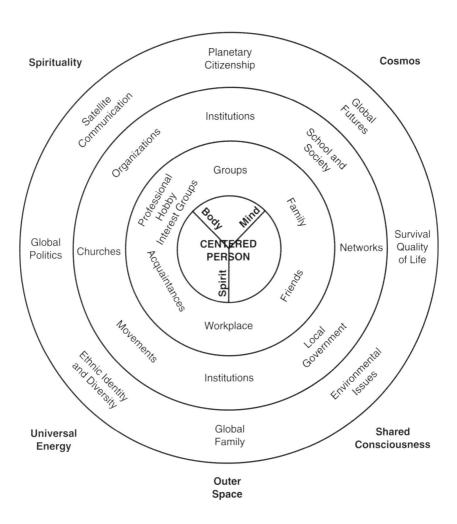

*Everything and everyone affects and is affected by everything
and everyone in an interactive, self-organizing system.*

Figure 2—Holistic Society: The Big Picture
The Person in the Process of Change

Association for Friendship with Foreign Countries is quoted: "What we really hope is that the government and people of the United States would understand the feelings of the people more. These are the sentiments of a billion people, not some policy concocted by a few people." Public rhetoric of leading officials, although not representative of the people of the United States, can inflame the sensitivities of culturally different and interfere with the efforts toward world harmony. Sensibilities of media figure in the formula.

Insight into the productive potential of polarizations is articulated in a quote from Ghandi (Tehranian 1984):

One must learn, then, to see a dynamic polarity rather than an inner contradiction in what at first looks like a basic inconsistency, such as that between fusion-in-the-mass and utter solitude, between sensual license and compulsive order, or between an utterly a-historical sense of living and inventories of assembled facts. (p. 63)

Tehranian (1984) has a list of challenges of modernization that sees the possibilities of the "dynamic polarity" envisioned by Ghandi. He suggests:

1. demonstration efforts (catch up)
2. fusion efforts (combine)
3. compression efforts (develop faster than industrialized nations)
4. preventive efforts (do all this at less human, material, environmental cost)
5. stylization efforts (whereby uniqueness of national identity unfolds as development proceeds). (p. 64)

Third World countries have choices in how to refuse to sacrifice their cultural heritage to modern exogenous values at the same time they work for worldly preeminence without crushing identity and tradition.

Summary

It is hoped that there has emerged from the discussion an argument for the importance of education and training that discover and stimulate levels of mentality capable of empathy that transcends personal experience and ideologies. A summation is reflected in a statement from an unknown writer: "Unity without diversity is uniformity; diversity without unity is chaos; justice is served when unity and diversity exist together in creative tension."

A tacit example of creative tension is in an article published in the *Journal of the International Organization of Journalists* (Zassoursky 1985), appealing for an increased role of the media in the interests of peace and international understanding. The fact that the article originates in the Soviet Union has significance as a symptom of encouraging possibilities for more open communication between journalists from politically different perspectives. The appeal is for: (1) the role of media in creating an atmosphere of international understanding, (2) reporting the problem of peace and disarmament, (3) utilizing the international exchange of information in the interests of understanding among nations, (4) excluding war propaganda and incitement to war by the media, and (5) preparing journalists in a spirit of peace and disarmament.

The problem of peace is everyone's problem. The media is in a preferred position to serve the cause. Education is in a preferred position to serve the evolution of all of human consciousness. The reality is a philosophical observation from the writing of Teilhard de Chardin: "Here we stand, ready to escape into the future with a joyful uncertainty."

Making the World Safe for Intuitives

It is by logic we prove but by intuition we discover.

—Henri Poincare

"Some day we'll find a way to make the world safe for intuitives." That statement, made to me by a ranking educationist, engraved itself on my mind ten years ago. It was intended to comfort me at a time of personal trauma over a sudden job loss. Now I am beginning to think of the statement as a sensitive perception, an intuitive leap, maybe a prophecy.

Anyone who has felt the creative power of a sudden flash of intuitive insight or a gradual building of connections between observations and new information into a system of intuitive certainty will recognize the need for a safe place for new ideas and new directions of action. The prospect of a world made "safe for intuitives" will probably be a real day brightener for minds with a high level of creative intuition. There are reasons to look with growing confidence toward such a prospect.

One of the reasons for confidence is the attention being paid to the concept of right-brain and left-brain processing differences described earlier in this book and reviewed here because of their particular relevance to the subject. A real boost in the understanding of individuality in human thinking patterns came with the work of Roger Sperry, M.D. (In Ornstein 1977). His experiments with persons who were seriously impaired with epilepsy showed that the right hemisphere of the brain and the left hemisphere of the brain could function independently of each other, and that they were inclined to process information in quite different ways. As many readers are aware, a major difference is described as right-brain intuitive thinking as opposed to left-brain logical thinking. Further, that one or the other style of thinking tends to be dominant in most individuals. A right-brain person will exercise intuition in the making of decisions. A left-brainer will be inclined to depend on logical reasoning.

Other dichotomies between the two hemispheres suggest that while "left-brain thinking processes information verbally and relates readily to quantitative, sequential patterns of thought, right-brain thinking processes more visually and relates to qualitative, spontaneous, systemic patterns. A personal experience provides a simple example of individual differences in learning and thinking styles. I became intrigued with learning to play a harmonica while observing a friend practicing her skills by following specific directions in a "How to Play A Harmonica" book. The notes and up-down arrows gave specific step-by-step directions. I bought a how-to book and an F-harmonica the same day and set about learning. It did not work for me. So I went alone to sit on a rock under a blue Colorado sky, closed my eyes, and experimented with the sounds and process. That was the system that worked for me at the beginning as a right-brain intuitive learner. Learning from the specific directions in the book is another way. There is much to be said in favor of integrated whole-brain learning.

Although it is readily agreed that the human brain and its functioning remain too complex and mysterious for anything like an absolute analysis, the scientific findings that began with Sperry and others (in Ornstein 1977), and that continue to unravel the secrets of brain, mind, and body integrations are giving the intuitive process a welcome validity. *Brain Mind Bulletin* edited by Marilyn Ferguson provides a regular update on progress in the understanding of those secrets. There is convincing substance to an argument on behalf of a position based on intuition when science is there to validate and confirm the basis (Sperry, a Nobel scientist). After all, how else does an intuitive defend a judgment? Most of traditional science, including the behavioral sciences, has had the limitation of assuming that if it can't be measured or counted, it doesn't really exist. That paradigm is making a significant shift.

In the past if it happened that a person turned out to be wired with a preference for right-brain thinking, what happened to his or her intuitive, creative ideas in a basically conforming authoritarian, hierarchical, left-brain organization or society? What happened to individuals with intuitive insight into solutions for solving problems, meeting challenges, and taking advantage of opportunities in an institutional or corporate bureaucracy when their slot in the system was marked "powerless"? Rather than recount the long list of examples of lost intuitive talents and the failure of many bureaucracies to open their doors to imaginative, innovative ideas, and intuitive decision making, it is more productive to look at some examples of developments in the valuing of intuitive, creative thinking.

A symposium on Creativity and Innovation in Bureaucracies was held in Washington, D.C. When I told friends that I had been invited to participate in that meeting, the common response was, "Isn't that a contradiction in terms?" When I reported further that the symposium was sponsored by the National Defense University and was being convened at Fort Lesley J. McNair in Washington, D.C., I sensed a further skepticism. However, the meeting became very much a reality, and represents a major example of the trend toward the recognition in high places of the importance of creative, productive thinking and decision making in organizations. About two hundred participants attended, including a majority from the military, a considerable number from administrative levels of business and industry, and a "delegation" of twelve or so colleagues of the Creative Education Foundation at the University of New York at Buffalo. For two days speakers and discussion groups addressed themselves to those natural reaches of the human mind identified for that program as creativity and innovation. Intuition may well be considered a companion term—the relationship is necessarily close.

Another example of the vigorous attention to the value of intuition, especially in the world of business and industry, is the emphasis on intuitive decision making. In the bestseller, *In Search of Excellence: Lessons from America's Best Run Companies,* Peters and Waterman (1982) cite companies whose management style and decision-making process include strong dependence on the value of intuition, risk taking, and action. Who can quarrel with factors that result in success at that level?

The Futurist, a publication of the World Future Society, endorses the futuristic character of the trend toward balance between intuition and reason in an article by Weston H. Agor (1983). Under the title, "Tomorrow's Intuitive Leaders," Agor claims that a new organizational climate is emerging amid the accelerating pace of technological and social change. Tomorrow's managers will make increasing use of an unorthodox decision-making technique—intuition—to steer their organizations through the upheavals ahead.

When Harlan Cleveland writes about the "Art of Leadership," he calls for visionary and integrative thinking. The global complexities and accelerating changes in modern society demand unprecedented growth in human consciousness and the quality of thinking. The intuitive ability to look into the future and to think in terms and images of interrelated systems becomes more critical as rapid growth and change make new, urgent demands on both leadership and follower-ship in families, in groups, in institutions, and throughout the global household.

Add one more example to the testimony in behalf of the value of intuition. The *Tarrytown Newsletter* (October 1983) features a review of the intuition and spirit of Native American thought. The three I's of Indian Education are said to be "intuition, imagination, and insight." An American businessman, quoted in the *Tarrytown Newsletter* says that operating out of impulse or intuition has long been known as an American characteristic. Yet in business during the last thirty years, the ever growing reliance on research indicates that our intuitive ideas are dying out. What passes for intuition today, for the most part, is not intuition at all, but hunch. Intuition is the revelation of a truth, a reality; hunch is nothing more than wish or chance. So how might we further define this attribute of the human mind that we think of as intuition and that is evidently coming to have so crucial a place in the ordering of human affairs?

Frances E. Vaughan (1979) identifies pure intuition as the knowledge that comes out of the experience of formlessness and silence, and distinguishes it from imagination. Imagination gives form to the formless and is conceptual in nature. Pure intuition, in these terms, may seem to be quite inaccessible to the average person. However, the intuitive process is said to be no different than the creative process in that anyone can tune in to either one in varying degrees, and that the potential for each can be readily cultivated and operationalized. Few people are aware of the extent of their intuitive powers. It has been said that we can know the physical world by means of our five senses and the spiritual world by the senses of our mind. Educational and social institutions with their emphasis on standard-ization, and the resulting limitations of authoritarian control, have dealt a serious blow to the natural expression of and trust in intuition.

The good news is that the recovery of intuitive perception is possible. Just as the creative thinking and problem-solving process can be developed through the practice of creative thinking strategies, so also can latent intuitive abilities be strengthened through practice and understanding. Awareness of techniques for awakening those abilities is a first step. Understanding the validity of some of the factors of intuition (dreams, extrasensory perception, artistic inspiration, etc.) is a close second. When intuition is awakened, the whole collection of experiences and knowledge stored in the unconscious mind can become available. A helpful book for anyone interested in intuitive thinking techniques is *Awakening Intuition* by Frances Vaughan (1979). Exercises in relaxation, open focus, imaging, concentration, visualization, and receptivity are described, and are a reminder that learning to use intuition is something like learning to be your own teacher. As with other psychological functions like feeling and sensations, intuition is an individualistic matter. The doors for knowing in an intuitive way can open all the way from sensory through abstract and imaginative to visionary perception.

One of the rewards of growth in the practice and validation of intuition is self-knowledge, possibly extending beyond the personal domain to include perceptions of one's self as a part of the universe along with other forms of life. The inner world of self and spirit can sense a relationship with cosmic space, and benefit from the exchange of inner and outer energies. The activation of intuitive right-brain power and potential can thus be brought into more productive balance with left-brain so-called rational, logical thinking.

The process of creativity, closely associated with right-brain dominance, is nurtured and enhanced by intuitive leaps of imagination. The sudden mental connections that come during periods of relaxation when the prepared mind inexplicably produces an "aha experience," are the work of intuition. Such periods of incubation are on record to have called up remote associations that resulted in startling new ideas in invention, art, problem solving, and breakthroughs in scientific principles (Cameron 1992, Fox 1995). The evolution of the human race probably owes its progress to the intuitive connections that result in great leaps of new knowledge and understanding.

A discussion of intuition would be incomplete without a reference to its relationship to humor. The moment when the mind makes the connection between two seemingly unrelated planes of thought, or makes the leap across space necessary to get the joke, that mysterious "mental somersault" depends on the tacit, intuitive understanding of the unspoken. It might be said that the more subtle the joke, the greater the level of intuition demanded to make connective sense of the disparate planes of thought.

A globe with all the problems of unifying the differences between persons, ideologies, and nations needs all the intuition it can get. Limiting the development of solutions to research and reason alone continues to fail. The threats to survival of such continuing failure are obvious. One cause for the expectation of greater understanding is the increasing attention to the need for balance between intuition and reason. Jonas Salk (*The Anatomy of Reality* 1983) brings a scientific authenticity to his argument for the cultivation in all peoples of their common human talent for the intuitive capacity to predict and anticipate consequences of actions that affect all of humanity in extensions of time forward.

The cultivation of the full range of human intellectual capabilities, especially the balancing of the arts of intuition and reason, are a growing responsibility of institutions of learning. It is becoming increasingly recognized that insight, imagination, and intuition have been neglected in Western education and its basically mechanistic society. Sylvester Morey (1983) makes an appeal for balanced, whole brain functioning. He says that intellect does not create; it only analyzes. We cannot expect solutions to come from intellect alone. If our youth could broaden themselves to the point where they could master intellectuality like the white man and still develop intuitively, like the Indian—they would bring balance and harmony into their own lives and the lives of those around them. (*Tarrytown Letter,* Oct 1983)

The unsettled and unsettling state of global affairs calls for global leadership with new talents. Salk (1983) in his discussion of intuition makes a relevant statement in summary:

> Human beings have a feeling, sensitivity, and understanding for where they are in the cosmos and in the world, in time as well as in space. There are some among us who feel and see more clearly than the rest; they are the ones who illuminate and reveal reality for others. This feeling, sensitivity, and vision give us our orientation and our sense of relationship to ourselves, to others, to the world, and to the cosmos. (pp. 18–19)

Here is an urgent call for intuitive growth and greater unity of consciousness and action for all of the world's people.

Iqbal and the "Intimate Immensities"

You are an eagle; therefore get you among the skies. Open your wings and pinions. Rise clear above the earth.

—Iqbal

Thus the individual and humankind are intimately linked as is the part to the whole. Man is linked to the cosmos as well as to all other human beings, and, in one way or another, human beings have feelings for each other whether they are remotely or closely related. Human beings have a feeling, sensitivity, and understanding for where they are in the cosmos and in the world, in time as well as in space. There are some among us who feel and see more clearly than the rest; they are the ones who illuminate and reveal reality for others. This feeling, sensitivity, and vision give us our orientation and our sense of relationship to ourselves, to others, to the world, and to the cosmos.

—Jonas Salk

Introduction:

Throughout the reading of Iqbal's *Javid-Nama,* I experienced an intense personal identity with the poetics of self and space that distinguish his writing, and I knew I was finding that quintessence of a thought long familiar and much treasured—the "intimate immensities." Its discovery has given a sense of reality to the otherwise incomprehensible vastness of the heavens. To find so emotional a response to a new poetic experience so absolutely, so immediately, and so intuitively has the feeling of something mystical. It is almost as if the system of universal energies caused a synchronistic connection, and brought the East with its organismic, holistic thought into partnership with the more familiar search for universal understanding of the West. A line from the *Javid-Nama* is relevant here: "For Westerners intelligence is the stuff of life: for Easterners love is the mystery of all being" (p. 57). I may flatter myself that I understand the thought which Iqbal's words suggest. That, at least, is my momentary "truth." Always assumed, of course, is the accompanying principle of uncertainty. In that somewhat amorphous state, the discussion of Javid-Nama is approached more as a synthesis of

201

the "intimate immensities" than as an analysis of literature, and somewhere between authority and apology.

A Person

It is small wonder that when Iqbal's writings and philosophies appeared fairly early in the twentieth century, he was said to have "stirred the dead into life." He wrote of "Secrets of the Self" and "The Mysteries of Selflessness" at a time when he had achieved academic, disciplined successes, having graduated from Cambridge in 1908, qualified for the bar in London, and done post-graduate work in Germany. His preoccupation with personal identity and human significance at its divine funda-mental could have come as a reaction to years of directed scholarship. His own his-tory of knowledge and service in a broad range of inter-connected disciplines of law, philosophy, religion, politics, economics, and literature placed him strategically for the systemic triumph of thought evident in his writing. His own personal place in this poetic drama, a spiritual journey, is a sensitive and cosmic reflection of a great mind, a great spirit, and a great spokesman for all who engage themselves in an active quest for the meaning of self in universe and universe in self.

A Style

Because it is the special style and language of the poet which have roused and raised new heights of understanding, they are of the first order of significance in the discussion. There were countless times when "my heart leaped up" in a sense of communion over a passage that touched a center. The repeated references to "this world, that is wrought of water and clay" has particular meaning, since I have been an enthusiastic wheel potter for a number of years. The pots produced are primitive in character, and probably best classified as of semi-professional quality. However, the sense of earthly belonging in the handling and forming of the clay gives one an advantage in sensory response out of the depths of remem-bered experience each time he speaks metaphorically of clay and water. There are many examples:

> He yearned for these to come forth from water and clay a cluster sprout-ing from the seed-bud of the heart. (p. 112)

The lustre of a handful of earth one day shall outshine the creatures of light. (p. 26)

...earth, through the star of his destiny one day shall be transformed into heaven. (p. 26)

Symbolic, also, to a potter is the recall of the sense of centering and the subtle, almost mystical sense of timing when all the separate properties and origins that make up the clay body have been brought together, blended, fused, and felt into a precise moment when intuition says that centering has been achieved and the earth is ready for forming. Iqbal has a tacit dimension that bespeaks the same sense of ordering, balancing, preparing, and purposeful entering of an event to effect change. He says, in "The Prayer":

> ...cease to be centreless, become stable,
> Create unity of thought and action
> That you may possess authority in the world.... (p. 139)

His use of the basic matters and energies of the natural world makes a profound connection for any who have felt the unspeakable closeness of the forces of earth and universe to the human psyche. He speaks as one who has internalized those forces into his personhood, and made himself one with the stars and seas in an exchange of identity, so that now they have message and meaning for him. He makes the meanings available to others. The wisdoms of the limitless universe weave themselves through his analogies and metaphors, and make resounding presence:

> Grant to this vagrant heart a resting-place, restore to the moon this fragment of the moon... (p. 23)

> A man who is a wanderer on the quest a fixed star with the constitution of a planet. (p. 39)

> White falcon, sharp of claw and swift to seize he takes for his counselor the silly sparrow. (p. 62)

Mood and imagery are here in the pen of a master:

> ...tempestuous wind, those night black clouds in their darkness the light-
> ning itself had lost lustre;
> an ocean suspended in their air,
> its skirt rent, few pearls pouring
> its shore invisible, its waves high-surging... (p. 73)

Synaesthetic description:

> ...mountain and plain embracing a hundred springtimes...fragrant with
> musk came the breeze from the hills,
> songs of birds conspiring together,
> fountains, and verdant herbs half-grown...
> the body was fortified by the emanation of that air. (p. 74)

Delicate picture-painting:

> ...they have made a way for waters into the desert
> upon the mountains the palm fronds are washed.
> Yonder two gazelles one after the other -
> see how they are descending from the hill,
> for a moment drink from the desert spring
> and then glance upon the traveller.
> The dew has softened the sands of the plain like silk
> the highway is not hard for the camel;
> the clouds ring on ring like the wings of the partridge. (p. 80)

and

> Yonder heights...so covered with snow as to seem a heap of silver
> beyond them stretches a diamond-shining ocean
> its depths even more translucent than its surface,
> undisturbed by wave or torrent
> in its nature an internal quiet. (p. 76)

The use of original terms and definitions:

> Earth fluttered before God in the agony of sunlight… (p. 26)

> If I could only see God's interlocutor again… (p. 78)

> Man as God's Vicegerent (p. 59)

> I am a sea; untumult in me is a fault… (p. 24)

The moods and images in this writing transport a nature-lover back to familiar visions and, in the context of the poetic drama, add philosophical dimensions. Not since the finding of Wordsworth and Whitman have the poetics of nature held so much personal intimacy.

Javid-Nama is rich with examples of the paradoxical "contraries" referred to in the writing of William Blake, leaving the reader in an expectant suspension of opposites and rehearsed in the androgynous realities of life's imprecisions:

> We…are in the world yet free from the world. (p. 83)

> Before the soul a mirror has been hung,
> bewilderment mingled with certainty… (p. 137)

> When he gives up the soul, his soul is truly his,
> otherwise his soul is his guest for but a moment or two. (p. 120)

Epigrammatic lines that puzzle and provoke:

> Faith is precious to the wise
> and to the ignorant it is contemptible. (p. 127)

> "You who are of the caravan, travel alone, yet go with all… (p. 141)

Neophytes to the writing of "Eastern weavers of subtleties" find challenge in the ambiguities:

The highways like travellers are on a journey,
Apparently at rest, secretly everywhere in motion. (p. 133)

Life, wherever it may be, is a restless search;
unresolved is this riddle—am I quarry, or is He? (p. 137)

Added to the sensuous imagery in many of the passages are the seductive sounds of words and place names. The name, Iqbal has, itself, a suggestion of mystery and power. To the Western ear, names like Mustafa, *Javid-Nama,* Ghazal, Zarvan, Qashmarud, Sorosh, Maulana Jamal et al. bring a soft mystery and music to some of the hard historian realities in the political references. There is also the talent for emotional shock when the lines make abrupt shift from the sublime to the vulgar:

You have in your throat melodies sweet and delicate.
How long will you croak like a frog in the mud? (p. 32)

A Format

The design chosen by Iqbal as a vehicle for presenting his message on human struggle is a drama representing himself as master inquirer and searcher. The didactics and moralities are presented by the cross-section of figures and personages encountered in the journey through the spheres of the Moon, Mercury, Venus, Jupiter, Saturn, beyond the spheres, and to the presence of God. His guide in the journey is the Sage of Rum, Jalal al-Din Humi, an admired poet. Most of the characters are based on actual political and spiritual leadership figures in the history of Islam and world affairs. A prayer and two preludes, in heaven and on earth, introduce the drama. The thirty-six characters give testimony, rebukes, exhortations, and prophecy on a broad spectrum of human and political issues.

The plan seems appropriate to the message, since it is more holistic than focused in its pattern. The itinerary has a quality of permissiveness about it, with distractions and unexpected themes interwoven. It is almost as if Iqbal were influenced by the line from one of Tagore's poems: "Where roads are made, I lose my way." Of course, he did not lose his way, and the culminating dictum of his journey is upbeat. From the "Song of the Angels," his perception of the destiny of human perfection is clear:

Consider one moment the meaning of Man: what thing do you ask of us?
Now he is pricking into nature, one day he will be modulated perfectly,
so perfectly modulated will this precious subject be
that even the heart of God will bleed one day at the impact of it! (p. 27)

A Message

The messages are many. For an anthropologist of creativity, they are, in most cases, a reinforcement of the substance of that discipline. A specific example of the isomorphism between the two sources is key:

1. From *Javid-Nama,* in "Prelude on Earth," spoken by Rumi, the guide:

Life means to adorn oneself in one's self,
to desire to bear witness to one's own being.
Whether you be alive, or dead, or dying -
for this seek witness from three witnesses.
The first witness is self-conscious
to behold oneself in one's own light;
The second witness is the consciousness of another,
to behold oneself in another's light.
The third witness is the consciousness of the God's essence,
to behold oneself in the light of God's essence. (p. 20)

2. And from the most comprehensive definition of creativity, according to Clark Moustakis:

Creativity is the experience of expressing and actualizing one's individual identity in an integrated form in communion with oneself, with nature, and with other persons. (p. 30)

The two mirror each other, except for the order in which the three components are placed. Iqbal places God third in the ordering. Moustakis gives nature second place. There is nothing to suggest that either thinker intended a hierarchy. Neither is it unreasonable to assume a hierarchy. Of greater significance is the fact that the term nature could be interpreted to include the entire human species, whether or not they had a conscious, articulated identity with God in a limited interpretation. The fact seems to be that there is a cross-disciplinary, cross-cultural agreement that human life and growth has requirements that are threefold, and that the process is synonymous with the creative spirit and heritage of man.

Many of the human qualities associated through observations and research with the creative personality are brought into special focus in Iqbal's exhortation to "tighten the know of the ego and hold fast to thy tiny being" in the process of becoming. The following excerpts are offered as examples of direct relationships with characteristic creativity factors of:

1. Energy and Aspiration

> We do not tolerate confinement to one station
> we are wholly and singly a yearning to soar
> every instant our occupation is to see and to quiver
> our labor is to fly without feather and wings. (p. 102)

> Reason is a chain fettering this present age;
> where is a restless soul such as I possess?
> for many ages Being must twist on itself
> that one restless soul may come into being. (p. 22)

2. Imagination and Revelation

> Suddenly I beheld my world,
> that earth and heaven of mine,
> I saw it drowned in a light of dawn…
> That light revealed every secret veiled
> And snatched the power of speech from my tongue.
> Out of the deep heart of the inscrutable world
> an ardent, flaming melody broke forth. (p. 140)

> Without revelation no wise man ever found the way,
> he died buffeted by his own imaginings;
> without revelation life is a mortal sickness,
> reason is banishment, religion constraint. (p. 23)

3. Self-concept

His concern is to taste the delight of rebellion
not to behold anything but himself;
for without rebellion the self is unattainable
and while the self is not attained, defeat is inevitable. (p. 131)

4. Divine Discontent

I do not know where my own station is,
I only know that it is apart from all friends
Deep within me rages a war without horsemen and armies
He well describes it who has vision like me
Men are ignorant of the conflict between unbelief and faith. (p. 72)

My soul is such, that for the joy of gazing
it every moment desires a new world. (p. 73)

in its breast the nine spheres cannot be contained;
when yearning makes assault upon a world
it transforms momentary beings into immortals. (p. 94)

5. Singularity and Altruism

Science derives pleasure from verification
love derives pleasure from creativeness
display is very precious to the verified,
to the creator solitude is very precious…
inflict not on the Creator the trouble of display. (p. 161)

The soul's substance resembles nothing else;
it is in bonds and yet not in bonds;
if you watch over it, it dies in the body,
and if you scatter it, it illuminates the gathering. (p. 119)

6. Change and Flexibility

Rechisel, then thine ancient frame;
and build upon a new being.
Such being is real being;
Or else thy ego is a mere ring of smoke! (p. 15)

If thou canst thus reshape thyself and pass
The test, thou art alive and praised or else
The fire of life is smoke and naught beside... (p. 16)

7. Risk taking

Life without prickings is no true life;
one must live with a fire under one's feet.
Such living is the destiny of the self
And through this destiny the self is built up... (p. 94)

8. Complexity and Ambiguity

It is this incessant conflict that purifies the spirit,
makes it firm, speedy, nimble,
it spreads its wings in the broadness of light. (p. 72)

Do not lose any time,
you who desire the resolution of every know:
for long you have been a prisoner in your own thoughts,
now pour this tumult out of your breast! (p. 93)

9. Awareness and Serendipity

The man who is fully aware of himself
creates advantage out of loss... (p. 117)

Many of the issues addressed by Iqbal in the context of his drama are much more apparent than the reflections on creative human potential. They are issues as relevant in the present as they were at the time of his writing. It is a reminder of the non-sequential, universality of human aspiration and the struggle for meaning in a system under a fearful acceleration of change. Iqbal's prophetic sensibilities anticipated many issues and dichotomies now under intensive social scrutiny, especially in the emerging disciplines of futures studies and general systems theory. Among the issues most frequently touched upon throughout the text are those of polarities seeking balance:

- Unity and diversity
- Holography and reductionism
- Logical reason and intuition
- Analysis and synthesis
- East and West diversities
- Science and the arts
- Creation and stagnation
- Time and space
- Transformation, emergence, and reincarnation
- Power and obedience
- Action and apathy
- The role of women
- Materialism and asceticism
- Selfhood and social influence

Iqbal made references to issues throughout the text quite randomly, rather than limiting each focus to a particular sphere. In this way, he represented the holographic, systemic nature of thought and knowledge which epitomizes his work. Each is part of the whole and, in the end, defies classification or space-time sequence.

The Intimate Self

Central to Iqbal's drama is his concern with human individuality, spirit, and emergence. Both the agony and the ecstasy of the individual center come under his sensitive searching. The dilemma of each person, striving and fired from within to discover his or her uniqueness and significance contradicts the need to escape the separateness of our life journey, once we discard the superficiality of socially imposed groups and classes. His words strike a sensitive chorus for anyone who has "taken the road less traveled." Even for the most socially motivated and involved, the frantic nature of the current zeitgeist can finally force the realization that "we can be so much together that we can die of loneliness." This theme and its "contraries" recur throughout his writing:

> Though the stars swarm in the selfsame sky
> each star is more solitary than the other,
> each one is desperate just as we are,
> a vagrant lost in an azure wilderness. (p. 21)

Further, the subconscious cry of highly creative, idiosyncratic children and youth with idiosyncratic needs:

> Bitterly I wept, but echo answered never;
> where may Adam's son find kindred spirit? (p. 21)

A prayer for intimacy casts knowledge in a role incomplete and belittled:

> Thou gavest me reason, give me madness too
> show me the way to inward ecstasy.
> Knowledge takes up residence in the thought,
> loves lodge is the unsleeping heart;
> so long as knowledge has no portion of love
> it is a mere picture-gallery of thoughts. (p. 23)

Solitude and company are given balance:

> Though you possess a soul illuminated as Moses,
> yet without solitude your thoughts remain barren."
> Not my eye only desired the manifestation of god;
> it is a sin to behold beauty without a company:
> What is solitude? Pain, burning, and yearning;
> Company is vision, solitude is a search... (p. 49)

Beyond present identity and achievement, the penultimate need is for enduring identity:

> This slave, impatient, conquering all horizons,
> finds pleasure neither in absence or presence.
> I am a momentary thing; make me eternal. (p. 23)

From this final passage, it would seem that Iqbal's purpose in his writing is an answer to a deep and undeniable urge to live on in the energies of his words and ideas, divinely inspired. He is describing the frustration within a creative person with a time reality in the future and with an idea whose time has not yet come. There is a small audience for prophets:

> He was true coin, but there was none to assay him,
> expert in theory, but none to prove him;
> a lover lost in the labyrinth of his sighs,
> a traveller gone astray in his own path. (p. 112)

Certainly Iqbal was one of the early "futurists." Many lines testify to his concepts of the immensities "beyond our region and beyond our time":

> ...the soul's light is upon a pathless journey,
> roves farther than the rays of sun and moon...
> ...Man's reason is making assault on the world,
> but his love makes assault on the infinite...
> ...Earthy, yet in flight he is like an angel;
> heaven is but an ancient inn upon his way;
> he pricks into the very depths of the heavens,
> like the point of a needle into silk...
> His sight becomes keen through observing phenomena
> so that he sees the Essence within the attributes.
> Whoever falls in love with the beauty of Essence,
> he is the master of all existing things. (p. 26)

> Wait until the day creation all is naked
> and has washed from its skirt the dust of dimension:

then you will see neither waxing nor waning in its being,
you will see yourself as of it, and it of you. (p. 30)

Immensities of Time and Space

"The dust of dimension" is but one of the countless references Iqbal makes
to the time and space principles of post-Newtonian physics. It would be of interest to know how much of Einstein's scientific theory of relativity was realistically
or mystically sensed when he wrote:

Boldly ride upon space and time,
break free of the convolutions of this girdle… (p. 33)

God's remembrance requires not nations,
it transcends the bounds of time and space… (p. 69)

Between us and the light of the sun there hang
how many veils of space fold upon fold… (p. 72)

For an instant I closed my eyes in the waters,
for a little in the depths I broke away from myself,
bore my baggage towards another world,
with another time, another space… (p. 81)

Lines from the *Sphere of Mars* by the Sage of Rum suggest the value of
excellence in physical and psychic sciences in the exploration of the immensities:

They have greater dominion over time and place
because they are cleverer at the science of space;
they have so penetrated into its essence
that they have seen its every twist and turn… (p. 81)

Iqbal's awareness of some of the developments of science was considerable;
however, in his discussion of Eastern and Western cultures he identified the East
with qualitative understandings and Western cultures with quantifications, num-
berings, and scientific precision, and then made clear the limitations of science:

> The task of science is to see and consume,
> the work of gnosis is to see and augment;
> science weighs in the balance of technology,
> gnosis weighs in the balance of intuition;
> science holds in its hand water and earth,
> gnosis holds in its hand the pure spirit;
> science casts its gaze upon phenomena,
> gnosis absorbs phenomena into itself.... (p. 90)

Which brings the discourse again to the world of intimate immensities.

In addition to the reflective, philosophical considerations of this work of Iqbal, there is the call for vigorous growth and self-transcendence. Reflection seems to energize his spirit to dynamics of action. He is a consistent model of the creative person rising to his utmost becoming through faith and daring. These passages are music to a Western mind finding that what was known intuitively—that creative powers are among the most unifying forces in the global family—is so conclusively demonstrated by so admired a poet of the East. The qualities of creativity are the same the world over, and are the qualities upon which the world depends for its leadership and emergence of individual and social growth and evolution. Iqbal knew the priorities:

> Only upon himself he has opened his eyes,
> yielded his heart to no man, is utterly free;
> swiftly he paces through the expense of being
> Man of reason, the soul is not contained in dimensions;
> the free man is a stranger to every fetter and chain,
> the free man rails against the dark earth
> for it becomes not the falcon to act like a mouse.... (p. 56)

In his appeal for the transcendence of identity and spirit in the human heart on the journey through many lives and incarnations, Iqbal adds to the context of exoteric humanism a component of practical and political consideration. He recounts events in Islamic history that recall the rise and decline of the Muslim community in the world view. His comparisons of East and West, laced through as they are with his dominating crusade for personal significance and service, becomes more a revelation of human unity of spirit than a conflict of ideologies. East and West can be seen moving toward a recognition of their human commonalities. His argument for unity is persuasive:

> I have seen the revolution of Russia and Germany,
> I have seen the tumult raging in Moslemdom,
> I have seen the contrivings of West and East
> prevent the destinies of West and East…

and

> Abandon the East, be not spellbound by the West
> for all this ancient and new is not worth one barley corn… (p. 140)

Summary

The vanity of attempting to respond to Iqbal's *Javid-Nama* in less than a lifetime becomes increasingly clear. His is a work of spectacular variety and vision. It binds the reader to time and space even as it sets him free of both. Passion and reason are immensely bestirred in the reading. Encounter with Iqbal's articulation of the intimate immensities has had these profound effects on my personal search for growth and understanding:

- A wider opening of the "doors of perception"
- The pleasure of poetics and their enduring images
- Fortifying of intimations of immortality and hints of reincarnations to come
- Renewed faith that a unity of differences is in the making between East and West
- Further evidence that science and the arts can become aware that it is their differences that make them interesting and important to each other
- Reinforcement of the validity of *Creative Studies* which seeks to identify, preserve, and recover the creative spark and power as part of the human, cosmic heritage
- Additional testimony to the concept that the universe is nowhere static, but in a continuing process of self-organization (Torrance, 1998).

This is a work across time and space. It was deliberate on the part of Iqbal to prepare a writing so profound and inspired in its vision and at the same time of such clarity that it would be a guideline into an enlightened future. In "The Prayer" he says:

> I, who despair of the great sages of old,
> have a word to say touching the day to come!
> Render my speech easy unto the young,
> make my abyss for them attainable… (p. 24)

Iqbal's intuitive genius has been too long unmarked by much of the Western world. Things take time. Now the human family is poised at a place of transformation as it approaches a new millennium. Old value systems of power and control, of superficial obedience and lip service to ancient laws, together with the failure of imperialism, capitalism, and communism as absolute models for the world, more than ever have been shown to deprive the human ego of the need for self-direction, renewal, and emergence to higher levels of consciousness. Educational and social systems have practiced a denial of the individual human spirit. Each single human spirit contains and affects the universal spirit. The world has need of it all.

There are signs of a transition from industrialized, materialistic, competitive value systems to a more balanced system adding values of human significance, unity, love, and intimate identity with the natural immensities. Iqbal's prayer was answered. He gave us a message:

> …loftier than the heavens is the station of man
> and the beginning of education is respect for man… (p. 60)

> When love is companioned by intelligence
> it has the power to design another world,
> Then rise and draw the design of a real world,
> Mingle together love with intelligence… (p. 37)

> Traveller, the soul dies of dwelling at rest,
> it becomes more alive by perpetual soaring… (p. 37)

> You are an eagle, therefore get you about the skies,
> open your wings and pinions, rise clear of the earth… (p. 63)

From selfhood to nation to universe, back and forth and throughout, change is constant and inevitable. Unity and action are stirred in all quarters of the globe by enlightened persons with faith and vision.

> You and I are waves of life's river,
> every moment this universe changes
> for life is a perpetual revolution
> since it is ever searching for a new world.… (p. 133)

Epilogue: An Urgent Message

One of the intentions of this book of readings is to beckon all students and scholars of creativity to join the leadership forces in a world engaged in the most radical change in human history. Because everything we do is affected by our habits of mind, a fundamental task across cultures is to prepare citizens who are capable of the higher order thinking patterns demanded by a complex, dynamic society.

Schools have the obligation to prepare students for active participation in democratically designed forms of government as well as in enlightened businesses, organizations, and institutions. Recognizable trends in the world of work are moving from closed, exclusive hierarchal management styles to systems of leadership that are inclusive and flexible enough to engage all the talents of the richly diverse work force. If new ways of systemic thinking are not specifically taught throughout the formal educational experience, training and development departments in business will have to assume the leadership that creates and models twenty-first-century thought and attitudes.

It is long past the time when labels, absolute numbers, and strict categorizations can be allowed to totally define anyone or anything. To do so is a denial of the rich complexities and systemic nature of all of life. If we were all able to perceive ourselves as a vital and creative force in our own right and at the same time realize that we are an essential factor in a total evolving, shared system, we could be on our way to new understanding of the realities of our world with its hope for greater equality, harmony, and peace.

It is a fact that creative thinking can be taught. The same is true for other related higher order thinking processes, including critical thinking, integrative thinking, paradoxical thinking, global, futuristic thinking, and systemic thinking. The need to add the teaching of thinking to other educational reforms is urgent, given the pace and scope of the global transformation in which the human family is engaged. Although confirmed traditionalists may perceive such a purpose to be idealistic, there is an undeniable reality in its possibilities. Awareness grows. Change happens. Paradigms do shift.

Leadership, both designated (titled) and undesignated (untitled) continues to emerge worldwide throughout the professions and the marketplace. The task is monumental but doable if human will and spirit serve. There is this wisdom to remember:

Excellence is possible if you
CARE more than others think is wise,
RISK more than others think is safe,
DREAM more than others think is practical;
EXPECT MORE than others think is possible.
       —Marilyn Zuckerman and Louis Hatala

References

Agor, W. H. 1984. *Intuitive management: Left and right brain management skills: How to make the right decision at the right time.* Englewood Cliffs, NJ: Prentice Hall.

Alpes, Joel R. 1984. World systems in change. *COMSAT* 15.

Argyris, C. 1985. Interpersonal barriers to decision making. In J. R. Hackman, E. E. Lawler III, and L. W. Porter, eds. *Perspectives on behavior in organizations,* 337–349. New York: McGraw Hill.

Arieti, S. 1976. *Creativity: The magic synthesis.* New York: Basic Books.

Arnspiger, J. C., Rucker, N. R., and Preas, M. E. 1969. *Personality in Social Process.* Dubuque, IA: H. C. Brown.

Bachelard, G. 1969. *The poetics of space.* Boston: Beacon Press.

Barthes, R. 1980. The brain of Einstein. In Maurice Goldsmith, Alan Mackay, and James Woudhuysen, eds. *Einstein, the first hundred years,* 93–96. New York: Pergamon Press.

Bateson, M. 1994. *Peripheral vision: Learning along the way.* New York: Harper Collins.

Bausinger, Herman. 1984. Media, technology and daily life. *Media, Culture, and Society* 6:343–351.

Berdes, George R. 1969. *Friendly adversaries: The press and the government.* Marquette University College of Journalism. Center for the Study of the American Press.

Benton, L. 1978. *Management for the future.* New York: McGraw Hill.

Besemer, S.P. 1995. How do you know it's creative? In M. Joyce, S. Isakson, G. Puccio, F. Davidson, and C. Coppage, eds. *An introduction to creativity,* 137–145. Acton, MA: Copley Publishing Group.

Beuys, J. 1998. *Creativity = capital.* Joseph Beuys Multiples Art Exhibition, Minneapolis, MN. Walker Art Center.

Blade, E. 1963. Creative science. In Myron A. Coler, ed. *Essays on creativity in the sciences,* 184–206. New York: New York University Press.

Bleedorn, B. 1984a. *Humor: lessons in laughter for learning and living.* Buffalo, NY: D.O.K. Publishers.

—————. 1984b. *Women in leadership: Impact of women's values on the future.* Unpublished Paper, Hubert H. Humphrey Institute for Reflective Leadership, University of Minnesota, Minneapolis, Minnesota.

—————. 1987. Creativity and innovation in bureaucracies: Stimulating and facilitating creative ideas upwards. *Value World* (Oct, Nov, Dec 1987, 4):4.

—————. 1988. *Creative leadership for a global future: Studies and speculations.* New York: Peter Lang Publishing Co.

—————. 1992. New think for the future: Educating the global brain. In T. Rickards, S. Moger, P. Colemont, and M. Tassoul, eds. *Creativity and innovation: Quality break-throughs,* 145–149. Delft, The Netherlands: Innovation Consulting Group TNO.

—————. 1993. Toward an integration of creative and critical thinking. *American Behavioral Scientist,* 37 (1):10–20. Thousand Oaks, CA: Sage Periodicals Press.

—————. 1995. Imagineering: Education and the creative process. In E. R. Krueger and F. A. Kulacki, eds. *Proceedings of Fourth World Conference on Engineering Education, Vol. 2,* 4–649. Minneapolis: University of Minnesota.

Botkin, J., Elmandjra, M. and Malitza, M. 1979. *No limits to learning: Bridging the human gap.* New York: Pergamon Press.

Botstein, Leon. 1997. *Jefferson's children: Education and the promise of American culture.* New York: Doubleday.

Bradford, D. L. and Cohen, A. R. 1984. *Managing for excellence: The guide to developing high performance in contemporary organizations.* New York: Wiley and Sons.

Bronowski, J. 1943. *A man without a mask.* London: Secker and Warburg.

—————. 1965. *Science and human values.* New York: Harper Row.

—————. 1978. *The origins of knowledge and imagination.* New Haven, CT: Yale University Press.

Burns, J. M. 1978. *Leadership.* New York: Harper and Row.

Bushrui, S., Ayman, I., and Laszlo, E. 1993. *Transition to a global society.* Oxford: One World Publications.

Buzan, T., and Buzan, B. 1994. *The mind map book.* New York: E. P. Dutton.

Cameron, J. 1992. *The artistic way. A spiritual path to higher creativity.* New York: G. P. Putnam.

Campbell, D. 1991. *Music: Physician for times to come.* Wheaton, IL: Quest Books.

Capra, P. 1990. The crisis of perception. *The Futurist* 24 (January-February): 64.

Clark, R. 1971. *Einstein: The life and times.* New York: Avon.

Cleveland, H. 1993. *Birth of a new world: An open moment for international leadership.* San Francisco: Jossey Bass.

—————. 1984. Leaders as first birds off the telephone wire. *Leading Edge Bulletin,* 5 (6, Nov):2.

—————. 1987. *The knowledge executive: Leadership in an information society.* New York: E.P. Dutton.

—————. 1997. *Leadership and the information revolution.* Minneapolis, MN: World Academy of Art and Science.

Csikszentmihalyi, M. 1993. *The evolving self: A psychology for the third millennium.* New York: Harper Collins.

Cunningham, B. F., and Torrance, E. P. 1965. *Sounds and images adult version form I.* Lexington, MA: Ginn and Company.

De Bono, E. 1970. *Lateral thinking: A textbook of creativity.* New York: Simon and Schuster.

——————. 1992. *Serious creativity: Using the power of lateral thinking to create new ideas.* New York: HarperCollins.

De Broglie, L., A. L. and Simon, P. H. 1979. *Einstein.* New York: Peebles Press.

DeMott, J. S. 1985. Here come the intrapreneurs. *Time* (Feb 5, 1985):36 .

Deutsch, K. W., Priestly, F. E., Brown, H., and Hawkins, D. 1958. *Science and the creative spirit: Essays on humanistic aspects of science.* Toronto, Canada: University of Toronto Press.

Donaldson, G., and Lorsch, J. W. 1983. *Decision making at the top: The shaping of strategic direction.* New York: Basic Books.

Drucker, P. 1969. *The age of discontinuity.* New York: Harper and Row.

——————. 1982. *Changing world of the executive.* New York: Times Books.

——————. 1989. How schools must change. *Psychology Today* 5 (May):18–20.

Einstein, A. 1950. *Out of my later years.* New York: Philosophical Library.

——————. 1954. *Ideas and opinions.* Edited by Carl Seelig. Based on *Mein Weltbild.* New York: Bonanza Books.

——————. 1990. In E. McGaa, Eagle Man. *Mother earth spirituality: Native American paths to healing ourselves and the world,* iii. San Francisco: Harper & Row.

Feather, F. 1979. Harmonic planning: A whole brained approach. *Business Tomorrow.* World Future Society.

Fellers, G. 1996. *Creativity for leaders.* Gretna, LA: Pelican Publishing Co.

Ferguson, M. 1980. *The Aquarian conspiracy: Personal and social transformation in the '80s.* Los Angeles: J. P. Tarcher.

Fox, J. 1995. *Finding what you didn't lose.* New York: G. P. Putnam.

Frank, P. 1947. *Einstein: His life and times.* Translated from a German Manuscript by George Rosen. Ed. and rev. by Shuichi Kusaka. New York: Alfred A. Knopf.

Fromm, E. and Xirau, R. 1968. *The nature of man.* New York: MacMillan

Fuller, R. B. 1977. *Operating manual for spaceship earth.* New York: Dutton

Fuller, R. B., and Dil, A. 1983. *Humans in universe.* New York: Mouton Press.

Galbraith, J. K. 1983. *The anatomy of power.* New York: Houghton Mifflin.

Galbraith, J. R. 1985. Organization design: An information processing view. In J. R. Hackman, E. E Lawler III, and L. W Porter, eds. *Perspectives on behavior in organizations,* 432–436. New York: McGraw Hill.

Gardner, H. 1983. *Frames of mind: The theory of multiple intelligences.* New York: Basic Books.

————. 1993. *Creating minds.* New York: Basic Books.

Gardner, J. 1968. *Morale.* New York: W. W. Norton.

Garnham, N., and Collins, R. 1985. Editorial. Media culture and society. *Sage Publications* 7 (Jan):1.

Gaunt, W. 1956. *Arrows of desire: A study of William Blake and his romantic world.* London: Museum Press, Ltd.

Gelb, M. 1995. *Thinking for a change: Discovering the power to create, communicate and lead.* New York: Harmony Books.

Gell-Mann, M. 1994. *The quark and the jaguar: Adventure in the simple and the complex.* New York: W. H. Freeman.

Gibson, J., Ivansevich, J., and Donnelly, J. 1982. *Organizations: behavior, structure, process.* Plano, TX: Business Publications.

Global Futures Digest: A Spectrum of Futures Research and International Development. 1983. Global Futures Network 1 (2).

Golding, P. 1974. Media role in national development: A critique of a theoretical orthodoxy. *Journal of Communication* 24:39–53.

————. 1977. Media professionalism in the third world: The transfer of an ideology. In James Curran, ed. *Mass communication and society.* London: Arnold.

Gorbachev, M. 1992. My final hours. *Time* (May 11, 1992).

Gregorc, T. 1983, Educator Gregorc maps out four thinking styles. *Leading Edge Bulletin* 3 (9, Jan):1–3.

Guilford, J. P. 1968. *Intelligence, creativity, and their total implications.* San Diego, CA: Robert R. Knapp.

————. 1977. *Way beyond the IQ: Guide to improving intelligence and creativity.* Buffalo, New York: Creative Education Foundation.

Hackman, J. R., Lawler III, E. E., and Porter L. W., eds. 1985. *Perspectives on behavior in organizations,* 586–598. New York: McGraw Hill.

Hackman, J. R., and Oldham, G. R. 1985. Redesign in organizational and social context. In J. R. Hackman, E. E. Lawler III, and L. W. Porter, eds. *Perspectives on behavior in organizations.* 586–598. New York: McGraw Hill.

Hagberg, J. 1984. *Real power: Stages of personal power in organizations.* Minneapolis, MN: Winston Press.

Handy, C. 1994. *The age of paradox.* Boston: Harvard Business School Press.

Harman, W., and Rheingold, H. 1984. *Higher creativity: Liberating the unconscious for breakthrough insights.* Boston: Houghton Mifflin.

Hart, M. H. 1978. *The 100: A ranking of the most influential persons in history.* New York: A & W Visual Library.

Hellman, H. 1980. *Idealism, aggression, apology, and criticism: The four traditions of research in international communication.* Caracas. IAMCR.

Hoffman, B. 1972. *Albert Einstein: Creator and rebel.* With the Collaboration of Helen Dukas. New York: New American Library.

Holton, G., and Elkana, Y. eds. 1982. *Albert Einstein: Historical and cultural perspectives.* Jerusalem Einstein Centennial Symposium. New Jersey: Princeton University Press.

Holy Bible. 1957. New Catholic Edition. Proverbs 17:22.

Iqbal. 1966. *Javid-nama.* Translated from the Persian with introduction and notes by Arthur J. Arberry. London: George Allen & Unwin Ltd.

Isaksen, S., et al. 1993. *Nurturing and developing creativity: The emergence of a discipline.* Norwood, NJ: Ablex Publishing Corporation.

Janowitz, M. 1975. Professional models in journalism: The gatekeeper and the advocate. *Journalism Quarterly* 52:618–626.

Janus, N., and Roneagliolo, R. 1979. Advertising, mass media, and dependency. *Development Dialogue* 1:81–97.

Janis, I. L. 1985. Group think. In J. R. Hackman, E. E. Lawler III, and L. W. Porter, eds. *Perspectives on behavior in organizations,* 378–384. New York: McGraw Hill.

Joyce, M., et al. 1995. *An introduction to creativity.* Acton, MA: Copley Publishing Company.

Kanter, R. 1977. *Men and women of the corporation.* New York: Basic Books.

—————. 1984. *The change masters: Innovation and entrepreneurship in the American corporation.* New York: Simon and Schuster.

Kastenbaum, P. 1987. *The heart of business: Ethics, power and philosophy.* New York: W. W. Norton.

Kazin, A., ed. 1976. *The portable Blake.* New York: Penguin Books.

Kellerman, B. 1984. *Leadership: Multidisciplinary perspectives.* New York Prentice Hall.

Kinsey Goman, C. 1989. *Creativity in business: A practical guide for creative thinking.* Menlo Park, CA: Crisp Publications.

Klonsky, M. 1977. *William Blake: The seer and his visions.* New York: Harmony Books.

Koestler, A. 1964. *The act of creation.* New York: Dell Publishing.

—————. 1967. *The ghost in the machine.* Chicago: Henry Regnery.

Land, G. 1973. *Grow or die: The principle of transformation.* New York: Random House.

Land, G., and Jarman, B. 1992. *Breakpoint and beyond: Mastering the future today.* New York: Harper Business.

Laszlo, E. 1992. The freedom of thought, expression and action in a just society. Paper presented at the Third International Dialogue on the Transition to Global Society: The Transition to a Just Society. Sep 8–12, 1992. Landegg Academy, Wienacht, Switzerland.

Lawrence, P., and Lorsch, J. 1969. Differentiation and integration in complex organizations. *Administrative Science Quarterly* 6:1–47.

Lee, Chin-Chuan. 1980. *Media imperialism reconsidered.* Beverly Hills, CA: Sage Publications.

————. 1982. The international information order. *Communication Research* 9:617–636.

Lehrer, J. C. 1980. Ours is the power to choose. In C. Sheppard, C. Stewart, and D. Carroll, eds. *Working in the twenty-first century,* 214–218. New York: John Wiley & Sons.

Lerner, A. B. 1973. *Einstein and Newton.* Minneapolis: Lerner Publications.

LeShan, L., and Margenau, H. 1982. *Einstein's space and Van Gogh's sky: Physical reality and beyond.* New York: Macmillan.

Likert, R. 1967. *The human organization.* New York: McGraw Hill.

Lorsch, J. W. 1985. Making behavior science more useful. In J. R. Hackman, E. E. Lawler III, and L. W. Porter, eds. *Perspectives on behavior in organizations,* 29–38. New York: McGraw Hill.

Maccoby, M. 1981. *The leader.* New York: Simon & Schuster.

Machado, L. 1980. *The right to be intelligent.* Elmsford, NY: Pergamon Press.

Manneheim, K. 1968. *Ideology and utopia.* New York: Harcourt.

Margenau, H. 1959. The scientific basis of value theory. In A. Maslow, ed. *New knowledge in human values,* 38–51. New York: Harper.

Maslow, A. 1959. Psychological data and value theory. In A. Maslow, ed. *New knowledge in human values,* 119–136. New York: Harper.

Mason, R. 1982. *Participatory and workplace democracy.* Carbondale, Illinois: Southern Illinois University Press.

Mayor, F. 1992. *Global vision.* Wienacht, Switzerland: Landegg Academy.

Mbigi, L., and Maree, J. 1995. *UBUNTU: The spirit of African transformation management.* Pretoria, South Africa: Sigma Press.

McDonough, P., and McDonough, B. 1981. A survey of American colleges and universities on the conducting of formal courses on creativity. *Journal of Creative Behavior* 21 (4):271–282.

McGhee, P. E. 1979. *Humor: Its origin and development.* San Francisco: Freeman.

Mestenhauser, J. 1997. Internationalization of higher education: A cognitive response to the challenges of the twenty-first century. Presentation made at the Ninth Annual Conference of the European Association for International Education, Barcelona, Spain. Nov. 20-23, 1997.

Millar, G. 1995. *E. Paul Torrance: "The creativity man."* Norwood, NJ: Ablex Publishing.

Mintzberg, H. 1976. Planning on the left side and managing on the right side. *Harvard Business Review* (Jul/Aug):49–58.

Mitchell, E. 1979. A look at the exceptional. In C. Tart, H. E. Puthoff, and R. Targ, eds. *Mind at large,* 1–10. New York: Praeger Publishers.

Morey, S. 1983. The three I's of Indian education: Intuition, imagination, insight. *The Tarrytown Letter* (Oct). Published By The Tarrytown Group-A Forum For New Ideas. Tarrytown House, East Sunnyside Lane, Tarrytown, N. Y.

Moustakis, C. 1977. *Creative life.* New York: Van Nostrand Reinhold.

Nadler, D., and Lawler, E. E. III. 1985. Motivation: A diagnostic approach. In J. R. Hackman, E. E. Lawler III, and L. W. Porter, eds. *Perspectives on behavior in organizations,* 67–78. New York: McGraw Hill.

Naisbitt, J. 1982. *Megatrends: Ten directions transforming our lives.* New York: Warner Books.

Nixon, Raymond. 1965. Freedom in the world's press: A fresh appraisal with new data. *Journalism Quarterly* 42:3–14, 118–119.

Noer, D. 1975. *Multinational people management: A guide for organizations and employees.* Washington, DC: BNA Books.

Ornstein, R. E. 1977. *The psychology of consciousness.* New York: Harcourt Brace Jovanovich.

Ouspensky, P. D. 1973. *The psychology of man's possible evolution.* New York: Vintage Books.

Parnes, S. 1981. *The magic of your mind.* Buffalo, NY: Creative Education Foundation.

Pascarella, P. 1981. *Industry week's guide to tomorrow's executive: Humanagement in the future corporation.* New York: Van Nostrand.

Peters, T. J., and Waterman, R. H. Jr. 1982. *In search of excellence: Lessons from America's best run companies.* New York: Harper & Row.

Porter, L., Allan, R., and Angle, H. 1985. The problem of upward influence in organizations. In J. R. Hackman, E. E. Lawler III, and L. W. Porter, eds. *Perspectives on behavior in organizations,* 358–368. New York: McGraw Hill.

Real, Michael. 1977. *Mass-mediated culture.* Englewood Cliffs, NJ: Prentice Hall.

Reiser, A. 1930. *Albert Einstein: A biographical portrait.* New York: Albert and Charles Boni.

Richards, M.A. 1964. *Centering in pottery, poetry, and the person.* Middletown, CT: Wesleyan University Press.

Richstad, J. and Anderson, M. H., eds. 1981. *Crisis in international news: Policies and prospects.* New York: Columbia University Press.

Ringham, E. 1985. Scaling the obstacles that still divide U.S. and China. Minneapolis *Star Tribune,* May 13, 1985.

Rivers, W. 1970. *The adversaries: Politics and the press.* Boston: Beacon Press.

Rosenbaum, M. and Sandowsky, A. 1976. *The intensive group: A guide. Therapy, sensitivity, encounter, self-awareness groups, human relations training and communes.* New York: Free Press.

Ruggiero, V. R. 1988. *The art of thinking: A guide to critical and creative thought.* New York: Harper and Row.

Russell, P, and Evans, R. 1992. *The creative manager: Finding inner vision and wisdom in uncertain times.* San Francisco: Jossey-Bass.

Saft, Stephen A. 1984. Focus. *COMSTAT,* 27–36.

Salencik, G., and Pfeffer, J. 1985. Who gets power and how they hold on to it: A strategic-contingency model of power. In J. R. Hackman, E. E. Lawler III, and L. W. Porter, eds. *Perspectives on behavior in organizations,* 417–429. New York: McGraw Hill.

Salk, J. 1983. *Anatomy of Reality: Merging of intuition and reason.* New York: Columbia University Press.

Sander, W., and Ziegler, R. 1977. A review of creativity and problem solving techniques. *Research Management* (July):34–42.

Sargent, A. G. 1981. *The androgynous manager.* New York: AMACOM.

Sayles, L. R. 1979. *What effective managers really do: And how they do it.* New York: McGraw Hill.

Schiller, Dan. 1985. The emerging global grid: Planning for what? *Media Culture and Society.* 7 (1):105–124.

Schram, Stuart., ed. 1967. *Quotations from Chairman Mao Tse-Tung,* New York: Bantam Books.

Schwartz, J. 1979. *Einstein for beginners.* New York: Pantheon Books.

Sexton, D., and Bowman-Upton, N. 1991. *Entrepreneurship: Creativity and growth.* New York: Macmillan.

Silber, M., and Sherman, V. C. 1983. *Managerial performance and promotability: The making of an executive.* New York: AMACON.

Skromme, A. 1989. *Memorization is not enough: The 7-Ability Plan.* Moline, IL: Self Confidence Press.

Suzuki, D. 1959. Human values in Zen. In A. Maslow, ed. *New knowledge in human values,* 94–106. New York: Harper.

Swede, G. 1993. *Creativity: A new psychology.* Toronto, Ontario: Wall and Emerson.

Tehranian, Majid. 1984. Communication and revolution in Asia: Western domination and cultural restoration in Japan and Iran. *KEIO Communication Review* 5.

Teilhard de Chardin, P. 1959. *The phenomenon of man.* New York.

—————. 1964. *Future of man.* New York: Harper & Row.

Tillich, Paul. 1959. Is a science of human values possible? In A. Maslow, ed. *New knowledge in human values,* 189–196. New York: Harper.

Toffler, A. 1980. *The third wave.* New York: Random House.

Torrance, E. P. 1966a. *Thinking creatively with pictures: Booklet A.* Princeton, NJ: Personnel Press.

——————. 1966b. *Torrance tests of creative thinking.* Bensenville, IL: Scholastic Testing Service.

——————. 1979. *The search for satori and creativity.* Buffalo, NY: Creative Education Foundation.

——————. 1979. *Your style of learning and thinking, Form C.* Georgia Studies of Creative Behavior, Department of Educational Psychology, University of Georgia, Athens, GA.

——————. 1980. Creativity and futurism in education: Retooling. *Education* 100 (4):298–311.

Torrance, E. P., et al. 1995. *Multicultural mentoring of the gifted and talented.* Waco, TX: Prufrock Press.

Torrance, P. 1995. *Why fly? A philosophy of creativity.* Norwood, NJ: Ablex Publishing Corporation.

Tuchman, G. 1978. Professionalism as an agent of legitimization. *Journal of Communication.* 28 (2):106–113.

U Thant. 1977. *View from the United Nations.* New York: Doubleday.

Vallentin, A. 1954. *The drama of Albert Einstein.* New York: Doubleday.

Vaughn, Frances. 1979. *Awakening intuition.* New York: Anchor Books.

Von Bertalanffy, L. 1959. Human values in a changing world. In A. Maslow, ed. *New knowledge in human values,* 65–74. New York: Harper.

——————. 1968. *General system theory.* New York: George Braziller.

Webster's third new international dictionary. 1968. Springfield, MA: Merriam Webster.

Wheatley, M. 1992. *Leadership and the new sciences.* San Francisco: Barrett- Koehler.

Wheatley, M., and Kellner-Rogers, M. 1996. *A simpler way.* San Francisco: Barrett-Koehler.

Whitrow, G. J., ed. 1967. *Einstein: The man and his achievement.* New York: Dover.

Williams, F. 1970. *Classroom ideas for encouraging thinking and feeling.* Buffalo, NY: D.O.K.

Wiseman, R. L. 1984. Methods for intercultural communication and research. *International Journal of Intercultural Relations* 8:4.

Zassoursky, Y. 1985. Peace: Role of the multi media. *The Democratic Journalist: Journal of the International Organization of Journalists* 3:85.

Zukav, G. 1979. *The dancing Wu Li masters: An overview of the new physics.* New York: William Morrow.

Zussman, I. R. 1983. Rorschach test correlates of humor appreciation. Dissertation, United States International University, San Diego, CA.

4/00 8

To order additional copies of this book,
please send full amount plus $4.00 for
postage and handling for the first book and
50¢ for each additional book.

Send orders to:

Galde Press, Inc.
PO Box 460
Lakeville, Minnesota 55044-0460

Credit card orders call 1–800–777–3454
Phone (612) 891-5991 • Fax (612) 891-6091
Visit our website at http://www.galdepress.com

Write for our free catalog.